VOLUNTARY
SIMPLICITY

VOLUNTARY SIMPLICITY

TOWARD
A WAY OF LIFE THAT IS
OUTWARDLY SIMPLE,
INWARDLY RICH

DUANE ELGIN

WILLIAM MORROW AND COMPANY, INC.

New York   1981

Library of Congress Cataloging in Publication Data

Elgin, Duane.
    Voluntary simplicity.

    Bibliography: p.
    Includes index.
    1. Simplicity.   I. Title.
BJ1496.E356   170   81-643
ISBN 0-688-03647-3   AACR1
ISBN 0-688-00322-2 (pbk.)

Printed in the United States of America

First Edition

1 2 3 4 5 6 7 8 9 10

BOOK DESIGN BY MICHAEL MAUCERI

*This book is dedicated
with love and appreciation
to Ann, Mary, Cliff, Ben, and Matt*

PREFACE

We have entered a time of transition as a human family. We are being pushed by hard necessity and pulled by enormous opportunity to fundamentally reconsider the ways in which we choose to live our daily lives. This book is about a whole pattern of practical changes that a growing number of people are making in their "ordinary" lives—changes that are conscious of, and responsive to, the pushes and pulls of our times. This innovative way of living is termed "voluntary simplicity."

We hear much about the individual being alienated, helpless, and powerless to make a difference in the face of massive institutions and massive forces, such as nuclear proliferation, environmental pollution, resource depletion, and loss of social cohesion. This book is premised on a different perspective—that the manner in which we live our ordinary lives *does* make a difference. Far from being helpless, we, as individuals working in cooperation with one another, are the only source of vitality that can breathe new life into our faltering civilizations. I view our personal empowerment not as a utopian wish but as a working reality that is already evident in the lives of many persons from all walks of life who have been actively experimenting with a path of voluntary simplicity. Thus, a major theme of this book is that while we do encounter enormous difficulties, we encounter even larger opportunities to create a more workable and meaningful future.

This is an eclectic and wide-ranging book. Yet, my overriding concern has been with how we can make small and practical changes in our everyday lives and thereby contribute both to the quality of our personal existence and to the well-being of the entire human family.

There are innumerable persons who have helped me along the way—either in the learning that led to the writing of this book, or in the writing process itself. I would like to acknowledge a few of the persons to whom I am particularly grateful: my father for his example of integrity, generosity, and patient craftsmanship; my mother for her example of curiosity, compassion, and zest for life; Daniel Berrigan for his example that taught that the way of love does not turn from life; Donald Michael for his example of enthusiasm for learning with an open mind and an open heart; Arnold Mitchell for his collaboration in early research on voluntary simplicity and for his helpful critiques of initial drafts of this book; Ann Niehaus for her abiding love and unconditional support; Ram Dass for his patient reading of early versions of this book and for writing the insightful preface; Frances Vaughan for her encouragement and enthusiasm for the work; Roger Walsh for his support and discerning reading of numerous versions of the manuscript; all of the people who responded to the grass roots survey (described in Chapter 2) for bringing, through their living example, a richly human dimension into this work; and Ronda Davé for her skilled computer analysis of the survey results.

Finally, I also appreciate the assistance of other persons who, in various ways, have helped this work along its path to completion: Barry Bartlett, John Brockman, Mary Elgin, Sally Furgeson, Bertil Ilhage, Kathryn Reeder, Mary Schoonmaker, Peter Schwartz, and Peter Teige.

—DUANE ELGIN

Menlo Park, California
November, 1980

CONTENTS

SECTION II: CONTEXT

SECTION III: ROOTS

APPENDICES

INTRODUCTION

by
Ram Dass

As one who in recent years has spent a great deal of time in the East, I've had the chance to view intimately a way of life which, in its simplicity, is very different from the style of living to which we in the West are accustomed.

Even as I write these words, I look out over a gentle valley in the Kumoan Hills at the base of the Himalayas. A river flows through the valley forming now and again man-made tributaries that irrigate the fertile fields. These fields surround the fifty or so thatched or tin-roofed houses and extend in increasingly narrow terraces up the surrounding hillsides.

In several of these fields I watch village men standing on their wooden plows goading on their slow-moving water buffalo who pull the plows, provide the men's families with milk, and help to carry their burdens. And amid the green of the hills, in brightly colored saris and nose rings, women cut the high grasses to feed the buffalo and gather the firewood which, along with the dried dung from the buffalo, will provide the fire to cook the grains harvested from the fields and to warm the houses against the winter colds and dry them during the monsoons. A huge haystack passes along the path, seemingly self-propelled, in that the woman on whose head it rests is lost entirely from view.

At a point along the stream there is laughter and talk and the continuous slapping of wet cloth against rock as the family laundry gets done. And everywhere there are children and dogs, each contributing his or her sound to the voice of the village.

Everywhere there is color: red chili peppers drying on the roofs and saris drying by the river, small green and yellow and blue birds darting among the fruit trees, butterflies and bees tasting their way from one brightly colored flower to another.

I have walked for some five miles from the nearest town to reach this valley. The foot path I have taken is the only means of exit from this village. Along the way, I meet farmers carrying squash, burros bearing firewood or supplies, women with brass pots on their heads, schoolchildren, young men dressed in "city clothes." In all of these people I find a quiet shy dignity, a sense of belonging, a depth of connectedness to these ancient hills.

It all moves as if in slow motion. Time is measured by the sun, the seasons, and the generations. A conch shell sounds from a tiny temple, which houses a deity worshiped in these hills. The stories of this and other deities are recited and sung, and they are honored by flowers and festivals and fasts. They provide a context—vast in its scale of aeons of time, rich with teachings of reincarnation and the morality inherent in the inevitable workings of karma. And it is this context that gives vertical meaning to these villagers' lives with their endless repetition of cycles of birth and death.

This pastoral vision of simplicity has much appeal to those of us in the West for whom life can be full of confusion, distraction, and complexity. In the rush of modern industrial society, and in the attempt to maintain our image as successful persons, we feel that we have lost touch with a deeper, more profound part of our beings. Yet, we feel that we have little time, energy, or cultural support to pursue those areas of life that we know are important. We long for a simpler way of life that allows us to restore some balance to our lives.

Is the vision of simple living provided by this village in the East the answer? Is this an example of a primitive simplicity of the past or of an enlightened simplicity of the future? Gradually, I have come to sense that this is not the kind of simplicity that the future holds. Despite its ancient character, the simplicity of the village is still in its "infancy."

Occasionally, people show me their new babies and ask me if that peaceful innocence is not just like that of the Buddha. Probably not, I tell them, for within that baby rest all the latent seeds of worldly desire just waiting to sprout as the opportunity arises. On the other hand, the expression on the face of the Buddha, who had seen through the impermanence and suffering associated with such desires, reflects the invulnerability of true freedom.

So it is with this village. Its ecological and peaceful way of living is unconsciously won and thus is vulnerable to the winds of change that fan the latent desires of its people. Even now there is a familiar though jarring note in this sylvan village scene. The sounds of static and that impersonal professional voice of another civilization—the radio announcer—cut through the harmony of sounds as a young man of the village holding a portable radio to his ear, comes around a bend. On his arm there is a silver wristwatch that sparkles in the sun. He looks at me proudly as he passes. And a wave of understanding passes through me. Just behind that radio and wristwatch comes an army of desires that for centuries have gone untested and untasted. As material growth and technological change activate these yearnings, they will transform the hearts, minds, work, and daily life of this village within a generation or two.

Gradually, I see that the simplicity of the village has not been consciously chosen as much as it has been unconsciously derived as the product of centuries of unchanging custom and tradition. The East has yet to fully encounter the impact of technological change and material growth. When the East has encountered the latent desires within its people, and the cravings for material goods and social position begin to wear away at the fabric of traditional culture, then it can begin to choose its simplicity consciously. Then the simplicity of the East will be consciously won —voluntarily chosen.

Just as the East still has its time of transition to move through before finding a new place of dynamic equilibrium and conscious balance, so too does the West face its own unique time of transition. In the West, there are many who have already begun the search for a more conscious balance, a simplicity of living that allows the integration of inner and outer, material and spiritual, masculine and feminine, personal and social, and all of the other polarities that now divide our lives. Since the decade of the 1960s, this search for integration has led many among a whole subculture to explore the learnings of the East. Yet, in attempting to partake deeply of the rich heritage of the East, many, myself included, have tended to diminish the value and relevance of our Western heritage.

My mind flashes back to 1968 when I returned from my first trip to India. Through the eyes of a renunciate I saw comfort and convenience, aesthetics and pleasure as the sirens seducing me back into the sleep of unconsciousness. So I moved into a cabin in the woods behind my father's house. Each day I bathed out of a pail of cold water, huddled in blankets against the night chill, slept on a thin mat on the floor, and cooked the same food of lentils and rice each day.

Not fifty yards away, in my father's house, there were empty bedrooms, electricity, warm showers, television, and tasty and varied hot meals cooked each day. I would look at that house in the evenings with disdain, which I now suspect was born mainly out of longing. I was running as hard as I could away from Western values even as I was studying in depth the *Bhagavad-Gita*, which says that one must honor one's unique life predicament; one cannot imitate another's. Though in time I surrendered slowly back into that sensual material ease of the West, I did so with some sense of being a fallen angel, of compromising with a technological society running out of control. I did not know where a skillful balance was to be found. I had been fortunate enough to deeply taste the most generous fruits of two richly developed cultural traditions. Often I felt them churning and pulling within my being as I searched for balance along the vast spectrum of potentials represented by these two perspectives. I felt the dualism within my being. I could not reject the West and embrace the East—both lived within me.

Similarly, many among the counterculture of the 1960s withdrew from the emptiness of the Industrial Disneyland of worldly delights (where even when you won, you lost) but did not halt their interior journey with an existential renunciation of the West. Many among a whole generation have turned within to the heart and have begun to move beyond intellectual alienation and despair to directly encounter the place where we are all connected, where we are all one. And from that place, many have felt drawn to life-styles in which their contact with their fellow human beings, with nature, and with God could be renewed.

A cycle of learning is being completed. The time of withdrawal is moving into a time of return. The exploration of new ways of living that support new ways of being is a movement that arises from the awakening of compassion—the dawning realization that the fate of the individual is intimately connected with the fate of the whole. It is a movement that arises from the recognition that our task is not only to be here, in the NOW; it is also to now be HERE. And where "here" is must include the fact that we are inhabitants of an aging industrial civilization that is in great need of the insight, perspective, and creativity that the journey to the "East" (to the interior) can bring upon return to the West.

The dualism inherent in our thinking process (which pits materialism against spiritualism, West against East), must be transcended if we are to be truly the inheritors of our evolutionary legacy and the children of a new age. From this perspective, the historic Western preoccupation with the intellect and with material consumption need not be viewed as "wrong" or "bad" or necessarily leading to our destruction. Rather, the Western orientation in living may be viewed as a necessary part of an evolutionary stage out of which yet another birth of higher consciousness— as an amalgam of East and West—might subsequently evolve. The industrial revolution, then, is part of a larger revolution in living. The West has made its contribution by providing the material basis of life needed to support the widespread unfolding of consciousness. The contribution of the East is the provision of insight into the nature of the conscious unfolding of consciousness. East and West require the learnings of each other if both are to evolve further and realize the potentials that arise in their integration and balance.

Yet, what does this mean in worldly terms? What are the practical, down-to-earth expressions of this integration of inner and outer, East and West, personal growth and social transformation? Are there ways of living that express this integrative intention? We must begin by acknowledging there are no "right answers" to these questions. The process of integration of East and West has only just begun to infuse the popular culture in the last few decades. We have only just begun to enter a new age of discovery. A vast new frontier beckons. The "answers" that we seek will be of our own making—they are still in the process of being discovered in our own lives. And yet, for many of us, merely saying this is not enough. We want to see more clearly the larger pattern into which our lives can fit more skillfully, and we also want to see more precisely how we might adapt our daily lives to fit harmoniously into this larger pattern of evolution.

What kind of person might assist in the delicate midwifery of revealing to us the nature of the worldly expressions of an integration of inner and outer, East and West? Certainly one would be required to have a foot in both the Eastern and Western perspectives. One must have cultivated in oneself at least the beginnings of a compassionate consciousness—a balance of head and heart. I think it requires people like E. F. Schumacher, the author of *Small is Beautiful* and *A Guide for the Perplexed*, who, with compassion and penetrating insight, challenged many of the traditional assumptions of Western industrial societies. And now, with this book on voluntary simplicity, we meet another of these beings, Duane Elgin. People such as Duane are neither afraid to immerse themselves in the problems and potentials of an advanced industrial civilization, nor to immerse themselves in the meditative journey. They find in this balancing process, neither despair nor pollyannish optimism, but an enthusiasm for the dance. They can reveal the complex dynamics of the existing world situation with a wisdom that reflects self-respect, integrity, compassion, and subtle discriminations of the intellect. Such beings look to the future and see through the smoke to the sunlight.

CHAPTER 1

VOLUNTARY SIMPLICITY

The world is profoundly changing, that much seems clear. We have entered a time of great uncertainty that extends from local to global scale. We are forced by pressing circumstances to ask difficult questions about the way we live our lives: Will my present way of life still be workable when my children grow up? How might their lives, and my own, be different? Am I satisfied with my work? Does my work contribute to the well-being of others—or is it just a source of income? How much income do I really require? Require for what? How much of my consumption adds to the clutter and complexity of my life rather than to my satisfaction? How does my level and pattern of consumption affect other people and the environment? Is there an alternative way of living that is more sustainable in an era of scarcity? Do I have the flexibility to adapt to a period of prolonged energy shortage and economic depression? In the face of scarcity, is there an alternative way of living that fosters cooperation and community rather than cutthroat competition and social fragmentation? Are there small changes that I could make in my own life that, with many others making similar changes, would result in a large difference in the well-being of others? What are my responsibilities to the other members of the human family who are living in grinding poverty? Am I missing much of the richness of life by being preoccupied with the search for social status and consumer goods? What is my purpose in life? How am I to take charge of my own life?

If these questions cause you some anxiety and self-searching, you are not alone. During the decade of the 1970s, a quiet revolution has been stirring at the grass roots level of virtually every Western industrial nation. People from all walks of life have been experimenting with alternative ways of living that touch the world more lightly, more gently, more compassionately. In their own unique manner, teachers, factory workers, lawyers, carpenters, farmers, students, and many more have been exploring alternative ways of living. For the most part, their experiments in living have been modest and have not attracted much attention: A city dweller plants his first intensive garden; a suburban family insulates its home, begins to recycle bottles, cans, and paper, and begins to shift its diet away from meat and highly processed foods; a student becomes a member of a consumer-owned food store; a lawyer learns carpentry as an alternative profession; a family decides not to buy a new car or a new television or a new dishwasher; and so on.

The majority of people who are undertaking these diverse and seemingly small experiments in simple living are not so much "purists" as they are "pioneers." They are persons who stand with a foot in two worlds—with one foot in an unraveling industrial civilization and another foot in a newly arising post-industrial civilization. These are the "in-betweeners"—people who are bridging two worlds and making the transition from one dominant way of living to another. Their way of living is an amalgam, a blending of the old and the new into a more workable and meaningful alternative to the deteriorating status quo.

The individual actions of these people may appear to be very modest responses to the serious concerns outlined at the start. Yet, actions such as these (recycling, changing one's diet, lowering one's level of consumption, etc.) represent an important beginning. The character of a whole society is the cumulative result of countless small actions, day in and day out, of millions of persons. Who we are, as a society, is the synergistic accumulation of who we are as individuals. A society cannot move toward greater frugality any farther or any faster than we, as individuals, will support in our own lives.

Small changes are beautiful. Small changes that seem insignificant in isolation can be great contributions when they are simultaneously undertaken by many others. For example, if only a few people intentionally conserve gasoline (or some other precious resource), the effect will be minuscule. However, if a majority of persons were each to intentionally conserve a small amount of gasoline, the aggregate impact would be enormous. As this example suggests, the small decisions of daily life have become an immensely important arena of social action.

Our passage through life is not a neutral process. How we live our lives matters greatly. Each of us makes a difference. Just as boats of various designs leave very different wakes in the water behind them, so too do various approaches to living send out different waves of reverberating influence into the world. The disruptive wake that has been left by nearly two centuries of aggressive industrialization now threatens to swamp Western industrial nations and perhaps even the entire earth. In our highly interdependent, increasingly vulnerable world, the process of daily living has become an important skill for us to learn. We can no longer afford to be oblivious to the impact of our way of living on the rest of the world. The food that we eat, the clothes that we wear, the work that we do, the technologies that we employ, the transportation that we use, the manner in which we relate to others, the "compassionate causes" that we support, the energy systems that we develop, the learning that we acquire, and many more are all vital to the well-being of the totality of life on this planet. Our daily lives are themselves a new frontier. If simplicity of living is integral to this new frontier, then what is the nature of simplicity?

Simplicity of living, if deliberately chosen, implies a compassionate approach to life. It means that we are choosing to live our daily lives with some degree of conscious appreciation of the condition of the rest of the world. I would like to share with you a personal example to illustrate the compassionate intention that underlies the intentional simplification of living.

Some years ago, I attended a conference with a number of leading thinkers who were exploring the notion of a transforming society. Although the meetings were of great interest and many grand pronouncements of the need for large scale social change were made, I remember none of what was said. Yet I do remember having lunch one day with Elise Boulding—a devout Quaker, feminist, sociologist, and compassionate advocate of the need for nonviolent, though fundamental, social change. At the end of the first morning's discussion, we emerged from conference rooms to encounter an enormous buffet heaped with fruits, cheeses, salads, meats, breads, and more. Having worked up a considerable appetite I filled my plate and sat down next to Elise. She had, without comment or display, selected for her lunch an apple, a piece of cheese, and a slice of bread. I was surprised that she had such a modest lunch when such a bountiful offering was available. I asked Elise how she felt, and though she reassured me that she was feeling fine, I was still puzzled. I persisted and directly inquired as to why she had taken such a small helping. In a few quiet sentences she explained that she did not want to eat what others in the world could not have as well. In this seemingly small incident I encountered a practical expression of the compassionate understanding that our individual well-being is inseparable from the well-being of other members of the human family.

It is interesting and instructive that I don't remember any of the ideas from that conference, but that I do recall what Elise had for lunch that day years ago—and why. Many lessons since then have had their roots in this experience: First, seeing that it is the example of each person's life, much more than his or her words, that speaks with power. Even the smallest action done with a loving appreciation of life can profoundly touch other human beings. Second, seeing that it is not so much our thinking about the intimate interconnectedness of the human family that makes a difference, but the actual experiencing of that connectedness that results in our acting to bring our personal lives into greater harmony with the needs of the human family. Third, seeing that all of us carry within ourselves the capacity for sensing appropriate action as we make our way through a complex and confusing world.

This small example illustrates the nature of a consciously chosen simplicity. It is the unpretentious merging of common sense and compassion in the immediate circumstances of daily life. Such an approach to living is enormously relevant to our times. Indeed, the widespread simplification of life is vital to the well-being of the entire human family. Why? Let's look at six compelling reasons.

First, we are running out of crucial nonrenewable resources. For example, we are exhausting the supply of cheaply available petroleum and natural gas. Given the critical importance of these resources for the global economy, common sense suggests that we simplify—that we deliberately conserve these precious resources rather than carelessly squander them through wasteful consumption.

Second, we are polluting ourselves into oblivion with massive discharges of wastes from industrial production. As the land, air, and water become fouled, not only do we disrupt our fragile ecology, we also endanger the genetic basis of life itself. Common sense suggests that we voluntarily simplify our material demands and thereby help to minimize environmental pollution.

Third, each year millions of persons in developing nations are physically and mentally disabled by the effects of prolonged malnutrition and poor health care. The welfare of the human family will best be served by insuring that all people are able to develop into healthy human beings capable of working productively to support themselves. Common sense suggests that the world's resources need to be shared more equitably in order to achieve this highly practical aim. Common sense also suggests that the more affluent peoples of the world intentionally simplify their material wants in order to release more of these desperately needed resources for those peoples who are still struggling to establish relative economic self-reliance.

Fourth, nuclear weapons are proliferating and the threat of atomic warfare over access to scarce resources (such as oil in the Middle East) is growing. Common sense suggests that the level of energy dependency that brings us to the brink of global nuclear war is inappropriate. Common sense also suggests that we moderate our energy demands and move toward greater self-reliance.

Fifth, in Western industrial nations in particular, millions of persons have searched for happiness through the single-minded pursuit of material wealth. Instead of happiness, many have found social alienation and spiritual impoverishment. Something is amiss—our lives are out of balance. We cannot attend to the depth and richness of life when we are largely preoccupied with the pursuit of material wealth and social status. Common sense suggests that if we simplify our lives—reduce the undue clutter and complexity—then it will be easier to find a more satisfying balance between the material and the spiritual aspects of existence.

Sixth, high rates of inflation are exerting unrelenting pressure on the poor and the elderly who live on relatively fixed incomes. In addition, the continuous escalation of prices is eroding away the very underpinnings of society (the integrity of its economic and political processes). Why is this happening? Although the mounting cost of imported oil and ever more costly defense outlays are important contributors to inflation, tangible sources such as these are not the sole cause. Another major source of inflation is our "inflationary psychology" that encourages a widespread, high-demand, live-for-today attitude. Instead of investing in the future, we are adopting a "buy now before prices get higher" attitude. Consequently, we tend to buy things before they are needed, replace old things before they are worn out, and buy other things in larger quantities than we normally would. This consumer psychology tends to be self-fulfilling and self-perpetuating. Common sense suggests that we need to consciously adopt an alternative approach—a conservation psychology—that will help to moderate inflationary pressures. If middle- and upper-income groups that have the most discretionary income were to consciously choose to live more frugally, it would have the greatest impact on the basic necessities of life: food, housing, energy, health care, clothing, and so on. These are the exact areas where prices are now escalating most rapidly and that impact upon the poor and the elderly most severely. Thus, simplicity of living fosters both a consumer psychology and a consumer behavior that respond constructively to some of the most important root causes of inflation.

What we see, then, is that there are many common sense reasons for choosing a life of greater simplicity: in response to the needs of impoverished millions in developing nations; in response to the needs of future generations who will inherit a wasteland if present growth trends continue; in response to the needs of our deteriorating global ecology on which we all depend; in response to our own needs for a satisfying and balanced existence; in response to the needs for a peaceful global society; and many more. None of these reasons are unfamiliar. We encounter evidence of these pushes toward greater simplicity virtually every day of our lives.

Although the conscious simplification of life has great relevance for our times, this orientation in living is not a new social invention. For more than 2,000 years the founders of the world's major spiritual traditions have taught that we are misdirecting our lives if we make the pursuit of material wealth and social status our overriding goal. Jesus urged us to "not store up treasures on earth" but, with a spirit of love, to share our wealth and our lives with others. Buddha urged us to consciously choose a balanced path through life—a middle way between the extremes of deprivation and indulgence. Other great teachers—Confucius, Lao-tzu, Mohammed, and many more—also taught the value of simplicity, clarity, unpretentiousness, and balance between the inner and the outer aspects of our lives.

In more recent times, the value of simplicity has been illustrated in the legendary self-reliance and frugality of the Puritans, in Thoreau's naturalistic vision at Walden Pond, in Emerson's spiritual and practical plea for "plain living and high thinking," and in the teachings of Gandhi, the spiritual and political leader of India's revolution of independence. Gandhi felt that true civilization consisted not in the multiplication of human wants, but in the voluntary simplification of these wants. The moderation of our wants increases our capacity to be of service to others, and in our being of loving service to others, true civilization emerges.

Simplicity of living has even more modern roots in the so-called "counterculture" movement that burst into prominence in the United States and in other Western nations in the 1960s. The counterculture was an eclectic assortment of people and causes held together by a "new consciousness" (which was not really a "new" consciousness but a very old consciousness re-emerging in a new social and technological setting). This is the consciousness spoken of, in one way or another, by Jesus, Buddha, Gandhi, and others. Pioneers of the new consciousness affirmed the dignity of the person and the preciousness of life. They also affirmed a commitment to both personal and social change and sought to combine them into a coherent way of living. In turn, many compassionate causes—from environmental activism to the civil rights movement to feminism to antinuclear activism, and many more—were embraced by these forerunners of a new culture.

During the 1960s the values of this pioneering culture had a considerable impact on national attitudes toward the environment, consumption, human equality, and global relations. However, by the early 1970s, it was clear that sweeping social changes were not going to materialize. An expansive period had passed. The United States was absorbed by the agony of Vietnam and Watergate, the culture was deeply polarized, a whole generation's trust in leadership had virtually collapsed, and the sense of national integrity and purpose had been shaken to the core. Not surprisingly, the national mood turned inward. People wanted to restore some semblance of "normalcy" to their lives after a decade of wrenching change.

For the millions of persons who had to varying degrees opened to the "new consciousness," the 1970s were a challenging time of finding a new integration and balance between the old and the new cultures. For the more persistent among this pioneering culture, the agenda shifted from transforming society to finding new ways of living that were practical and useful expressions of the new consciousness. Public activism gave way to exploring new ways of living at the grass roots level of society. Instead of continuing the seemingly fruitless struggle to change dominant institutions, many among this forerunner group began to concentrate on their immediate lives—the domain where they had genuine control and could make a visible, if seemingly small, difference. At the local level, countless small experiments in living began to flourish.

For many reasons, simplicity of living was integral to these experiments in new ways of living. Simplicity was a way to increase personal autonomy—by consuming less a person could lessen his or her dependency on a dehumanizing economy. Simplicity was also viewed as a way to help conserve resources and protect the environment from undue pollution. Not surprisingly, then, many of the labels used to describe these experiments in new ways of living reflect the role of simplicity; for example: "the frugality phenomenon," "ecological life-styles," "conspicuous conservation," the "conserver society," "creative simplicity," "simple living," and others.[1]

Although the decade of the 1970s also saw the beginnings of public debate on notions such as "limits to growth," "soft energy paths," "small is beautiful," and the "human potentials movement," the grass roots experiments in simplified living went largely unnoticed. This lack of cultural attention to innovations in living is understandable. The larger society was far too preoccupied coping with proliferating problems to pay much attention to the small (and seemingly inconsequential) experiments in living that were quietly blossoming within the cracks and crevices of society. Without mass protests or major media events to mark its progress, the growth of simplicity of living could unfold virtually unnoticed. Acts done skillfully and cleanly cause little stir or notice. The squeaky wheel gets the grease of public attention. Where people are learning to take responsibility for making their lives contribute to the workability and meaningfulness of the whole, there is no need for fanfare to announce their small, but cumulatively significant, actions.

As we move into the decade of the 1980s, I think it unlikely that this practical revolution in living will remain hidden at the grass roots level of societies. Although the number of persons actively experimenting with a life of conscious simplicity is small (probably less than 10 percent of the adult population in the United States as of 1980), there are immensely powerful forces at work that seem destined to bring this way of living into the awareness of the larger society. Simplicity of living is being driven both by the push of necessity (the need to find more sustainable ways to live), and by the pull of opportunity (the realistic possibility of finding more satisfying ways to live).

This emerging way of life is being pushed also by a powerful demographic wave. In the 1960s the baby-boom generation was beginning to pass through its college years; by the 1980s this generation will begin to mature into middle age and will occupy positions of authority and power. The so-called counterculture of the 1960s thus moves to the position of a subculture in the 1970s, and then offers the potential, at least, of becoming the dominant cultural orientation in the decade of the 1980s and beyond. I do not view this as a turning away from the industrial era but as a creative attempt to begin the process of moving beyond it. Rather than an attempt to turn back the clock to retrieve the past, this orientation in living implies using all of our skills, ingenuity, and compassion to move into the future constructively.

For many reasons, then, I think the many scattered experiments in living that blossomed during the 1970s will begin to coalesce into a coherent, alternative way of life in the 1980s.

What are we to call this alternative way of living? We have seen that it embraces both inner and outer dimensions of life, and that it has roots in ancient spiritual traditions as well as in modern social change movements. What phrase might suitably or appropriately characterize this way of living? As a researcher exploring the nature of social change, I puzzled over that issue for nearly five years before I encountered in 1974 a short article entitled "Voluntary Simplicity," written by a man named Richard Gregg. Although the article had been written decades earlier (1936), it seemed highly relevant to our times. Why? The way of living Gregg described intended the integration of both inner and outer aspects of life, it affirmed the role of simplicity, and it was written by a man whose learning drew deeply from both Eastern and Western cultures (Gregg had been a student at Harvard and had lived in India as a student of Gandhi). Here is a portion of what Gregg said concerning voluntary simplicity:

> Voluntary simplicity involves both inner and outer condition. It means singleness of purpose, sincerity and honesty within, as well as avoidance of exterior clutter, of many possessions irrelevant to the chief purpose of life. It means an ordering and guiding of our energy and our desires, a partial restraint in some directions in order to secure greater abundance of life in other directions. It involves a deliberate organization of life for a purpose.[2]

I am immensely grateful to the late Richard Gregg for providing a phrase that seems to evoke the most essential qualities of this emerging way of life. At the same time, I feel no special attachment to the phrase, nor do I feel that it has any special virtue —it is merely a label and a somewhat awkward label at that. The phrase "voluntary simplicity" is useful, I think, because it contains within it a seed description of this way of living. To explain, let's look at it one word at a time.

First, what does it mean to live more "voluntarily"? To live more voluntarily means to live more deliberately, intentionally, purposefully. To bring these qualities into our lives we must live more consciously (thus, there is an intimate connection between the new consciousness and living more voluntarily). We cannot be deliberate when we are distracted from our critical life circumstances. We cannot be intentional when we are not paying attention. We cannot be purposeful when we are not being present. Therefore, crucial to acting in a voluntary manner is being aware of ourselves as we move through life. This requires that we not only pay attention to the actions we take in the world "out there" (the outer world), but also that we pay attention to the person acting "in here" (the inner world). To the extent that we do not notice both inner and outer aspects of our passage through life, then our capacity for voluntary, deliberate, intentional, purposeful action will be commensurately diminished. In earlier times, when our actions had a limited impact upon the world, our conscious attention to ourselves (and those actions) could remain a spiritual luxury for the few. Now, however, as our actions have reverberations of global dimension, the capacity for conscious action has become a social necessity for the many.

Second, what does it mean to live more "simply"? To consciously bring greater simplicity into our lives does not mean that we must live in a primitive or rudimentary manner. Voluntary simplicity is an aesthetic simplicity because it is consciously chosen. Few people will choose deliberately to make their lives ugly when they instead can choose to bring a functional beauty and integrity into their lives. Yet, how we simplify is a very personal affair. We all know where our lives are unnecessarily complicated. We are all painfully aware of the distractions, clutter, and pretense that weigh upon our lives and make our passage through the world more cumbersome and awkward. To live with simplicity is to unburden our lives—to live more lightly, cleanly, aerodynamically. It means establishing a more direct, unpretentious, and unencumbered relationship with all aspects of our lives: consuming, working, learning, relating, and so on. Simplicity of living means meeting life face to face. It means confronting life clearly, without unnecessary distractions, without trying to soften the awesomeness of our existence or mask the deeper magnificence of life with pretentious, distracting, and unnecessary accumulations. It means being direct and honest in relationships of all kinds. It means taking life as it is—straight and unadulterated.

When we combine all these ideas, we can see there are many possible ways to define "voluntary simplicity." Here is a sampling of definitions of voluntary simplicity that strike a resonant chord within me: a manner of living that is outwardly more simple and inwardly more rich; an integrative way of living that balances both inner and outer aspects of our lives; a deliberate choice to live with less in the belief that more of life will be returned to us in the process; a path toward consciously learning the skills that enable us to touch the world ever more lightly and gently; a way of being in which our most authentic and alive self is brought into direct and conscious contact with every aspect of living (working, relating, consuming, etc.); a way of living that accepts the responsibility for developing our human potentials, as well as for contributing to the well-being of the world of which we are an inseparable part; a paring back of the superficial aspects of our lives so as to allow more time and energy to develop the heartfelt aspects of our lives. Clearly, there are many different ways to define the notion of "voluntary simplicity." We are free to discover and create definitions of our own.

This way of life is not a static condition to be achieved, but an ever changing balance that must be continuously and consciously made real. Voluntary simplicity in this sense is not simple. To integrate and maintain a skillful balance between the inner and outer aspects of our lives is an enormously challenging and continuously changing process.

Since one of the principal qualities of voluntary simplicity is that of an unfolding balance between the inner and outer aspects of our lives, it is impossible to define it by pointing to any particular extreme (such as necessarily living in poverty or a rural setting). The intention of this way of life is not to dogmatically live with less. It is a more demanding intention of living with balance. This is a middle way that moves between the extremes of poverty and indulgence. Simplicity, then, should not be equated with poverty.

Poverty is involuntary whereas simplicity is consciously chosen. Poverty is repressive; simplicity is liberating. Poverty generates a sense of helplessness, passivity, and despair; simplicity fosters personal empowerment, creativity, and a sense of ever present opportunity. Poverty is mean and degrading to the human spirit; simplicity has both beauty and a functional integrity that elevate our lives. Poverty is debilitating; simplicity is enabling.

Are there more visible or concrete expressions of voluntary simplicity that clarify what living in this manner means? There are; however, it is important to remember that the phrase "voluntary simplicity" refers to a way of experiencing the integration and balance of the inner and outer aspects of life. And it is from this direct experiencing that there arise the worldly behaviors and attitudes characteristic of this intention in living. As we turn to look at the worldly expressions of this way of life, it is important to not forget the deeper roots in human experience from which these expressions originate. Recognizing this, let's examine a sampling of the worldly behaviors that tend to accompany this way of life. People who intentionally simplify their lives:

- tend to lower their overall level of personal consumption —buy less clothing (pay more attention to what is functional, durable, aesthetic, and less to passing fads and seasonal styles); buy less jewelry and other forms of personal ornamentation; buy fewer cosmetic products, particularly those designed to mask one's physical appearance; observe holidays in a non-commercialized and loving manner;

- tend to alter their patterns of consumption in favor of products that are durable, easy to repair, nonpolluting in their manufacture and use, energy-efficient, functional, aesthetic;

- tend to shift their diet away from highly processed foods, meat, and sugar and toward foods that are more natural, healthy, simple, and appropriate for sustaining the inhabitants of a small planet;

• tend to reduce undue clutter and complexity in their personal lives by giving away or selling those possessions that are used seldom and could be used productively by others (for example, clothing, books, furniture, appliances, tools, etc.);

• tend to use their consumption politically by boycotting goods and services of firms whose actions and policies are considered unethical;

• tend to participate in the recycling of metal, glass, and paper as well as to cut back on consumption of items that are wasteful of nonrenewable resources;

• tend to participate in consumer- and/or worker-owned enterprises (cooperatives) that meet needs ranging from food, clothing, child care, repair shops, bookstores, and others;

• tend to pursue "contributory livelihood" or work that directly contributes to the well-being of the world and simultaneously allows one to more fully use his or her creative capacities in making that contribution;

• tend to develop personal skills that contribute to greater self-reliance and thereby reduce dependence upon experts to handle life's ordinary demands (for example, skills such as carpentry, plumbing, appliance repair, intensive gardening, various crafts, and others);

• tend to prefer smaller scale, more human-sized living and working environments that foster a sense of community, face-to-face contact, and mutual caring;

• tend to alter male/female roles in favor of nonsexist patterns of relationship;

• tend to be more open to nonverbal forms of communication: greater body contact, greater eye contact, more space in communication for periods of silence;

• tend to participate in, and find support from, extended families of both biological and spiritual dimensions;

• tend to work on developing the full spectrum of their potentials: physical (for example, running and yoga), emotional (learning the skills of intimacy and sharing with others), mental (developing both sides of the brain—both rational and intuitive faculties), and spiritual (allowing the totality of one's life experience to become a meditation);

• tend to participate in holistic health-care practices that emphasize preventive medicine, the healing powers of the body when assisted by the mind, and health as more than the absence of disease;

• tend to involve themselves with "compassionate causes"— such as ending world hunger, promoting global nuclear disarmament, protecting the environment, promoting a moratorium on the killing of whales and other endangered species —and employ compassionate means (nonviolence) in the realization of those causes;

• tend to change their pattern of transportation in favor of taking public transit, participating in a car pool, driving smaller cars, living closer to work, riding a bike, or walking;

• tend to employ appropriate technologies wherever possible —this can range from a preference for using solar power instead of nuclear to using simple, resource-efficient devices rather than complex, resource-wasteful devices (for example, a regular knife instead of an electric one, an ordinary toothbrush instead of an electric one, and so on);

• tend to question the appropriateness of traditional public education in a rapidly and radically changing world, and to participate in alternative schools.

The range and diversity of even this partial list of changes that tend to accompany a life of conscious simplicity make it clear that no simple formula can define its worldly expression. Given human diversity, there can be no single, "right and true way" to live more voluntarily and simply. Every person has his or her own unique manner of expressing this way of living. As persons and their surrounding life circumstances change, the worldly expressions will also change. This selectivity and diversity is central. Gregg, for example, was insistent that the nature, manner, and degree of simplification was something that each person should decide for himself or herself: "Simplicity is a relative matter depending on climate, customs, culture, and the character of the individual." [3]

Still, in the popular imagination it is difficult to dispel the romantic image of Thoreau's cabin in the woods. As a consequence, when the notion of voluntary simplicity is first encountered, there is a tendency to imagine a hardy person or couple who have turned away from material progress, moved to a rural setting, and chosen a life of isolated and austere self-sufficiency. Although this romanticized image may be easily grasped, it does not paint an accurate picture of voluntary simplicity. Why?

First, the deliberate simplification of our lives should not be equated with turning away from progress. To the contrary, simplicity is crucial to progress, for without simplicity we will be overwhelmed by massive social and material complexity. To simplify is to bring order, clarity, and purpose into our lives. These qualities are not opposed to progress; rather, they are crucial foundations for progress. Voluntary simplicity, then, is not a path of "no growth" but a path of "new growth" (growth that includes both a material and a spiritual, or interior, dimension). Furthermore, simplicity of living has immediate relevance for aging industrial economies such as that of the United States: In consuming fewer nonessentials, we release the investment capital necessary to rebuild our faltering economies in ways that are more appropriate to our radically changing circumstances.

Second, simplicity should not be equated with isolation and

withdrawal from the world. To the contrary, a majority of those choosing to simplify their lives are not trying to drop out and go it alone; rather, they are seeking the support and participation of other people. Instead of withdrawing from the world, most people are busy building their personal network of friends, extended family, work associates, and others who share a similar intention.

Third, a life of greater simplicity should not be equated with living in a rural setting. Instead of a "back to the land" movement, it is more accurate to describe voluntary simplicity as a "make the most of wherever we are" movement. A majority of those choosing to simplify their lives do not live in the backwoods or small rural towns; they live in the bigger cities and suburbs.

Just as there is no "cookbook" approach that can narrowly define the outer expressions of voluntary simplicity, so too with its inner dimension. Yet, there are patterns of attitudes that seem characteristic of many who adopt this way of life. A sampling of these attitudinal changes is shown in the table on pages 39–40.[4] To place them in perspective, they are shown side by side with contrasting attitudes characteristic of the industrial era. This table reveals that voluntary simplicity is not a variation on the industrial era theme, but a new and coherent pattern of attitudes and values that move beyond the industrial era.

The emergence of this way of life could foreshadow a change even greater than the shift that occurred in the transition from the Middle Ages to the industrial era. Every aspect of life would be touched: consumption patterns, living and working environments, political attitudes, organizational forms, international relations, environmental policies, education, the uses of the mass media, and many more.

We have made a brief journey into exploring the way of voluntary simplicity. In our making this journey the question naturally arises: "How does all this affect each of us?" Even though simplicity of living may be a rational response to our

CONTRASTS BETWEEN INDUSTRIAL WORLD VIEW AND WORLD VIEW OF VOLUNTARY SIMPLICITY

INDUSTRIAL ERA VIEW	VOLUNTARY SIMPLICITY VIEW
• The overriding goal in life is material progress.	• The central intention in life is that of evolving both the material and spiritual aspects of life with harmony and balance.
• Much emphasis is placed on conspicuous consumption; the "good life" is dependent upon having enough money to buy access to life's pleasures and to avoid life's discomforts.	• Much emphasis is placed on conservation and frugality— using only as much as is needed. A satisfying life arises with balanced growth in cooperation with others.
• Identity is defined by material possessions and social position; identity is thought to be either static or only slowly changing.	• Identity is revealed in the process of living; identity is experienced as fluid, being born anew in each moment.
• The individual is defined by his or her body and is ultimately separate and alone.	• The individual is experienced as both a unique *and* an inseparable part of the larger universe; who "we" are is not limited to our physical existence.

• The universe is viewed as material and largely lifeless; it is proper for us, the living, to exploit the lifeless universe for our own ends.

• The universe is experienced as a vast living organism; it is appropriate to act in ways that honor the preciousness and integrity of all life.

• Much emphasis is placed on self-serving behavior (get as much for myself as I can while giving no more than is required in return).

• Much emphasis is placed on life-serving behavior (give as much of myself to life as I am able and ask in return no more than I require).

• "Cutthroat competition" prevails; compete against others; strive to "make a killing."

• "Fair competition" prevails; cooperate with others; intend to earn a living.

• There is a "lifeboat ethic" in global relations.

• There is a "spaceship earth ethic" in global relations.

• The welfare of the whole is left to the workings of the "free" market and/or federal bureaucracy.

• Each person takes responsibility for the well-being of the whole and directly participates in promoting the overall welfare.

• There is a high level of dependency upon experts and specialists.

• Much emphasis is placed on becoming more self-reliant and self-governing.

• Much emphasis is on autonomy and mobility.

• Much emphasis is on connectedness and community.

pressing circumstances, we hesitate to act. We find it difficult to overcome our inertia. We feel anxious or threatened or depressed or fearful when we consider how our lives might be altered by consciously embracing the intention of simplicity. We hope that our problems are temporary or that a technological solution that does not disturb the status quo will soon be found. Yet, the problems of widespread starvation, nuclear proliferation, environmental deterioration, resource depletion, overwhelming bureaucratic complexity, and many more are not destined to go away soon. The human family is in the grip of a whole pattern of forces that will, within a few short decades, either devastate or else fundamentally transform the nature of life on this planet. The outcome will depend to a considerable extent on whether we in the wealthier nations of the West are willing to consciously simplify our lives. If we are willing to simplify, then who is in charge of this process? Who is responsible for seeing that this time of civilizational transition is skillfully negotiated?

Just as we tend to wait for our problems to solve themselves, so too do we tend to wait for our traditional institutions and leaders to provide us with guidance as to what we should do. Yet, our leaders are bogged down, trying to cope with our faltering institutions. They are so enmeshed in crisis management that they have no time to exercise genuinely creative leadership. We may keep waiting for someone else. The message of this book is that *there is no one else. You are it. We are it.* Each of us is responsible. It is we who, one by one, must take charge of our lives. It is we who, one by one, must act to restore the balance. We are the persons who are going to have to work through this time of enormous civilizational challenge.

We are empowered to respond creatively to this time of historic transition when we know that we are not working or learning alone. In the following chapter we will see—in the living example of many persons from all walks of life—that there do exist workable and satisfying responses to our difficult times.

SECTION I

PEOPLE

CHAPTER 2

LIVING ON THE NEW FRONTIER

What is it like to live more voluntarily and simply? What are the politics of this way of life? What satisfactions and dissatisfactions accompany this way of living? We can learn about these and other concerns by turning to the firsthand experiences of hundreds of persons who have actively been involved with a life of conscious simplicity. First, some background is necessary to describe the grass roots survey from which these descriptions of personal experience were derived.

While working as a social scientist and "futurist" at the Stanford Research Institute in the mid-1970s, I did a great deal of research on grass roots experiments in more ecologically sound ways of living. In an era of growing resource limits, environmental deterioration, and spiritual malaise, this seemed an important area of personal and social inquiry. Hoping to learn more about this emerging way of life as well as to share our personal learning and research, Arnold Mitchell (a former colleague) and I published an article describing our understanding of the notion of voluntary simplicity in the summer, 1977, issue of the *Co-Evolution Quarterly*[1] (this journal is the successor to the *Whole Earth Catalog* and its readership includes many who consciously have been exploring this way of life for a number of years). Here was an opportunity to speak directly to, and hear directly from, some of the pioneers of a new way of life.

Consequently, we included a questionnaire in our article on voluntary simplicity (shown in Appendix II).

In the year and a half after this article was published, more than 420 questionnaires and over 200 letters (totaling more than 1,000 pages) were received. This was much more than a statistical survey in which percentages were the final concern. Nearly every letter offered a short, yet revealingly honest, journey into the lives of an individual or a family. Many were inspiring and empowering. Some were light and humorous. A few were despairing. Overall, it was an enormous gift to be allowed to learn through their personal experiences about the worldly expression of voluntary simplicity. I read each of the letters at least four times and the qualities that continued to come through were those of humanness, humor, compassion, and courage. These letters truly represented a celebration of both unity and diversity.

This grass roots survey was not intended to be a random sampling of national attitudes toward voluntary simplicity. Its purpose was to provide an opportunity to learn from persons already involved with this way of life. Other surveys will surely reveal different emphases concerning what is meant by voluntary simplicity. Nonetheless, the general pattern of findings drawn here has an integrity and coherence that is derived from the collective experience and insight of many hundreds of persons from all walks of life. This survey allows us, I think, to draw useful conclusions regarding this approach to living. Here, then, is some useful background information about the respondents:

- The people who responded came from all walks of life and included lawyers, teachers, social workers, students, government bureaucrats, firemen, carpenters, factory workers, retired couples, white-collar workers, and more.

- Responses were received from forty-two states in the United States as well as from several European countries, Canada, and Australia.

• People from a broad age spectrum (from seventeen to sixty-seven) responded to the survey. The age of the average respondent was approximately thirty years, and 75 percent were under the age of thirty-five. This reveals that the respondents were younger than the national average and were drawn disproportionately from the "baby boom" generation of the post-World War II era.

• Nearly all respondents were white.

• Not surprisingly, overall income levels tended to be somewhat lower than that of the general U.S. population. However, single individuals had income patterns closer to national averages whereas families had a markedly lower income relative to the national norm. More than two thirds of the respondents had incomes under $12,000 a year (although high rates of inflation make such figures less of a meaningful guide).

• Most were highly educated—roughly 70 percent had completed college.

• A majority (56 percent) lived in cities and suburbs, somewhat less than a third (32 percent) lived in rural areas, and 13 percent lived in smaller towns.

• Most grew up in relatively affluent homes (71 percent indicated a middle-class economic background and 22 percent an upper-class background).

• A conservative estimate of the length of time the average person had been living in this manner was six years as of 1977.

From just this much information we can draw some important insights regarding voluntary simplicity. First, the wide geographic distribution of responses indicates that this way of life is not a regional phenomenon but includes persons throughout the United States and other Western nations. Second, the fact that a majority of persons lived in urban environments indicates that this is not a predominantly "back to the farm" movement. Third, the fact that virtually all who responded were white and had childhood backgrounds of relative affluence indicates that the early adopters, or innovators, are not likely to come from those groups that are heavily discriminated against (those whose childhood experience has been that of poverty are much less likely to become forerunners in choosing a way of life that they may perceive to be a perpetuation of that poverty). Fourth, the fact that these respondents earned a moderately wide range of income suggests that within limits, the manner in which one's income is used is as important as the size of income earned. Fifth, the relatively high levels of education of this forerunner group indicates they are not unskilled and poorly educated dropouts from society but well-educated and skilled persons who are searching for alternative ways of living and working that are more sustainable and satisfying. Sixth, the fact that the average length of time persons had been involved with this way of living was six years (as of the time of the survey) makes it unlikely that we are examining a short-lived life-style fad.

With this as background, let's turn to explore the first-person accounts of voluntary simplicity. A representative sampling of comments across a broad range of issues has been drawn from over 100 of the more than 200 letters received. In order to insure the privacy of these individuals and yet reveal some of the flavor of their lives, each quotation is identified by the person's sex, age, marital status, degree of urbanization of residence, and geographic locale.

What Is Voluntary Simplicity?

In the first chapter we explored various definitions of voluntary simplicity. A common thread among these definitions was the importance of integrating both inner and outer aspects of our lives into a more workable and meaningful approach to living. Now let's turn to a group that is practicing what it preaches and see how they define this way of life for themselves:

Voluntary simplicity has more to do with the state of mind than a person's physical surroundings and possessions.
(woman, twenty-three, single, small town, east)

Simplicity meant I fit easier into the more ecological patterns, hence was more flexible, more adaptable, and ultimately more aware of the natural spiritual path before me; less nonsense in the way.
(man, thirty, single, small town, west)

As my spiritual growth expanded and developed, voluntary simplicity was a natural outgrowth. I came to realize the cost of material accumulation was too high and offered fewer and fewer real rewards, psychological and spiritual.
(man, twenty-six, single, small town, south)

I don't think of it as voluntary simplicity. I am simply going through a process of self-knowledge and self-realization, attempting to better the world for myself, my children, my grandchildren, etc.
(woman, thirty-eight, married, suburb, east)

. . . to me, voluntary simplicity means integration and awareness in my life.
(woman, twenty-seven, single, city, south)

In realizing true identity (a continuing process), voluntary simplicity naturally follows.
(man, age unspecified, living together, small town, west)

Ecological consciousness is a corollary of human consciousness. If you do not respect the human rights of other people, you cannot respect the Earth. The desires for material simplicity and a human-scale environment are results of an ecological consciousness.
(man, twenty-six, single, small town, west)

> I can't call us living simply but rather living creatively and openly . . .
> (man, thirty-one, married, rural, west)

> Voluntary simplicity is not poverty, but searching for a new definition of quality—and buying only what is productively used.
> (man, twenty-eight, married, rural, west)

> We laugh that we are considered a "poverty" family as we consider our lives to be rich and full and completely rewarding—we are living in harmony with everything. I know for myself the source of "richness" or "poverty" comes from within me . . .
> (woman, forty-one, married, rural, west)

Clearly, each person has his or her own unique description of the nature of voluntary simplicity. At the same time there is a strong thread of shared common sense that runs through these various definitions. This diversity is important, as many said they were wary of any narrow definition of voluntary simplicity. Some felt that a rigid definition would be dogmatically applied and would promote a self-righteous, simpler-than-thou attitude.

Another concern expressed in the letters was that voluntary simplicity—as a fundamental change in *way* of life—would be trivialized by the mass media and portrayed as a faddish and superficial change in outward *style* of life only. Here are two illustrative comments:

> This is a country of media hype and VS is good copy. The media is likely to pick up on VS terminology and create a movement. I hope they won't. The changes we're talking about are fundamental and take lots of time . . . If it is made into a movement it could burn itself out. I hope it spreads slowly. This way the changes will be more pervasive. Voluntary simplicity is the kind of thing that people need to discover for themselves.
> (man, twenty-seven, single, rural, midwest)

Make a movement out of a spontaneous tendency like voluntary simplicity and the best aspects of it (and the individuals) will elude you.

(woman, thirty, living together, rural, west)

Many of the persons who began to experiment with simplicity of living during the early part of the 1970s said they did not view themselves as part of a social movement—at least not in the traditional sense of that term. At that time, there was no broadly based consensus that established simplicity of living as a social movement per se. Instead, people said, they were acting mostly on their own to bring their lives into a more harmonious balance with the needs of the world. As they found others who shared this perception and intention, there naturally arose a sense of social cohesion. The grass roots birth of voluntary simplicity thus seems more a spontaneous alignment of many individuals who, in a great variety of seemingly independent actions, were harmoniously expressing a shared intention. Overall, then, it seems more accurate to characterize the historical growth of voluntary simplicity as a natural alignment of many independent persons rather than as a conscious social movement.

Why Choose Voluntary Simplicity?

Why would an individual or couple adopt a way of life that is more materially frugal, ecologically oriented, inner directed, and in other ways removed from the traditional ways of life of Western society? Here is a sampling of the reasons given:

I believe in the imminent need for the skills and resources I am developing now. I am not sure how it will come about, whether economic collapse, fuel exhaustion, or natural disaster, but whichever it is, I will need (and my family) all

of whatever self-sufficiency I or we can develop.
(man, twenty-nine, married, rural, west)

I believe voluntary simplicity is more compassionate and
conducive to personal and spiritual growth. I live this way
because I am appalled that half the planet lives in dire
poverty while we overconsume. And people think they are
"Christian." I think it is "spiritual" to make sure that everyone has adequate food, shelter, and clothing and take
care of the planet.
(woman, twenty-five, married, big city, midwest)

I sincerely believe that voluntary simplicity is essential to
the solution of global problems of environmental pollution,
resource scarcity, socioeconomic inequities and existential/
spiritual problems of alienation, anxiety, and lack of meaningful life-styles.
(man, thirty-two, married, suburb, south)

I have less and less to blame on other people. I am more
self-reliant. I can both revel in the independence and be
frustrated by my shortcomings—but I get to learn from
my own mistakes. Each step is progress in independence;
freedom is the goal.
(man, twenty-six, married, small town, east)

The main motivation for me is inner spiritual growth and
to give my children an idea of the truly valuable and higher
things in this world.
(woman, thirty-eight, single, small town, east)

I feel more voluntary about my pleasures and pains than
the average American who has his needs dictated by Madi-
son Ave. (my projection of course). I feel sustained, ex-
cited, and constantly growing in my spiritual and intellectual
pursuits.
(woman, thirty, living together, rural, west)

Why VS? I see it as the only moral, economic, rational, humanistic goal. Besides, it's fun.
(man, twenty-three, single, small city, midwest)

It was the injustice and not the lack of luxury during the Great Depression that disturbed me. I took up this way of life when I was seventeen. I remember choosing this simplicity—not poverty—because: 1) it seemed more just in the face of deprivation—better distribution of goods, 2) more honest—why take or have more than one needs? 3) much freer—why burden oneself with getting and caring for just "things" when time and energy could be spent in so many other more interesting and higher pursuits? 4) but I wanted a simplicity that would include beauty and creativity—art, music, literature, an aesthetic environment —but simply.
(woman, sixty, married, suburb, west)

Our interest in VS dates to overseas tours with the U.S. embassy in underdeveloped nations—we know firsthand what the problems are.
(woman, sixty-one, married, suburb, east)

I felt the values involved in consumerism to be false, useless, and destructive. I prefer to appear as I am. People are complex enough to understand without excess trappings. I was also influenced by the values of the feminist and ecological movements.
(woman, twenty-five, married, suburb, south)

Increasing my self-sufficiency seemed the only honest way to effectively make my feelings, actions, and life congruent.
(man, twenty-seven, married, rural, east)

It is a highly rewarding way to live. It forces you into a relationship with a basic reality . . . It also forces you to deal with some direct anxieties and rely on and be thankful to a benevolent deity. It succinctly points out your

frailty and clearly delineates your dependencies. It also reinforces your strength and independence.

(married couple, thirty-seven and thirty-two, rural, west)

I wanted to remove my children from the superficial, competitive (east coast) value system. Wanted a family venture to draw us closer and a community that was stable.
Also wanted to provide the children with a learning experience that exposes them to alternatives to the "rat race"
system, plus I wanted out from the typical pressures of
maintaining material acquisitions that were meaningless to
me.

(woman, thirty-six, single, rural, west)

Overall, the most common reasons given for choosing to live
more lightly were to find a more skillful balance between one's
inner experience and its outer expression in work, consumption,
relationship, community, etc.; to search for a workable and
meaningful alternative to the emptiness of a society obsessed
with material consumption and display; to provide one's children with more humane value systems and life experiences that
are appropriate to the emerging world they will have to live in;
to find a much higher degree of independence and self-determination in a mass society of alienating scale and complexity;
to establish more cooperative and caring bases for human relationships; to acknowledge and, in small but personally meaningful ways, begin to reduce the vast inequities between rich and
poor persons around the world; to cope in a personal manner
with environmental pollution and resource scarcity; to foster
nonsexist ways of relating; to develop the personal skills and
know-how to survive a time of severe economic and social disruption; and to create the personal circumstances of life in which
one's feelings, thoughts, and actions can come into alignment.
Importantly, in reviewing these motivations for choosing a path
of deliberate simplicity, we see that people are not simply pro-
testing a set of conditions; they are busy in the process of sup-

porting themselves, learning about viable alternatives, and then expressing those alternatives in the context of their daily lives.

The Path to Voluntary Simplicity

What is the pathway from the industrial era way of life to voluntary simplicity? Is this way of life chosen abruptly or does it evolve gradually? Here is a sample of comments:

> . . . we are moving toward a life of greater simplicity from within and the external changes are following—perhaps more slowly. We are seeking quality of life—and a path with heart.
> (woman, age unspecified, married, suburb, west)

> Voluntary simplicity must evolve over a lifetime according to the needs of an individual . . . the person must grow and be open to new ideas—not jump on a bandwagon, but thoughtfully consider ideas and see how they relate to themselves . . .
> (woman, twenty-one, single, small city, midwest)

> [Voluntary simplicity is] a thorough life-style that only works through full commitment and takes many years to grow into.
> (man, twenty-nine, married, small town, west)

> VS began unfolding in my life as a process. It was an inarticulate but seemingly sensible response to emerging situations—and one response after another began to form a pattern, which you identify as voluntary simplicity. VS for me was the result of a growing awareness plus a sense of social responsibility.
> (man, thirty-one, married, small town, west)

> To me, VS as a life-style is not something you take up in one moment, but occurs over a period of time due to: 1) consciousness raising; 2) peer group support; 3) back-

ground; 4) inner-growth interest, and many other factors —my wholehearted commitment to a certain spiritual path finds outer expression in a simple, gentle, humane life-style.
(woman, twenty-eight, single, suburb, west)

It wasn't a slam-bang, bolt-from-the-blue, overnight change. I'm still growing and learning. The most important goal I have is inner development with a good blend of living with the here and now on this planet.
(man, twenty-five, married, small town, east)

I consciously started to live simply when I started to become conscious . . . Living simply is in the flow of things for me.
(man, thirty, married, rural, east)

My ideas and my practice of voluntary simplicity have been and I hope will continue to be a gradual process of evolution and growth. From early adolescence on I tended to prefer simplicity . . .
(woman, twenty-one, single, small city, midwest)

Various flirtations with yoga, meditation, drugs, and radical politics gave me exposure and some personal experience with "inner growth" possibilities. I began living my life freely, following no preconceived roles, and gradually discovered my overriding interest in quality: the environment, life, the universe.
(man, twenty-nine, married, small town, east)

I became interested in VS . . . primarily because of ecological concerns. However, since then my interest has become concentrated more on metaphysics, self-realization, etc., with the same end results.
(woman, thirty-eight, married, big city, midwest)

Voluntary simplicity is an individual thing . . . it has to be something that springs from the heart because it was always there, not something you can be talked in to by

persuasive people, or something that is brought on by financial necessity. . . . This is not something we do because we want to be different, or because we're rebellious to convention, but because our souls find a need for it.
(woman, thirty, married, big city, Canada)

Overall, the journey into this way of life seems to be a relatively slow, evolutionary process—one that unfolds gradually over a period of months and years. The initial stages of this living experiment are a time of exploring and testing; a time of moving back and forth between traditional and innovative patterns of living and consuming. Gradually, a person or family may find they have made a number of small changes and acquired a number of slightly different patterns of perception and behavior, the sum total of which adds up to a significant departure from the industrial era way of life. One conclusion that I draw from these letters is that if change is too abrupt, it may not have the staying power to last. It seems better to move slowly and maintain a depth of commitment that can be sustained over the long haul.

The letters also revealed that the transition into this way of life is a personally challenging process. It may be accompanied by a period of intense inner turmoil and feelings of uncertainty, self-doubt, anxiety, despair, and more. Life changes of this dimension seldom are made without deep soul-searching. The support of friends, family, and work associates is of great importance for transforming a stressful and difficult process into a constructive and shared adventure.

The path toward voluntary simplicity is further revealed in people's descriptions of how they consciously altered their daily lives.

> . . . quit smoking, stopped eating meat, now run about eight miles a week, stopped shaving legs, stopped using scented products, stopped buying stylish haircuts, buy less clothing, buy looser freer clothing, regularly take vitamins, gave away a lot of things, eat 90 percent more fruits and

vegetables, meditate, walk a lot, read humanistic psychology, study Sufism, feel strong affinity for all animals, weave, write . . .

(woman, thirty-three, single, big city, west)

I quit my forty-hour-a-week slavery and got a twenty-hour-a-week job that I love (working in a library). I started learning how to grow food in the city and make compost. I became conscious of what I was eating and how I was spending my money. I started learning to sew, mend, and shop secondhand, and I've stopped eating meat.

(woman, twenty-three, married, small city, west)

I do not own anything more than I need. The things that I do own are selected on the basis of their utility, rather than their style or the fact that they are currently faddish. I attempt to make things last. . . . I am nursing my car past 100,000 miles. I am doing political work, notably in opposition to nuclear power. . . . I am planning to build my own house, and the plans include small-scale technology aimed at promoting self-sufficiency, such as passive solar design, a greenhouse, composting toilets, windmills, etc.

(man, thirty, single, suburb, west)

Changes include smaller house, wear clothes longer (except when in court; I'm a trial lawyer, feel it necessary to "play the role" when actually engaged in formal professional activity), recycle and buy secondhand when possible, bike and hike . . . live with a nice lady, have more time for children . . . human relationships, though fewer, are closer.

(man, forty-two, living together, rural, east)

I am doing what Bucky Fuller calls "doing more with less." He also speaks of education as the process of "eliminating the irrelevant," dismissing all that is not furthering our chosen articulation of value—eliminating wasteful speech as well as costume, dietary habits as well as information addictions that do not further the evolution into that simple (not to say "noncomplex" but only "noncomplicated") life of adaptive progress to more and more diversified environments.

(man, twenty-seven, single, small city, east)

I recycle cans, bottles, and newspapers. We're very careful with water. . . . I buy used and handmade things as much as possible. . . . We've always been frugal in the way we furnish our house. We've never bought on time, which means we buy fewer things. We wear other people's hand-me-downs and we buy used furniture when possible. . . . A large percent of our spending goes for classes (music, dance, postgraduate courses for my credential), therapy, est, and other human potential experiences.

(woman, forty-seven, married, big city, west)

We have a car but seldom use it, preferring to use bicycles because of a car's pollution and energy consumption. I am not into fashion and attempt to wear things till they are worn out—buy mostly serviceable work-type clothes, sometimes secondhand from friends. . . . Am vegetarian . . . belong to a food cooperative . . . everybody contributes four hours per month to working at the store/restaurant. This co-op forms an important hub in our community for most alternate social and spiritual activities. Learning about gardening . . . buy tools and appliances that are durable . . . avoid buying plastic and aluminum whenever possible. No throwaways . . . I attempt to use my buying power politically . . . strongly support appropriate technology . . . strongly motivated to understand myself and others—involved in meditation for awareness . . . the spiritual search component is the major driving force in my life . . . I always try to acquire new self-help skills: sewing, car repair, etc.

(woman, twenty-five, living together, city, Canada)

Greater simplicity frees time, energy, and attention for personal growth, family relationships, participation in compassionate causes, and other meaningful and satisfying activities. In turn, the greater satisfaction derived from these nonconsumerist pursuits tends to diminish our need for predominantly material sources of satisfaction. A self-fulfilling cycle is set in motion that transforms both our approach to consumption and the intentions with which we participate in life.

Inner Growth and Voluntary Simplicity

The term "inner growth" refers to a process of learning a natural quietness of mind and openness of heart that allows our interior experiencing to become apparent to us. It is a process of going behind our day-to-day labels and ideas about who we think we are in order to make friends with ourselves and the world. Here are some illustrative comments regarding the importance of inner growth to voluntary simplicity:

> I don't believe a person can make the commitment necessary to maintain this life-style without a spiritual-psychological motivation.
> (man, thirty-three, single, small town, south)

> It seems to me that inner growth is the whole moving force behind voluntary simplicity.
> (woman, thirty-eight, single, suburb, west)

> My life is suffused with joy, and that transforms even the ordinary day-to-day unpleasantries that come along. I've had a lot of years of growth pains and for a long time I got lost in the pain and suffered; but I've learned to let go more easily now and even the hard stuff that comes along doesn't overpower the joy.
> (woman, thirty-five, married, rural, west)

> My husband and I . . . feel that our inner growth at this

time is a daily way of life—tailored to our own particular situations. We know from life that one does not step in the same stream twice . . . thus, one keeps observing and relating to situations as they flow . . .
(woman, fifty-five, married, small town, west)

I consider the whole picture one of positive personal growth that I inadvertently (luckily?) set in motion through trial and error and suffering. And now I sense a momentum established that I could not now "will" to halt.
(woman, thirty-three, single, big city, west)

I consider every moment a chance for growth. To pay attention and learn is my meditation.
(man, twenty-seven, married, rural, east)

In the opinion survey, people were asked if they were "now practicing or actively involved with a particular inner-growth process." The results, presented below, are striking (keep in mind that the percentages can exceed 100 since a person was asked to check those that apply and it was not uncommon for a person to be engaged in more than one growth process).

- Meditation (e.g., Zen, Transcendental Meditation) 55%
- Other (e.g., biofeedback, "intensive journal," visualization) 46%
- Human Potential (e.g., Gestalt, encounter) 26%
- Traditional Religion (e.g., Catholicism, Judaism) 20%
- None 12%
- Psychoanalysis (e.g., Freudian, Jungian) 10%

A number of key findings emerge from this question. First, an overwhelming majority (88 percent) of the respondents indicated they were presently involved with one or more inner-growth processes. Second, more than half of the respondents (55 percent) indicated involvement with some form of meditative discipline. In fact, meditation appears to be the most prominent inner-growth process correlated with a life of conscious simplicity. Third, a near majority (46 percent) were involved with other, often highly personalized, inner-growth processes. The category "other," as described in the letters, runs the gamut from keeping an intensive journal to the use of biofeedback, hatha yoga, jogging, and many more. This diversity reflects the innovative spirit of this group. Fourth, although traditional religion is not unimportant with 20 percent actively involved, still it is not the primary focus for a group that is so strongly psychologically and spiritually oriented.

Inner growth is even more important to a path of voluntary simplicity than the foregoing statistics suggest. A number of persons who declined to identify themselves as being involved in any particular growth process explained why with comments such as these:

> I don't know what label to put on my inner-growth process . . . I get high on a beautiful sunrise, a night when I sit alone on a chunk of granite and gaze up at billions of stars. . . . So what would you call it? I like to sit alone on a rock and just open my mind up to everything—would you call it meditation? And I do believe in God and Christ but for sure am not into traditional religion.
> (man, twenty-four, single, rural, midwest)

> I am not actively involved in any particular growth process but I'm always aware of the Spirit and how I'm part of it— gleaning what I can from traditional religions, yoga, and the insights provided to a clearer head since I've begun living more simply.
> (man, twenty-two, single, rural, south)

> I'm 75 percent spiritually oriented though I haven't found a particular "path" outside of living simply and with love and searching.
> (woman, eighteen, single, suburb, east)

> I practice meditation and have a strong spiritual emphasis in my life that draws mainly from Christianity and Bud-

dhism but also all other religions, and I do not practice any of them in any strict sense. I would call myself very strongly religious, but independent.
(woman, twenty-five, married, big city, midwest)

. . . tried Zen, but it was wrong pace—but work constantly on self in a small, personalized manner.
(man, twenty-four, single, rural, west)

I do not deny taking ideas from many sources but the result is fairly eclectic. The fact that most people I know do not fit me into a category seems to support this. So, my process would be individualistically developed inner growth: that which suits me personally.
(woman, twenty-six, single, big city, west)

The letters indicate a basic dilemma: When one's entire life is the inner-growth process, how can any one piece be singled out and labeled as "the practice"? The category "none" thus includes an undetermined, but substantial, number of persons for whom the inner-growth process is really "all" (and paradox smiles again).

Some indicated that they felt the category "inner-growth" was too limiting and asserted that activities from political action to artistic creation to running should be considered legitimate vehicles of inner-growth:

I am a radical and a feminist and believe that leading a VS life-style and continuing political struggle is a form of personal growth left out of your analysis.
(man, twenty-nine, single, rural, west)

The inner-growth you write of may be artistic, scientific, or social action, not just "spiritual."
(man, twenty-eight, single, small city, west)

Athletics is played down unjustifiably. For me, human potential has a physical as well as spiritual meaning. Distance running produces a lot of the same vibrations that meditation evokes.

(Man, twenty-nine, married, small city, west)

In short, just as there is no single "right" way to outwardly live more simply, so too there is no single "right" way to engage in the process of interior growth. This way of life requires adherence to no particular religious dogma or ideology. Voluntary simplicity is a way of life that is compatible with Christianity, Buddhism, Hinduism, Taoism, Sufism, Zen, and many more traditions. The reason for this compatability with diverse spiritual traditions is that this way of life encourages a more conscious and direct encounter with the world. And it is from a conscious and direct encounter with life that there naturally arise the perennial experiences at the heart of all the world's great spiritual traditions (this important notion is discussed further in Chapters 6 and 10). Voluntary simplicity, then, is openhanded with regard to various spiritual traditions. It is compatible with the notion that there can be as many traditions as there are persons in the world.

The Importance of Relationships

The involvement with inner growth so characteristic of voluntary simplicity may suggest an inward turning away from worldly relationships. To the contrary, it is the very deepening of insight through the inner quest that reveals the entire world as an intimately interconnected system. The interior journey is indispensable in revealing that we inhabit an ecological reality. In an ecological reality—where everything is related to, and connected with, everything else—the quality and integrity of interpersonal relationships are of intense concern. Or, as Martin Buber said: "All real living is meeting." This too is reflected in the letters:

We value our relationships more highly than anything else.
(man, twenty-nine, married, small city, west)

I feel good about everyday things, place more value and get *much* satisfaction from interpersonal relationships.
(woman, nineteen, single, suburb, west)

I feel this way of life has made my marriage stronger as it puts more accent on personal relationship and "inner growth."
(man, twenty-seven, married, rural, east)

We are intensely family oriented—we measure happiness by the degree of growth, not by the amount of dollars earned.
(man, thirty-one, married, small town, east)

Satisfactions—growth through relationships with others and continuing personal contacts—the circle expands as more interests develop.
(man, twenty-nine, living together, small town, east)

We see some friends just grow old and tired of fighting [to maintain this way of life] especially when not backed up by solid love connections. It's been our fortune (and that of most successful VSers we know who last into their late thirties and forties) to have good "love" or "family" lives.
(man, thirty-four, married, rural, Canada)

This is not to portray a utopian situation of idyllic quality. These are very human people. Many have confronted the fact that movement toward a fundamentally different way of life—involving change in both inner and outer worlds—can be challenging for relationships, even when there is a joint commitment to change. The varied nature of the stresses that may accompany movement toward voluntary simplicity is revealed in the letters:

I expect to become more voluntarily simple in the future

as I become more ingenious about dealing with differences in life-style preferences of my husband and myself and more firm about saying no to outside demands.

(woman, fifty-seven, married, suburb, west)

It is sometimes difficult or frustrating to live fully VS because my partner is not as fanatically committed as I am to personal-growth exploration, nonconsumerism, and conservation. Satisfactions, however, are innumerable—I feel better physically, spiritually, and mentally . . .

(woman, twenty-eight, married, suburb, west)

I feel that I am alone with no support. Oh, some of my friends think that the things we are doing are admirable in a patronizing sort of way. Most people just think we're a little "nuts." I need some support. My wife is a somewhat reluctant supporter.

(man, thirty-six, married, big city, west)

My father and mother are supportive of our life-style, his parents are critical and don't understand—they are very money oriented. The kids sometimes worry that we are poor and compare themselves with their more conventional classmates.

(woman, twenty-nine, married, rural, west)

My choice of life-style, I feel, cannot infringe so much on my almost grown children's desires that it makes them miserable and rebellious. If they had all been toddlers when we began living this way, it would have been easier.

(woman, thirty-six, single, rural, east)

Clearly, movement toward voluntary simplicity is not without its tensions and stresses. For couples, the most frequently mentioned source of tension within a relationship arose when one partner was content with traditional patterns of living, consuming, relating, and working whereas the other partner wanted to explore nontraditional alternatives to one or more of them. For couples with children, the most frequently mentioned source of stress arose when the children were in their teens as parents began to make a shift toward living more simply. The children then sometimes felt themselves in a double-bind between their previous adaptation to a more traditional identity (shared by their peer group) and an emergent identity being explored by their parents (who obviously are powerful role models).

Despite these stresses, relationships were described overall as an important source of nurturance, love, encouragement, reality testing, and support. Often this sense of support extended beyond one's immediate family or friends to include a larger community of persons with whom there was a sense of kinship or spiritual bonding.

Community Support

Many persons in this poll reported they felt tolerated by the larger community and actively supported by a smaller group of friends and associates. This is not surprising when we consider that many began adopting this way of life in the late 1960s and early 1970s—a time when the mood of most Western nations was not strongly or consciously supportive of a trend toward voluntary simplicity. Here is a sampling of the spectrum of experience reported in the letters.

> As for community support—I get both jeered at and cheered at—and some people even join in.
> (woman, fifty-five, married, small town, west)

> My motivations are understood by very few; I accept the responsibility for my actions.
> (man, twenty-seven, married, rural, east)

> I am greatly enriched by my life-style but sometimes feel

alienated from society because of it. I consider it takes strong determination to stick to VS convictions; sometimes frustrating because there are so many American dreamers.
(woman, twenty-seven, single, small town, west)

I thought that the rural community would be a mecca of higher consciousness and have generally a spiritual atmosphere. Wrong! I have a problem finding people I have enough in common with that I can communicate with, but when I do, it's really dynamite!
(man, thirty-three, single, small town, south)

It is scary to live with less because for so long our society has said that money, possessions, and a career lead to security and happiness. I have a lot of support to make changes because of a tremendous community of people who are doing the same thing. The advantage is feeling more inner peace, increased self-acceptance, and community support.
(woman, twenty-nine, single, big city, midwest)

Probably we will lead lives of greater simplicity to the degree that others in greater numbers in the society also start to do so. Community support is important.
(woman, thirty, married, big city, west)

The relative lack of community support was mentioned by many persons as being important in their rate of adoption and degree of experimentation with alternative ways of life. Many of the pioneers of voluntary simplicity did not feel substantial support from the larger community or culture, but there is reason to think (as we will discuss in Chapter 4) that mainstream values are shifting dramatically in a direction that is highly congruent with deliberate simplicity of living. If so, the sense of community support—so important in empowering individuals to move from sympathetic leanings to active involvement—could be growing rapidly.

The Politics of Voluntary Simplicity

The political orientation of this group represents a clear break with mainstream Western politics. An unambiguous message runs through the letters: this is a strongly independent group of persons. The survey results reveal that their political perspectives do not fit within the traditional spectrum of right wing/conservative and left wing/liberal.

Among the respondents from the United States, only 1 percent labeled themselves as Republicans. Some 28 percent said they were registered Democrats, but many included comments such as "out of lack of choice," or "would switch to something better." This indicates there is no deep sense of affiliation with the Democratic party.

Roughly 60 percent of the sample placed themselves either in the category of "independent" or "other" and 11 percent declined to give any political orientation. The truly experimental character of the politics of this group is reflected in their responses to the category "other." Here people could write in their own political perspective. This brought responses such as: *cooperativist, feminist, nonviolent activist, whatever works at the time, Libertarian, eclectic, decentralist, conservative anarchist, nonviolent leftist,* and *apolitical but the weather may change.*

A majority of those pioneering a life of conscious simplicity are not strongly identified with any traditional political dogma. What seems to bind this group together is not political ideology but an appreciation for the dignity and preciousness of all life. Virtually nowhere in the letters was there any reference to traditional political ideologies—whether capitalist, communist, or socialist. Rather, there was a sense that a whole new perspective or political orientation is emerging that will begin to bridge between left and right, East and West, inner and outer, rich and poor, masculine and feminine.

Let's turn to the letters to get more of a firsthand sense of the political concerns and attitudes of this group:

. . . our system causes us to be very political . . . We are not a centralized movement . . . Our concerns are for each other's survival. We communicate better than government and business. The "movement" is in reality a conscious choice of individuals—not a centralized program . . . we are passing free ideas around, becoming independent through cooperation—young, old, brilliant, salt of the earth, revolutionary, conservative. We are the shakeout of the system, about to show the system how to improve itself. We communicate by learning and teaching. Call it the People's University, not a movement . . .

(man, thirty-five, married, suburban, east)

I am spending more and more of my time in various forms of community building and feel there are no political organizations, ideologies, or labels with which I am continually comfortable—except maybe voluntary simplicity.

(man, thirty-eight, single, small city, west)

Different aspects of VS have the potential of touching small parts of everyone's life-style, and it is this feature that I feel gives hope to the movement. VS has the potential of working on people like a chain reaction once the first spark is lit. On the other hand, I also see great potential for ecological disaster, social and political unrest and ruin. I make no bets; I live from day to day and do what I can.

(woman, twenty-eight, married, suburb, west)

The fire ignited by combining life-style and politics is truly liberating and a joy to experience. Revolutions are made of such stuff .   .

(man, twenty-six, single, small town, west)

I don't think our lives will be very satisfying if we are divided and live in fear of others, regardless of what we may be able to accomplish with our inner lives. Thus, if we are seeking genuine VS, we will have to operate in a way that will help others to gain awareness of their higher self-interest in what is happening to our planet and to ourselves as human beings.

(woman, fifty-five, married, small town, west)

For several key reasons, apathy seems less widespread among those adopting voluntary simplicity than among the general population. First, these people are taking control of their own lives, and although it may seem limited, this domain of control is real. In small, but cumulatively significant, ways they are exercising and experiencing their own empowerment and competence.

Second, there is a pervasive realization that even if we wanted to, there is literally no place where we can go to escape or drop out. In an ecological reality—where everything is intimately connected with everything else—there is not the option of being apolitical. Once we acknowledge our capacity to consciously experience the plight of the world, there is no place where we can go to retreat into our former ignorance.

Third, intentionally living with less is politically radicalizing. This clearly emerged in the survey as those with higher incomes tended to be more traditional in their political perspectives, while those with lower incomes were more innovative and experimental. When people deliberately choose to live closer to the level of material sufficiency, they are brought closer to the reality of material existence for a majority of persons on this planet. There is not the day-to-day insulation from material poverty that accompanies the hypnosis of a culture of affluence.

In a variety of ways, many survey respondents said they did not want to drop out of political processes so much as alter the nature of their participation in them. In general, people seemed to be putting much of their political energy into local- and global-level concerns rather than into national-level concerns. Examples of local involvement mentioned in the letters ranged from attempting to change building codes that inhibit the use of innovative materials and building design to developing consumer and worker-owned cooperatives that are responsive to the needs of the local community. Examples of global involvement ranged from working to end starvation in the world to promoting international nuclear disarmament and aiding endangered species. I do not interpret this shift of attention to greater emphasis on the local and global level as a turning away from the problems of the nation-state. Rather, it seems an attempt to find a more skillful balance of attention in a world fast becoming a global civilization and simultaneously confronting many problems that seem most readily dealt with at a local level.

How are we to make sense out of this emerging political perspective? This is such an important issue in our troubled times that it is useful to take a brief detour in our journey through the firsthand experiences with voluntary simplicity. I think that we are seeing the emergence of a political perspective that is first and foremost concerned with the ecology of all life on this planet. This is not a new approach to living. For example, more than a century ago the early European settlers in the United States encountered a profoundly ecological perspective in the culture of the American Indians. Illustrative of this view of life is the oration that Chief Seattle delivered in 1852 to his people as they gave up their ancestral lands to the white people. In part, he said:

> This we know. The earth does not belong to man; man belongs to the earth. This we know. All things are connected like the blood which unites one family. All things are connected. Whatever befalls the earth befalls the sons of the earth. Man did not weave the web of life, he is merely a strand in it. Whatever he does to the web, he does to himself.[2]

This ancient and profoundly ecological orientation toward all of life is now re-emerging in our political and social processes. One graphic example of this is revealed in the Greenpeace Movement—mentioned by a number of respondents as having their support. It is the intention of this movement to stop the slaughter of whales, dolphins, and other highly intelligent sea mammals that are being hunted into extinction. These are not armchair activists. Greenpeace crew members are placing themselves in boats between the killer ships and whales. Their lives are their political statement. With this as background, it is revealing to note the parallels between the oration of Chief Seattle and the following statement of Greenpeace philosophy:

> Ecology teaches us that humankind is not the center of life on the planet. Ecology has taught us that the whole earth is part of our "body" and that we must learn to respect it as we respect ourselves. As we feel for ourselves, we must feel for all forms of life—the whales, the seals, the forests, the seas.[3]

The Greenpeace philosophy also provides a useful description of how the political concerns of those embracing voluntary simplicity may become manifest as greater levels of nonviolent activism:

> The Greenpeace ethic is not only to personally bear witness to atrocities against life; it is to take direct action to prevent them. While action must be direct, it must also be nonviolent. We must obstruct a wrong without offering personal violence to its perpetrators. Our greatest strength must be life itself, and the commitment to direct our own lives to protect others.[4]

Many letters from the voluntary simplicity survey emphasized the importance of learning nonviolent means of resolving conflict. This too is consistent with an ecological political orientation. However, as the Greenpeace example suggests, pacifism should not be equated with passivity. A number of persons indicated they had participated in various nonviolent social protest movements of the 1960s and early 1970s. Thus, an ecologically oriented, nonviolent activism seems to characterize the political orientation of a majority of the survey respondents.

In summary, where the traditional political perspective of Western industrial nations has tended to emphasize national interests, material concerns, and the legitimacy of violence in the conduct of foreign affairs, the emerging politics tends to emphasize planetary interests, a balanced regard for both material and spiritual concerns, and the importance of nonviolent means of resolving disputes.

One example of this emerging political orientation is the "New World Alliance." The alliance is a recently formed coalition of persons from all walks of life who are encouraging the birth of a new politics in the United States. Here is how the alliance describes its objectives:

> The New World Alliance seeks to break away from the old quarrels of "left-against-right" and help create a new consensus based on our heartfelt needs. It emphasizes personal growth—and nurturing others—rather than indiscriminate material growth. It advocates "human scale" institutions that function with human consideration and social responsibility. It draws on the social movements of the recent past for new values like ecological responsibility, self-actualization and planetary cooperation and sharing. It draws on our conservative heritage for values such as personal responsibility, self-reliance, thrift, neighborliness and community. It draws from the liberal traditions a commitment to human and civil rights, economic equity and social justice. We call this synthesis "New World" politics.[5]

Should this kind of integrative political orientation continue to grow and infuse the larger culture, it will surely result in a profound transformation in the conduct and character of our political processes.

Contributions of Feminism

Feminism has made important contributions to both the growth and the character of voluntary simplicity. In saying this, I do not mean to equate feminism with a life of conscious simplicity. There are many women who have broken free of traditional sexual stereotypes but continue to embrace other stereotypes of Western industrial societies—particularly those concerning the nature of material success and social status. A feminist orientation, therefore, does not guarantee sympathy for voluntary simplicity. However, a substantial majority of those choosing a life of deliberate simplicity expressed a strong affinity for the spirit of the feminist movement. Here are some illustrative comments from the letters:

> I am becoming tuned to these ideas and life-style changes, partly as a feminist who sees a need for more bridges from the new age to feminism. . . . Behind this, of course, the relationship of our alienation/destruction of our mother, the earth, is parallel to our alienation/control of our mothers, the women.
> (woman, thirty, married, big city, Canada)

> I am a feminist—the women's movement gave me the strength and knowledge and confidence in myself and abilities to attempt this lifetime and life-style adventure. . . . I am especially supportive of women who want to "try their wings" and serve as an example of what a woman can do when she rejects prescribed roles and does "her own thing."
> (woman, thirty-nine, living together, rural, east)

> I took up voluntary simplicity after leaving my last (hopefully) male-dominated relationship, where I was supported financially by a man. A year of feminism and consciousness-raising . . . convinced me that I would never be free to even know a man truly, unless I could be free of dependency. . . . So supporting myself, seeing how I really wanted to spend my waking hours, coupled with the concept of right livelihood, ecological awareness, yoga study, all led in one direction.
> (woman, thirty-four, single, rural, west)

Another part of VS is more equally shared roles of men

and women. Even though we have a child (which is often
the determining factor in the traditional mother-stay-home,
father-go-to-work family) we are attempting to not put
ourselves in those roles . . . Between us, we share child
care, meal fixing, cleaning, shopping, and money earning,
while making sure our other needs are met (crafts, classes).
For people without children, this is even more so the case.
(woman, twenty-two, living together, small town, west)

. . . it is a way of life that made sense to me—nonmaterial-
istic, focused on people, cooperative, nonsexist.
(woman, twenty-seven, married, big city, midwest)

Major changes include elimination of the "man is the chief
breadwinner and boss" hangup.
(man, thirty-eight, married, suburb, west)

How has the feminist movement contributed to the growth
of voluntary simplicity? First, feminism, by its example, has encouraged people of both sexes to explore alternative ways of
living and working. When any person or group empowers themselves to act in ways that move beyond traditional roles and
expectations, an example of cultural liberation is provided that
all can emulate and translate into their unique circumstances.
The liberation of women from sexual stereotypes thus has relevance far beyond women and sexual roles—it is a significant
example of cultural liberation that applies to many other limiting stereotypes of traditional Western industrial societies.

Second, the large numbers of women who have freed themselves from long-standing sexual stereotypes have provided
powerful role models for the liberation of men as well. In liberating men from the need to perpetuate their half of the polarity
of sex-based roles, feminism offers both men and women the
freedom to be more authentically who they already are. This
has important implications for the historically male-dominated
orientation of Western industrial societies where the proof of
"manhood" has often been equated with the ability to succeed

in the material world. For many men, consumption has served purposes far beyond that of meeting genuine material needs. High earnings and high consumption have also been used as evidence of masculine competence, potency, and social status. With changes in male-female roles, other criteria of "success" can begin to emerge—criteria that are more balanced across both masculine and feminine qualities.

Western industrial cultures have tended to reinforce selectively what might be termed "masculine" qualities—aggressiveness, competitiveness, rationalism, a dissecting approach to the world, a materialistic orientation—while suppressing so-called feminine qualities. Although a "masculine" approach to living has been a potent force in contributing to the success of the industrial revolution, it is ultimately one-sided and unbalanced. Many important "feminine" qualities—including the capacity to nurture others, to be receptive, to maintain a felt sense of the wholeness of all life, and to subjectively appreciate a way of living that places a high value on feeling and emotion—have not been integrated completely into Western cultures.

With a more balanced integration of "masculine" and "feminine" qualities, our cultures would tend to become less aggressive, contain less disguised competition, be more receptive and open, have more supportive friendships, have a greater mixing of roles among men and women in accordance with innate interests and capacities, be able to nurture and care for others to a greater degree, place greater value on feeling and emotion, express greater concern for unborn generations, and have a stronger sense of the intimate interrelatedness of life. This integration and balance seems crucial. If a one-sided "masculine" orientation—with its competitive, aggressive, dissecting, and materialistic approach to living—continues to dominate our perceptions and actions as a culture, we will scarcely be able to live in relative peace and harmony with the rest of the life on this planet. If we are to become whole persons in a cohesive culture, we must consciously integrate more "feminine" qualities into our lives. Importantly, a path of conscious simplicity involves for many the integration and balance of both "masculine" and "feminine" qualities into a coherent approach to living.

Voluntary Simplicity and Contributory Livelihood

As mentioned at the beginning of the chapter, those who answered the survey had a variety of work backgrounds ranging from professionals to blue-collar and white-collar workers to students, and many more. Although for some, work seemed to provide little more than a source of income, for most, it constituted a vehicle for participating in the world and a major source of satisfaction in living. Here are some illustrative comments from the letters:

> To me, the central reality of VS is the unity and inter-relatedness of all aspects of my life. While my work has often been scheduled and distinct from the rest of my life, the more I get into the VS life-style the more I take my work home with me and involve all aspects and experiences of my life in my work. Work is something I do to make a living, but if it's not the kind of work that is also filling my need to feel that I'm contributing in a positive way to the welfare of at least some small part of humanity, I will find some way to make it contributory or find other work. It's like the Eastern perspective that a healthy life is all a meditation. The more you get into that kind of perspective, the more natural VS is, the easier it is to instinctively do what is going to be good for others and make you happy, and the more consistent and fulfilling your life is going to become.
>
> (man, thirty-eight, single, small city, west)
>
> It's important for people to realize that this life-style places no real boundaries between "work" and "play." "Work" is enjoyed and becomes simply a different activity than "play."
>
> (woman, nineteen, single, suburb, west)

I live in grateful simplicity. The search for money (for its own sake) interferes in "loving work." For a time it seemed the solution was partial, a compromise between aesthetics and economics—between self-expression and survival. Now it seems that as artificialities are dropped, aesthetics becomes simple and natural—as life energy is released from survival and defense mechanisms, it enters a flow of abundance.

(man, twenty-nine, single, suburb, midwest)

In work it takes another kind of energy and self-caring for "sanity" (rather than externally determined "success") to move away from the path that would take me "to the top." I know pretty clearly what the "top" is as defined by my colleagues. What I'm searching for is the "top" as defined by me.

(woman, twenty-eight, living together, small city, midwest)

I recognized that the larger American culture did not sustain me with its consumerism and small jobs in large corporations.

(woman, thirty, living together, rural, west)

Commercialism is making people live on only the periphery of their whole beings. Things don't make you whole and happy, they can divide and disorientate. Putting all of oneself in a task makes you real—whole!

(woman, sixty-five, single, big city, midwest)

What is the attitude toward work that is reflected in these comments? My sense is that if we give less than our wholehearted participation to our work, then our sense of connectedness to life itself will be commensurately diminished. Work that is not strongly contributory may yield the income to feed our endless search for gratification, but such work seldom provides us with a sense of genuine contribution and satisfaction. Therefore, work that is largely self-serving will generate by its very nature a sense of alienation and unsatisfactoriness. However, when our work is life-serving, then our energy and creativity can flow cleanly and directly through us and into the world without impediment or interruption.

Overall, people seemed to view work as having at least four functions: first, as a means of supporting oneself in activity that is meaningful and materially sustaining; second, as an opportunity to support others by producing goods and services that promote a workable and meaningful world; third, as a context for learning about the nature of life—using work as a medium of personal growth; and fourth, as a direct expression of one's being—as a celebration of one's existence in the world. Clearly, work is viewed as much more than a source of income. It is a primary vehicle through which we contribute to, and participate in, life.

The drive to find meaningful work, coupled with the shortage of such work in today's economy seems to be an important force behind a small-business boom involving a number of those choosing to simplify their lives. Among the various businesses mentioned in the letters that have been started with a voluntary simplicity orientation were restaurants, bakeries, bookstores, used-clothing stores, auto repair shops, bicycle repair shops, child-care centers, alternative health-care centers, various craft shops, grocery stores, alternative schools, and more. This skilled and highly motivated group seems to have ample talent to initiate a grass roots rebirth of entrepreneurship in local communities across the country. This same spirit of compassionate entrepreneurship seems to be infusing the traditional workplace as well and is evident in the rising demand for democratization of the economy and for meaningful work.

Satisfactions and Dissatisfactions

Given the demands and stresses of this way of life, it would not be voluntarily chosen unless it was a satisfying way to live.

Here is an illustrative sampling of responses to a question asking people to describe their satisfactions and dissatisfactions with voluntary simplicity:

> Dissatisfactions of VS are minute, not because they don't exist, but because they are part of the process—not obstacles but bumps on a road that I choose to follow.
> (man, twenty-seven, single, big city, midwest)

> Satisfactions are the fulfillment of the heart. Dissatisfactions are the rumblings of the mind.
> (man, twenty-eight, single, rural, west)

> The most satisfying thing is that you can see life right in front of your nose—feel it all around you—running through you and continuing on. It's such a natural occurrence . . . You gain access to parts of life that are otherwise inaccessible.
> (woman, twenty-three, married, rural, east)

> Satisfactions: I am my life. Dissatisfactions: There is always dissatisfaction; it precedes change.
> (man, twenty-seven, married, rural, west)

> Satisfaction is internal (not wanting and not rejecting), and I feel it when I am in touch with Reality or God. . . . I always get what I need. This renders my dissatisfactions irrelevant and meaningless (although I forget this often). So I can't bring myself to list my dissatisfactions because they're only a form of unfounded self-pity . . .
> (man, thirty, married, rural, east)

> There are no dissatisfactions, only difficulties, which can and will be overcome.
> (woman, thirty-eight, married, suburb, east)

> Satisfactions: Life is a lot simpler—I no longer spend twenty-four hours a month shaving legs and curling hair and god knows how long driving back and forth to Safeway. Life is infinitely cheaper—releasing money for the real

luxuries of life. Dissatisfactions: outward appearances suggest poverty, and this culture is very discriminatory toward the poor . . .

(woman, twenty-eight, married, rural, west)

The greatest satisfaction derives from increasingly seeing the truth of one of the tenets of simplicity—my needs are always met, although my desires take a beating. . . . I begin to see that my satisfactions and dissatisfactions actually arise more from my attitude than circumstances. This for me is one of the most important aspects of voluntary simplicity . . . the state of consciousness associated with it.

(woman, thirty-two, single, city, west)

My life is less cluttered with "things" that control and befuddle me. Dissatisfactions? Only that it's sometimes the harder way to do something . . . I can't rely on fast food, fast service, fast buying. Everything takes longer—cooking, buying, fixing. But it's worth it—most times.

(woman, twenty-seven, married, rural)

The satisfactions are of sharing and caring; of putting forth your best effort regardless of the results; of simply being happy . . . the rewards are immeasureably greater than those of possession or individual accomplishment. After a brief period of remorse for giving up the comfort and recognition that may have been attained, dissatisfaction with life seems to be experienced more infrequently and less intensely than before. As desires become fewer; frustration diminishes. As life becomes less ego-centered, it becomes more enjoyable.

(man, thirty-one, married, small town, west)

A most satisfying life in that we have a very close family relationship (our children are grown). We see that the children have developed values which are simple and allow for coping flexibly with the changing world. Using our own ideas and hands to make our way in both professions and homelife is an exhilarating (and sometimes tiring) way to live.

(woman, forty-seven, married, suburb, west)

Satisfactions and dissatisfactions: The two sure go together! I can be so elated one day and down in the dumps when the progress is slow the next. Extrinsic joys are: 1. a marriage that works, 2. creating my own joys, 3. making my own music, 4. seeing my spiritual life blossom. Sorrows are just the bottom of the sine wave—when progress is slow.

(man, twenty-five, married, small town, east)

Satisfaction: Much more flexibility to move, grow, and generally bend with the winds. Continual improvement of my relationship with the universe. . . . In short, after thinking about it a minute, my life has only improved since I began to consciously simplify everything. Aside from some complaints about others not understanding my life-style (my problem, not the life-style's) and a certain difficulty at making money (again, my problem) I have *no* complaints . . . I feel more successful, wealthy, and healthy than I ever felt. And I mean wealthy in all senses.

(man, thirty, single, small town, west)

There are infinite satisfactions—primarily because I have consciously chosen to direct my life toward this life-style— I am opening myself to growth, change, freedom of expression, caring for others. The major dissatisfaction—growth is painful!

(woman, twenty-eight, single, suburb, west)

The pervasive sense of satisfaction expressed in these letters is, I think, a direct result of people's learning to take control of their lives. This control can assume many forms: learning basic skills that promote greater self-reliance (gardening, carpentry, repair skills, etc.), choosing work that is contributory and challenging, consuming in ways that respect the rest of life on this planet, participating in compassionate causes, and many more. A growing capacity for self-determining action contributes to the individual's sense of personal competence, dignity, and self-worth.

A positive spiral of learning and growth unfolds from approaching life in this manner. As we become empowered to take charge of our own lives, we sense that no one is to blame other than ourselves if our experience of life is not satisfying. And, in continually opening to and meeting that challenging responsibility, a sense of freedom, aliveness, and satisfaction naturally emerges. This approach to life stands in sharp contrast to that exemplified by the industrial era. How?

The overriding objective of the industrial era has been to maximize one's personal pleasures while minimizing one's personal discomforts. Life has been lived as a constant process of "pushing" (trying to push away from discomforts) and "grabbing" (trying to acquire or to hold on to that which gives pleasure). With the loss of inner balance that accompanies a largely habitual "pushing" and "grabbing" approach to life, a deeper pain ensues—that of becoming aware of the ultimate unsatisfactoriness of the pleasure-seeking/pain-avoiding process itself.

By choosing balance we can more easily negotiate a skillful path through the world. Instead of a continual movement back and forth between pleasure seeking and pain avoiding, we can view life as a continual process of learning and challenge that will always include some measure of both pleasure and pain. By allowing both to be present in our lives, we find that we need be dominated by neither and instead can consciously choose a path that promotes our harmonious participation in the web of life. What is changing, then, is not the existence of pleasures and pains but rather the manner in which we choose to respond to these perennial aids to our learning. The material pleasures of a balanced existence may be fewer, but the overall satisfaction with life is, for many, greater.

Conclusion

There are several conclusions that I draw from this survey of people choosing a life of conscious simplicity. First, voluntary simplicity is not a utopian dream but a present reality. This is a down-to-earth, practical, and realistic manner of living that has already taken root in a number of Western developed nations. Further, given the emphasis on self-reliance and self-determination, it seems likely that these early roots will have a tenacious foothold in these cultures.

Second, the pioneers of an alternative way of living demonstrate by their living example that we can each begin to take control of our own lives. We are not powerless in the face of civilizational breakdown. We are not helpless. We can take charge of our lives and create a more workable and meaningful existence.

Third, voluntary simplicity means much more than greater material frugality. Like spokes that reach out from the hub of a wheel, this way of life radiates outward from an inner core of human experience to touch every facet of life in distinct and discernible ways.

Fourth, voluntary simplicity is in its springtime of growth. Consequently, its contemporary expression does not represent the culmination of this way of life; rather, it represents its initial blossoming. A vast amount of work and learning yet remains before the potentials of this way of living will be fully apparent.

Fifth, there are no fixed rules or norms that define this way of life. The worldly expression of voluntary simplicity is something that each person must discover for himself or herself in the context of his or her unique circumstances.

Sixth, this way of life does not represent a withdrawal from the world. Some may mistake the unwillingness of this forerunner group to participate in the aggressive exploitation of resources, the environment, and other members of the human family as a retreat from the world. Yet far from withdrawal, a path of conscious simplicity promotes our penetrating and intimate involvement with life. With conscious and direct involvement comes clarity. With clarity comes insight. With insight comes love. With love comes mutually helpful living. With mutually helpful living a growing civilization is made possible. Thus, rather than abandoning the world, those choosing a life of conscious simplicity are, I think, pioneering a new civilizing process.

Seventh, these pioneers of an alternative way of living reveal that "small is beautiful" when it comes to the process of making changes in our lives. Small changes that are seemingly inconsequential when viewed in isolation are of revolutionary significance in their cumulative impact. It is these many, small changes that will accumulate, bit by bit, into a thorough transformation of our collective manner of living.

We have been examining the attitudes and experiences of a pioneering group of people engaged in a practical transformation in living. Is this way of living relevant to the majority in Western industrial societies? Is it likely that this way of life will grow in the future? We will explore these two key questions, but before we do so we require additional perspective. Therefore, the following chapter considers the nature and dynamics of our time of civilizational challenge. Having considered this important issue, we will return in Chapter 4 to consider the relevance and growth potential of voluntary simplicity.

SECTION II

CONTEXT

CHAPTER 3

CIVILIZATIONS IN TRANSITION

Are Western industrial nations approaching the "end of an era"? If the present era of single-minded attention to, and pursuit of, material progress is coming to an end, then what will that ending be like? If we now encounter a time of fundamental transition, then what will the path ahead be like? Do we face a smooth ride into a transformed future? Or, is it a rough road that we now confront? If the latter, then how rough might it get? If we do face a time of civilizational transition, then how long might such a transition take? Will this be a fast apocalyptic process? Or, will we move ahead at a slow and grinding pace? What kind of society would result if we do more than strive to preserve the status quo? Alternatively, what would it be like to live in a society that is transforming itself? What is the role of simplicity of living in all this?

These are some of the questions that I want to address in this section. In responding to these questions, I will share my best guess as to the pathways that lie before us. Although my estimate is based on a decade of futures research, it is important to remember that this can be no more than a guess. The future is genuinely uncertain. It is uncertain because we know so little about the synergistic consequences of the powerful forces that now converge around us. It is also uncertain because of the enormous difference that our individual choices will make in shaping the eventual outcome. With this acknowledgment of inescapable uncertainty, I will forthrightly present my best guess of the terrain of social evolution that lies squarely before us.

Just as we humans are mortal, so too are our civilizations. One of the primary lessons of the industrial era has been that for all our technological power, we are not above nature but within it. Being within nature, we cannot escape the natural rhythms of birth and decay that characterize all living things. Just as the seasons inexorably pass, so too do civilizations pass through their seasons of growth and decline. In my judgment, Western industrial civilizations have already passed through their seasons of growth and have entered a period of decline that will likely, though not inevitably, lead to eventual breakdown. As painful and difficult as this process may be, it is as natural as the passing of summer into autumn and beyond.

The outward signs that signal our entry into a period of civilizational discord and decline are many; they include a loss of compelling social purpose, a loss of social cohesion, overwhelming bureaucratic complexity, an eroding economy, and special interest group politics that override the public interest. These signs reveal the presence of civilizational autumn and indicate that life has begun to flow more and more slowly through our aging industrial societies. The vitality of spring can return, I think, but not before we have passed through a hard winter of civilizational crisis and have consciously discovered a sense of social purpose that again draws out our wholehearted and enthusiastic participation in life.

When viewed from this perspective, it seems no accident that a life of voluntary simplicity has entered its springtime of growth at the same time that Western industrial civilizations have entered their autumn of initial decline. Those who consciously simplify their lives will, I think, provide a crucial source of vitality for promoting the creative rebirth of our fragmenting industrial societies.

These are strong assertions and I would like to share my reasons for making them. We can begin by examining a description of civilizational growth that moves through four seasons, or stages.

Four Stages of Civilizational Growth

It is psychologically demanding to seriously consider the prospect of profound civilizational transition. Such a transition is not an abstract possibility that is apart from ourselves—we are the persons who are destined to live through it. Consequently, to venture into this realm of inquiry may bring—as it has for me— much psychological discomfort. All of the hopes and fears that lie in uneasy, though quiet, repose in our everyday lives become starkly visible as we consciously encounter the depth and scope of change that lies dead ahead.

Our anxiety about fundamental civilizational change is lessened when we realize that it is part of a natural and, indeed, purposeful process. To see the organic character of our social evolution, we need some organizing framework to separate the deeper currents of change from the surface turbulence that occupies so much of our public attention. We also need to expand our perspective beyond the present and embrace both past and future growth as part of a larger pattern. One view of the larger pattern of civilizational change is simply, though usefully, suggested by the following four-stage description of the life cycle of civilizational growth.

Although there are fairly rigorous underpinnings to this model of growth, I will not discuss them here but instead refer you to Appendix III. Here it is sufficient to note that the origins of this model of growth derive from two principal sources: economic theory (expanding the "law of diminishing returns" to characterize the growth dynamics of an entire society), and systems theory (which is used to describe the behavioral properties of social systems as they grow to enormous size and complexity).

FOUR STAGES OF GROWTH IN THE LIFE CYCLE OF WESTERN INDUSTRIAL CIVILIZATIONS *

Stage I	Stage II	Stage III	Stage IV
High Growth	Full Blossoming	Initial Decline	Breakdown
"Springtime"	"Summer"	"Autumn"	"Winter"
Era of Faith	Era of Reason	Era of Cynicism	Era of Despair
High social consensus; strong sense of shared social purpose	Social consensus begins to weaken with fulfillment of shared social purpose	Consensus very weak. Special interest group demands grow stronger than shared social purpose	Collapse of consensus; multiple and conflicting social purposes
Bureaucratic complexity is low; activities are largely self-regulating	Bureaucratic complexity is mounting rapidly; activities are increasingly regulated	Bureaucratic complexity mounts faster than the ability to effectively regulate; bureaucracies begin to falter	Bureaucratic complexity is overwhelming; bureaucracies are out of control; society begins to break down

* "A growing civilization may be defined as one in which the components of its culture are in harmony with each other and form an integral whole; on the same principle, a disintegrating civilization can be defined as one in which these same elements have fallen into discord." Arnold Toynbee, *A Study of History*.[1]

STAGE I: HIGH GROWTH

This is the "springtime" of civilizational growth. It is an era of faith in basic values. The majority of people share a coherent and compelling image of future potentials for growth. This is a period of great vitality, creativity, innovation, and experimentation as people seek to realize those potentials. The established social order has great legitimacy and is sufficiently uncomplicated so as to be comprehensible to the majority. People have a relatively high degree of access to their leaders. Activities are self-regulating to a significant extent. There is an implicit faith in the appropriateness of seeking a higher material standard of living as a paramount personal and social goal.

STAGE II: FULL BLOSSOMING

This is the "summertime" of growth for industrial civilizations. The material promise of the industrial view of the world reaches its fullest blossoming in this period. As the social order becomes increasingly complex and the need for rational management grows, this becomes an era of reason more than faith. The time of entrepreneurial creativity has passed and we have moved into a period of managed creativity. Creativity is still present, but it is increasingly channeled into acceptable institutional forms. The bursts of vitality and innovation of Stage I have been replaced by a more methodical process of planning and implementation. With the rapid growth in the size and complexity of all institutions—in both government and business—people find themselves increasingly removed from access to leadership and often feel dwarfed by these massive institutions. Yet, this seems a small price to pay for the extraordinary benefits and achievements that accompany this period of growth. Growth continues throughout the entire period but at a steadily decreasing rate. As we approach the end of this period, the industrial era goals are increasingly fulfilled and social consensus weakens commensurately.

STAGE III: INITIAL DECLINE

This is the "autumn" of growth for industrial civilizations. With the fulfillment of the promise of the industrial era, social consensus begins to dissolve. Special-interest group demands begin to grow stronger as the sense of shared social purpose grows weaker. Not surprisingly, this is an era of cynicism and skepticism. Faith in the appropriateness of the historical civilizational agenda of ever increasing material growth is eroded. The entire culture is losing both its drive and its sense of direction. The dream of material abundance and ease is rapidly becoming a nightmare of unexpected problems and overwhelming bureaucratic regulation. The powerful engine of economic and technological growth is running out of steam. The "social glue"—a compelling sense of social purpose—that has held the industrial culture together is rapidly dissolving. Institutions in every sector of society are faltering under the weight of mounting bureaucratic complexity. Leaders are so bogged down in coping with institutional crises that they have little time to reflect on the larger pattern of forces at work. The visionary capacity of the culture is being rapidly exhausted as leaders are unable to rise above the demands of crisis management and envisage an alternative course of social activity that will again draw out the enthusiastic participation of the citizenry. Unexpected problems are cropping up everywhere. At the same time, the pervasively bureaucratized society is losing its resilience and is becoming more vulnerable to disruption. Faith in the basic soundness of institutions is eroding, and trust in the leadership to solve problems is rapidly declining. Some people seek representation by special interest groups in an attempt to insure their own well-being, even though it may be at the expense of the larger social welfare. Leaders are more tolerated than actively supported.

People feel divorced from their leadership and powerless to make fundamental changes. The costs of running the massive bureaucracies that dominate every sector of society are mounting rapidly. The performance of the whole social apparatus is declining.

STAGE IV: BREAKDOWN

This is the "winter" of growth for industrial civilizations. It is an era of despair as all hope that things can return to their former status is exhausted. All of the problems of Stage III are present, but the problems are now more intense. Social and bureaucratic complexity has reached overwhelming levels. The society and its institutions are no longer comprehensible and are increasingly out of control. Social consensus and a shared sense of social purpose have all but vanished. Political and social relations are in chaos. With the collapse of consensus, multiple and conflicting social purposes compete with one another for dominance. There is a rapid turnover of leaders, ideologies, and policy solutions; yet, nothing seems to work for long. Every attempt to restore some semblance of order is quickly overwhelmed by mounting levels of disorder. Leaders govern virtually without support. The regulatory apparatus that held the faltering social system together in Stage III is now unable to cope with the overwhelming complexity, the loss of social legitimacy, the unexpected problems that abound, and the absence of compelling social purpose. The remaining creativity, vitality, ingenuity, and resiliency of the entire social apparatus are being rapidly exhausted in a grinding downward spiral into bureaucratic confusion and chaos. The situation has become intolerable and untenable. The need for fundamental change is inescapable.

Where Are We Now?

If we accept these four stages of growth as a rough though useful approximation of the life cycle of industrial civilizations, the issue immediately arises: "Which stage of this life cycle are we in now?" To respond to this question, I will use the United States as my principal example. In my judgment, the United States, at the beginning of the 1980s, is somewhere in the Stage III region of Initial Decline.

What evidence is there to support the assertion that the United States has entered this stage? The United States as well as the entire human family now confronts a number of critical problems.[2] In order to suggest our present status relative to these four stages of civilizational growth, I list below a sampling of these critical problems. As you look at this list, place your attention, not on any particular problem, but on the *overall pattern* of problems. Many different types of problems are considered: economic, political, social, environmental, psychological, and so on. It is an eclectic assortment, but it powerfully suggests the present status of Western developed nations in particular and the human condition in general.

CRITICAL GLOBAL PROBLEMS:

• Nearly 1 billion persons on this planet live in absolute poverty. In human terms, absolute poverty is ". . . a condition of life so limited by malnutrition, illiteracy, disease, high infant mortality, and low life expectancy as to be beneath any rational definition of human decency."[3]

• In 1975 there were slightly more than 4 billion people in the world (by comparison, in 1930 there were only 2 billion). By the year 2000, the global population is expected to increase to more than 6 billion. Eighty percent of this population growth is expected to occur in the poorer, less materially developed nations. Most of those born in these countries will, if present trends continue, live in urban slums and shantytowns, have a meager and unbalanced diet, have little access to productive work, and be deprived of medical care and education.

• The gap between rich and poor nations is already large and is growing wider. The following statistics begin to suggest the size of this gap: in 1975 the roughly 3 billion persons in the poorer countries earned less than $400 per capita, while the roughly 1 billion persons in the wealthier nations earned more than $4,300 per capita—more than a tenfold disparity between rich and poor countries. Furthermore, the gap is widening rapidly into a chasm: Over the next twenty years it is expected that if present trends continue, for every $1 increase in the GNP of poorer nations, there will be a $20 increase in the GNP of wealthier nations. So, not only are the rich nations ten times richer, they are expected to become even richer at a rate twenty times faster than the poorer nations.

• At least 15 million children under the age of five die of starvation each year (roughly one child every two seconds). Many millions more will suffer from physical and mental impairment because of prolonged malnutrition.

• Arsenals of both nuclear and conventional weapons are proliferating; huge amounts of critically needed resources, both human and material, are being diverted into weapons production.

• The vulnerability of developed nations is mounting as reliance on highly complex and interdependent technologies grows in areas such as transportation, energy, and communications.

• Terrorism is growing rapidly as an instrument of political action.

• Cheaply available nonrenewable energy resources are being rapidly exhausted and we face the prospect of chronic and severe energy shortages in the coming decades.

• Toxic wastes are being poured into the environment and

we are beginning to encounter outbreaks of cancer and genetic damage that may reach massive proportions.

• We are depleting the ozone layer of the upper atmosphere and this, in turn, threatens to harm animal and plant life on earth.

• We are burning huge quantities of coal, and in doing so, we are releasing an undue amount of carbon dioxide into the atmosphere which is creating a greenhouse effect that may seriously disturb the long-run stability of the global climate (which, in turn, could drastically reduce global food production at a time when food requirements are escalating and thereby intensify international stresses to the breaking point).

• "Acid rains" from coal burning are destroying freshwater ecosystems, damaging the soil, reducing crop yields, impeding the growth of forests, contaminating drinking water, and eroding stone buildings.

• Overfishing and pollution of the world's oceans have led to a leveling off in annual fish catch at the same time that the demand for food from the world's oceans is increasing.

• We have disrupted the fragile ecology of large land areas suitable for farming resulting in "desertification," which is now claiming huge tracts of land.

• In many Third World countries there are growing shortages of wood as a basic fuel—this is already having a significant impact on the roughly one quarter of humanity that depends upon wood for cooking and heating.

• Perhaps as much as 20 percent of the earth's plant and animal species will become extinct by the year 2000 because of loss of habitat and pollution.

• Shortages of clean drinking water are becoming more and more common in many parts of the world (for example, over half of the people in the poorer Third World countries do not have safe water to drink).

CRITICAL UNITED STATES PROBLEMS:

• Trust in government leadership to cope with proliferating problems is virtually nonexistent.

• The visionary capacity of our leaders seems exhausted at the same time that we desperately require a renewed sense of social purpose and social direction.

• We confront chronic and severe economic problems (unacceptably high levels of inflation, unemployment, and trade deficits). Furthermore, the overall productivity of the U.S. economy is slowing markedly—we seem to have exhausted our creativity within present ways of doing things.

• We have allowed many of our crucial bureaucracies—corporations, federal agencies, universities, hospitals, etc. —to grow to such size and complexity that they are no longer comprehensible either to the persons they serve or to those whose job it is to manage them.

• Enormous fiscal problems plague these same institutions and even a brief economic depression could collapse the whole intertwined structure.

• There is widespread worker dissatisfaction with jobs that are unfulfilling, unchallenging, and that provide little opportunity to contribute to the well-being of others.

• We confront enormously difficult problems in the manufacture, transport, use, and disposal of nuclear materials.

• We face the likely prospect of critical shortages of strategic raw materials (for example, chromium, manganese, and cobalt) that are essential to the building of everything from aircraft and automobiles to computers.

• There is much evidence that we are an overstressed and overtranquilized society.

• There is serious crime in our public schools as well as teen-age alcoholism and drug abuse that in some areas reaches epidemic proportions.

• The quality and relevance of public education is declining rapidly.

• We have systematically excluded the aged from meaningful participation in our culture.

• A majority of persons feel alienated and powerless to make a difference in coping with the problems that abound.

• There has been a precipitous decline in the perceived trustworthiness of big business to be responsive to either the needs of the consumer or the needs of our fragile global ecology.

• Public participation in political processes is exceedingly low and we are a seriously uninformed electorate.

This is by no means a complete listing of our critical problems. Yet it is sufficient to provide a sense of the urgency of our situation. In looking over this list, I draw several conclusions. First, these problems are enormous in size (often involving millions of people), complexity (of bewildering difficulty to comprehend and resolve), and severity (failure to cope with any one of them will insure much human suffering). Second, we face many different kinds of problems: technical problems (such as energy and resource shortages), normative problems (such as challenges to the appropriateness of the historic social purpose of unending material progress), and process problems (such as trying to cope with overwhelming levels of bureaucratic complexity). Third, these problems are not isolated from one another but comprise a tightly intertwined pattern of problems that reach from local to global scale. As a consequence, they cannot be successfully dealt with through a one-by-one approach; these problems require a pervasive shift in our overall pattern of living. In sum, we confront a fundamental challenge of the workability and meaningfulness of Western industrial civilization.

Some may examine this evidence and conclude that we are already in a Stage IV condition of civilizational breakdown. Yet, I think we have some distance to travel before reaching that condition. Despite the pervasiveness and severity of the problems we confront, there remains, I think, a great deal of resiliency in our society. The United States may be rapidly depleting its reserves of adaptive potential, but it has not yet in my estimation exhausted them.

Others may look at these same problems and conclude that the collective challenge they pose is exaggerated—insisting that our present condition of social distress is an abnormal condition soon to be brought under control. Yet, I think the array of difficulties we confront are of such obvious seriousness that we can only conclude that the United States, and perhaps many other Western industrial nations, has passed through its summer of growth and has entered the Stage III region of Initial Decline.

It is important that we not equate this stage of civilizational maturity with failure. To the contrary, movement into the region of Initial Decline is evidence of the successful realization of the underlying goals and drives of the industrial civilization. We have arrived at Stage III by completing Stage II—the era of Full Blossoming of potentials. Entry into Stage III is thus a signal of completion of Stage II. Our eventual success or failure will be determined, not by the fact that we have entered a period of decline, but by what we do in response to our movement into that period. We will be successful if we are able to move beyond our time of civilizational decline and find a new beginning—a fresh start— that provides us with a revitalized sense of civilizational purpose.

There is no one to blame for our movement into a stage of civilizational decline. Who can be blamed when the problems we face are intrinsic to the whole intertwined structure in which we all participate? The attitudes and behaviors that arose in realizing the potentials of the industrial era were fitting for that era. Now these same attitudes and behaviors are becoming increasingly ill-suited for carrying us into the future. No one is at fault for this larger condition, as it is intrinsic to our entire structure of activity. Although no one is to blame, we are all responsible for where we go from here. (Blaming others is, I think, an unproductive diversion of our creative energy—it encourages us to avoid taking responsibility for our part in creating a more workable and meaningful society which, in turn, makes it more likely that we will actually move into the Stage IV region of civilizational breakdown).

We can put our current situation into a larger perspective by turning to the work of the eminent historian, Arnold Toynbee. In his massive analysis, *A Study of History,* Toynbee examined the cycles of growth of all major civilizations throughout recorded history.[4] He concluded from his study that a civilization begins to disintegrate when it loses the capacity to respond creatively to successive challenges. He also concluded that this failure of creativity often followed a period of great civilizational achievement.

When we examine Western industrial nations and acknowledge their two centuries of unparalleled material achievement, then it is not surprising to think that we too might now encounter a time of diminished creativity. Indeed, the stages-of-growth analysis suggests that the burst of creative energy exemplified by the industrial revolution is now exhausting itself. After acquiring a civilizational self-image of seemingly invincible mastery, we find ourselves suddenly unable to manage even our own affairs let alone begin to cope with the global problems that abound. In turn, it is a demoralizing experience to find ourselves unable to cope through traditional means that have been so successful in the past.

Toynbee is clear in asserting that a civilization is not bound to succumb to a time of loss of creativity and self-determination. If a civilization continues to decline, the people themselves bear the responsibility for that decline. When the traditional leadership and institutions have exhausted their creative potentials, the responsibility for civilizational revitalization is turned squarely back upon the individual citizens of society.

Thus, it is not necessary that we move deep into the Stage IV region of civilizational breakdown. Our movement into the last stage of decline is not inevitable unless we collectively acquiesce, through complacency and inaction, to such a civilizational path. By not choosing an alternative path, we make a profound choice to continue along our historical trajectory of growth and to see the industrial revolution through to its most extreme, and most devastating, conclusion.

The Rate of Descent into Civilizational Breakdown

If we do not heed the not-so-subtle warning signals provided by Stage III, how long might it take the United States (our prime example) to move into the Stage IV region of breakdown? Clearly, this is impossible to predict with accuracy. Although I have used a smooth curve to portray movement through the four stages of growth, I do not think our journey down the backside of the growth curve is likely to be equally smooth. Just as our ride up the front side of the growth curve had many bumps, plateaus, and sudden jumps, so too will similar variability characterize our movement into the Stage IV region.

Although it is impossible to predict precisely when we might move into the Stage IV region, this is such an important issue that I would like to venture a rough estimate of timing. In order to gauge the timing of movement from Stage III to Stage IV, we have to back up and look at the relative speed with which we have been moving through the earlier stages of growth.

The United States entered the Stage I period of high industrial growth in the early 1800s—a period commonly accepted as the starting point for rapid industrialization for the United States. The Stage I period of high growth continued, I think, until the 1930s. The period between the Great Depression and the beginning of the Second World War seems to mark the transition from Stage I to Stage II. In the post-World War II period, the United States entered a period of managed growth and the fullest realization of industrial potentials. This—the time of greatest blossoming for industrial civilization—was the height of Stage II. For a brief decade or two it seemed as though material progress would be unending. This dream rapidly faded in the turbulent and traumatic period stretching from the mid-1960s through the mid-1970s. During this decade much of the vigor and vitality of Stage II was exhausted. By the late 1970s, the United States had begun, I think, to move into the Stage III of initial decline. The economy was beginning to malfunction seriously, the political apparatus was rapidly losing its legitimacy, the sense of social cohesion was dissolving, the environmental damage from rapid industrialization was beginning to mount, the availability of cheap energy and raw materials was coming to an end, and, in many other ways, the closing of an era of growth was increasingly evident.

If we have, as of the 1980s, moved into the Stage III region of initial decline, then it reveals that the pace of change has been picking up speed. It took more than a century to move through the Stage I region of growth, but it took less than half a century to move through the Stage II region. Based upon estimates such as this (as well as other futures research in which I have participated), my best guess is that the United States will move into the Stage IV region of civilizational breakdown no later than the 1990s. The actual pace of change could be slower or faster. Destabilizing events (such as war in the Middle East leading to a cutoff of oil to industrial nations) could rapidly propel us into Stage IV. Although I think it less likely, it is also conceivable that we could muddle along for several more decades before entering a time of civilizational breakdown. The important point is *not* the exact timing of transition into Stage IV; rather it is that the amount of time we have to mount a creative, grass roots response to our rapidly changing conditions is very short. We have no room for complacency.

The Stage IV Challenge

I do not view Stage IV as a time of abrupt and apocalyptic change. Nor do I think that entry into Stage IV implies the immediate or automatic breakdown of society. Instead, I think it much more likely that Stage IV will be characterized as a period of disharmony, discord, disynchronization, and fragmentation that could extend over a period of decades.

Despite the severity of the problems that I anticipate will accompany Stage IV, this does not mean that the productive capacity of the economy will be physically devastated or that the nation will be turned into a wasteland. Indeed, the outward physical appearances could suggest that nothing quite so momentous was happening. The offices, homes, factories, roads, and other landmarks of a secure physical existence will still be in place (barring a devastating nuclear war or natural catastrophe). Further, I assume that there will still be sufficient resources available to support a materially frugal existence. What this means, then, is that *the most fundamental challenge that arises in Stage IV is an invisible crisis: a loss of social cohesion around a compelling civilizational purpose that draws out our enthusiastic participation in life.*

We humans can bear many hardships when the burden of those hardships is felt to be meaningful, productive, and somehow contributing to the well-being of others. However, feelings of futility and despair begin to infuse our daily lives when, with no sustaining sense of purpose, we enter a period of great psychological stress and material hardship. Without a sense of meaningful participation in life, we begin to lose our bearings, we begin to wander, we become disoriented.

An overriding challenge of Stage IV is the need to find a new common sense—a new sense of reality, human identity, and social purpose that respects and responds to our radically changing global circumstances. Finding this new common sense amidst the turbulence and disarray of the Stage IV conditions of civilizational breakdown—which involves the breakdown of social consensus—is likely to be a drawn-out, messy, and ambiguous process of social learning. Whether we make skillful use of our tools of mass communication will be critical, I think, in determining how readily we can arrive at a new and widely shared common sense.

Overall, I do not anticipate a quick or easy resolution to the difficult conditions of Stage IV. Rather, I think it much more likely that we will confront an extended period of social turmoil that will eventually bare the very soul of Western industrial cultures. Only when we have exhausted the hope that the golden era of industrial growth can somehow be revived will we collectively venture forward. Yet, if we (as individuals) fail to begin our grass roots adaptation to these profoundly changing circumstances, we (as a society) will be ill-prepared as the mounting force of this challenge hits us. Unable to assimilate so much change all at once, the social fabric could be violently torn apart and become so chaotic that the possibility of maintaining a democratic social order could vanish. Then, either anarchy or, more likely, a highly managed society could result.

We cannot go back, nor can we continue indefinitely along our historic path of growth. We must begin the process of creative adaptation. Patient and persistent efforts are essential. There will be no quick fixes for our global predicament. Indeed, I think we may be several decades into the next century before we pass through this dark night in our life cycle of civilizational growth and emerge again in the awakening springtime with a revitalized sense of social purpose.

Two Outcomes from a Period of Civilizational Breakdown

A time of civilizational Breakdown can be viewed as either an ending or a beginning. On the one hand, if we maintain an exclusive identification with the Western industrial view of the world and are thereby unable to make the creative adaptation demanded by this evolutionary watershed, then the Stage IV conditions will seem like the end of civilization. On the other hand, if we can see beyond the breakdown of the industrial view of the world and sense the enormous opportunity that lies beyond, this difficult time of transition will be viewed as the beginning of a new springtime of civilizational growth.

Thus there are two outcomes that could most plausibly emerge from the Stage IV conditions of civilizational breakdown. One is a stagnating civilization in which human creativity is paralyzed in the web of an authoritarian bureaucracy. The other is a revitalizing civilization in which creativity is released from bureaucratic bondage by the self-determining and self-organizing efforts of millions of individuals acting in cooperation with one another. These two pathways are summarized below:

TWO PATHWAYS INTO THE FUTURE:

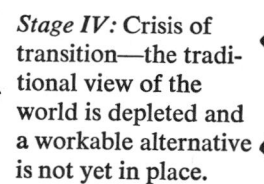

Stage III: Growing exhaustion of the industrial world view and accompanying social order.

Stage IV: Crisis of transition—the traditional view of the world is depleted and a workable alternative is not yet in place.

• *Revitalization*—People embrace the challenge; a time of compressed social invention and high creativity.
• *Stagnation*—People retreat from this time of challenge and seek security in a highly managed social order.

Given these two contrasting outcomes from a Stage IV condition, how might we come to select one path or another? What are the transition dynamics that will tend to lead us toward either stagnation or revitalization? In the following tables I have attempted to summarize some of the most important factors that, I think, would tend to take us in one direction or another.

SCENARIO I:

A PATH TO CIVILIZATIONAL STAGNATION

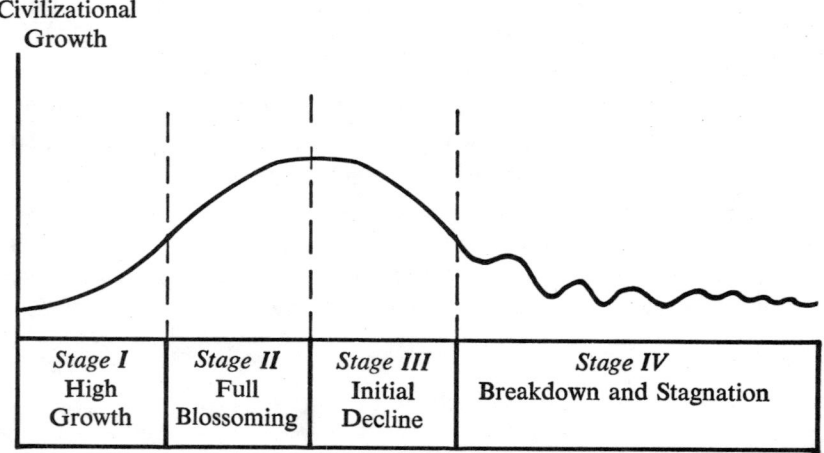

Civilizational
Growth

Stage I High Growth	Stage II Full Blossoming	Stage III Initial Decline	Stage IV Breakdown and Stagnation

Given Stage IV conditions, there are a variety of factors that could powerfully contribute to stagnating civilizational growth; for example:

> • *Psychological Responses*—The majority of individuals are slow to accept the magnitude of the civilizational challenge.[5] Instead of experimenting with alternative ways of living and working, they dissipate creative energy in a variety of responses: 1. *Denial*—some insist that this is not a time of fundamental civilizational transition, that the current distress is merely a short-term aberration and that things will soon return to "normal"; 2. *Indifference*—other people feel helpless to make a difference and simultaneously assume, with blind trust, that someone must be in control,

so "why bother"; 3. *Blame*—others assume that some group "out there" must be to blame for these problems; consequently, much creative energy is expended in looking for and punishing various scapegoats; 4. *Escape*—others, having acknowledged the seriousness of the situation, look for a way for themselves and their friends to escape: Some attempt to return to the land to live in isolated self-sufficiency, others, particularly the wealthy, search for secure enclaves in which to "ride out the storm"; 5. *Resignation*—others have a fatalistic acceptance of what seems an unstoppable process of disintegration; they feel a sense of defeat and despair; they feel powerless to initiate a creative response and unable to hold back the inevitable breakdown of society.

• *Mass Media*—The mass media, particularly television, are used as an ever more sophisticated source of passive entertainment. Television continues to divert public attention from the pressing realities of the world. Immature programming tends to mask the reality of the situation and generates a false sense of normalcy. The major media corporations continue to place short-run profit making above the rapidly changing and growing needs of the public interest. Critical issues ranging from political fragmentation to world hunger are pushed aside in favor of more traditional and more profitable programming. In-depth and continuing exploration of alternative ways of living and working do not appear. Social learning is retarded and distorted. Democratic processes continue to falter as the citizenry increasingly loses the race with mounting social complexity.

• *Grass Roots Organizations*—Grass roots organizations that might have brought an infusion of creativity and innovation are two few, too late, and too weakly connected with the larger society to make any substantial impact. People are forced to rely almost exclusively on traditional bureaucracies for coping with the situation.

• *Cultural Consensus*—The culture has no collective intention beyond that of survival. With no compelling agenda beyond survival concerns, people hold on to traditional ways of living rather than squarely confront this time of civilizational challenge. Nations adopt a lifeboat ethic in global relations and turn away from responsibilities to the larger human family. With no clear agenda beyond maintaining a faltering and fragmenting civilization, the culture loses its drive and sense of direction. The social order is severely buffeted by competing interest groups that battle for dominance with increasing intensity. The remaining trust and goodwill of the social order is rapidly depleted.

With these forces at work and with little prior adaptation, the society is quickly overwhelmed and social relations collapse into chaos. From this chaotic conditon there emerges a highly managed social order that attempts to impose stability and order upon the situation. Historic freedoms, both political and economic, are "temporarily" suspended. Massive though deadening bureaucracies attempt to manage virtually every facet of life. Though well-meaning, they pre-empt local responsibility and raise the level of dependency on these bureaucracies. The outcome is an arrested civilization—one that is paralyzed into dynamic inaction. The social order is expending all of its creative energy in just maintaining the status quo. As everyone struggles desperately to hold on, the whole social order sinks deeper into the bureaucratic stranglehold. The "winter" of industrial civilization appears to stretch into an endless future.

SCENARIO II:
A PATH TO CIVILIZATIONAL REVITALIZATION

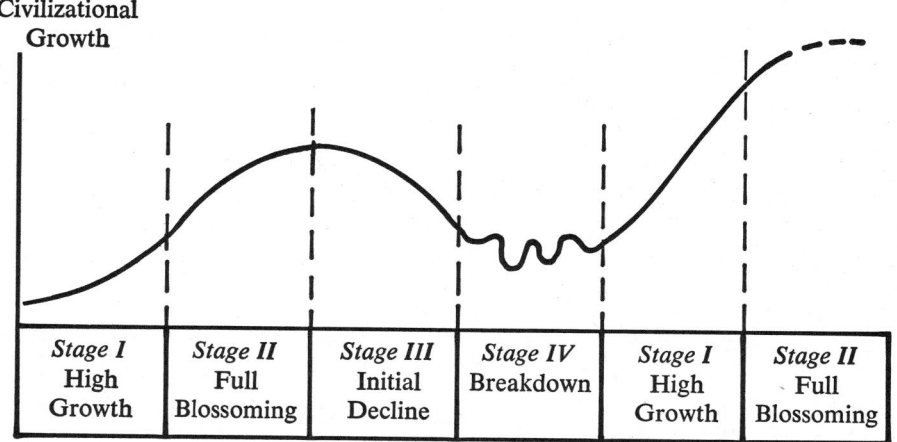

Civilizational
Growth

Stage I High Growth	Stage II Full Blossoming	Stage III Initial Decline	Stage IV Breakdown	Stage I High Growth	Stage II Full Blossoming

Given Stage IV conditions, there are a variety of factors that could powerfully contribute to a revitalization of civilizational growth; for example:

- *Psychological Responses*—A period of intense social learning begins as people acknowledge their fears, anxieties, sorrows, anger, and other legitimate feelings that accompany any significant passage in life. With this acknowledgment, people are empowered to come into a conscious and direct relationship with life as it is. In turn, people are thereby enabled to rapidly move through the psychological responses of denial, indifference, blame, escape, and resignation. As a growing number of persons accept our time of civilizational challenge, an enormous wave of pent-up creativity is released.

- *Mass Media*—The mass media are used as an ever more

sophisticated tool for active social learning. The use of
television is fundamentally reoriented toward revealing the
hard realities of our situation. The needs of the public interest are placed above the short-term profit pursuits of the
mass media. Mature programming awakens the culture
from complacency and infuses daily life with a sense of
urgency and purpose. Whole new areas and forms of programming emerge (for example, ongoing and in-depth exploration of alternative ways of living and working as manifest in the lives of real people; alternative future paths for
civilizational growth; exploring the make-up and character
of the human family; etc.). Social learning is greatly accelerated. Democratic processes are revitalized as citizens
are empowered to cope with mounting social complexity
and to participate in decision-making.

• *Grass Roots Organizations*—Grass roots organizations
are growing at every level, from local to global. These
organizations assist in empowering people to take charge
of their own lives. At the local level, these organizations
are taking charge of activities formerly pre-empted by centralized bureaucracies: education, housing, crime preven-
tion, child care, health care, employment, job training, and
more. Strength and resiliency are brought into society as
local organizations promote self-help, self-organization,
community spirit, and neighborhood bonding into cohesive
units. Thus, the impact of faltering central bureaucracies
is cushioned. These grass roots organizations are numerous
enough, have arisen soon enough, and are effective enough
to provide a genuine alternative to centralized forms of bureaucratic control. At the global level, these grass roots
organizations bridge across nation-state boundaries and
provide a source of global cohesion and consensus that
otherwise would be lacking. These organizations also assist
in raising public consciousness regarding issues of global
concern: nuclear proliferation, world hunger, energy scarcity, a growing gap between rich and poor nations, and so on.

• *Cultural Consensus*—With widespread acceptance of the Stage IV conditions, with the use of the media as potent tools for active social learning, and with grass roots organizations proliferating, there rapidly emerges a new cultural consensus. The culture moves beyond the historic agenda of self-serving material progress to a new agenda of life-serving participation in promoting the well-being of the entire human family. A spaceship earth ethic is adopted in global relations. Developed nations become fully participating partners in the process of global revitalization. Despite enormous social stresses, there is an overriding sense of social purpose that provides sufficient social glue to hold society together. A sense of human dignity, mutual aid, goodwill, and trust is growing as people gradually learn new ways of living and working that are both sustainable and satisfying.

With these forces at work, the collapse of the social order is averted. There has been sufficient prior adaptation to allow the larger society to begin to redirect its unfolding in a more sustainable and satisfying direction. New ways of living and working (developed by creative minorities) meet with the sympathy of the majority and the overall social agenda begins to shift. This is a very demanding period, requiring the utmost in commitment and personal responsibility. Yet, the adversity of the situation is viewed by most as purposeful. Consequently, a majority of persons willingly participate and contribute to their fullest. Problems still abound but there is a widely shared sense that they are no longer insurmountable. A new springtime of civilizational growth is emerging.

Let's examine the nature of these two outcomes—stagnation and revitalization—in greater detail. Because Chapter 8 is devoted to exploring the nature of a revitalized civilization (premised on the widespread choosing of a life of intentional simplicity), I will comment here only briefly on this outcome.

A stagnating civilization results when we encounter the Stage IV region of Breakdown (with its accompanying economic, social, political, and environmental problems) and are ill-prepared to cope with it. With little prior adaptation, and few visible examples of alternative ways of living and working that might creatively respond to the situation, people retreat into the seeming security of a highly managed social order. Stage IV is thereby viewed as a chaotic condition that should be replaced by predictability, order, and security as quickly as possible—even if the cost to economic and political freedoms is high. As people turn to paternalistic bureaucracies to manage social affairs that they think they are unable to manage for themselves, the vitality of the social order is strangled in a web of bureaucracy. The will and creativity of the entire civilization is ensnared in a mountain of regulation and red tape. People feel increasingly dependent upon, and yet isolated from, this growing bureaucracy.

A wartime psychology prevails—but it is a war without a visible opponent. In reality, we are at war with ourselves and our fear of the unknown challenge that lies beyond the industrial era. As we retreat again and again from that challenge, the vitality of our civilization is increasingly locked into just maintaining the faltering status quo. In an evolutionary sense, our civilization is not going anywhere despite the frenetic activity. There is much "sound and fury signifying nothing." What might life be like in a stagnating civilization? Here are some guesses.

Democratic processes would be "temporarily" suspended to allow more "rational" and simplified forms of crisis management. The executive branch would have virtually absolute power to govern in ways that are not constitutionally responsible to the citizenry. This would not likely be a military dictatorship intended to brutalize people; rather, it would be a softer form of authoritarianism that emerges from the well-meaning actions of an anonymous elite working through vast bureaucracies. Wages and prices would be tightly controlled. Gasoline and many consumer goods would be rationed. Access to some modes of transportation would be tightly regulated. A black market would flourish. Many basic industries would be nationalized or run under close government supervision. Population migration into favored areas would be restricted. In many cities, the "city-boss" leadership of an earlier era would again become commonplace, thereby turning many cities into virtual "fiefdoms." Many affluent communities would be turned into small police states as they hire private police forces to protect their property and wealth from the increasingly desperate and resentful poor. Disparities between rich and poor would ostensibly be narrowing, but the reality would be more akin to an implicit caste system that tends to isolate rich and poor and perpetuate inequalities. Acts of political terrorism would be commonplace. Leaders in both government and business would tend to withdraw into faceless bureaucracies to protect their anonymity. Government surveillance of persons or groups who threaten the prevailing "law and order" would be widespread. The monitoring of individual activities would become increasingly sophisticated and would employ centralized data banks and new generations of computer technology. To relieve the stress and despair of life, new types of mood-altering drugs would come into increasingly legitimate social use. The mass media would be restricted in the scope and content of their programming. A stagnating, somber, fearful, and ingrown social order would be emerging—one that would be increasingly isolated from the reality of the larger global situation. Developed nations would spend a disproportionate share of scarce national resorces on bolstering their military power as they attempt to protect their wealth from the growing demands of the world's poor for a more equitable use of resources and productive capacity.

The nature of the adaptive process whereby we could sink into a condition of stagnation is well illustrated, I think, by the following laboratory experiment (I don't know whether this gruesome experiment was ever actually conducted; nonetheless, it graphically illustrates the process at work). In this experiment, a frog was placed in a beaker of boiling water. Not surprisingly, the frog immediately jumped out. However, when the frog was then placed in a beaker of cold water that was slowly warmed to boiling temperature, the change was sufficiently gradual that the frog adapted in increments, making no attempt to escape. By the time the frog instinctively realized the danger, it was too late. Weakened, he could no longer jump out. So, he died. In a similar process of adaptation, developed nations (whether capitalist, communist, or socialist) could succumb to a "living death" as the will and creativity of people are totally absorbed in deadening bureaucracies that attempt to cope with massive problems. Virtually no one, I think, would consciously choose such a civilizational outcome. Therefore, it will emerge, not from conscious choice, but from unconscious acquiescence to the seemingly rational necessities for coping with the state of national emergency that characterizes Stage IV.

The second outcome that I think could likely emerge from the Stage IV condition is that of a grass roots revitalization of society. In order for revitalization to occur, a significant minority must be well prepared to cope with the difficult conditions of civilizational breakdown. In turn, the creative minority could provide many visible examples of a wide diversity of alternative ways of living and working. In doing so, they could demonstrate to the larger society that there exist genuine alternatives beyond acquiescence to the dictates of deadening bureaucracies. The coherent alternatives of the few could help to transform the chaos of the many into a revitalizing path of civilizational growth.

A revitalizing outcome assumes that a majority of people would view the Stage IV conditions as a time of compressed social invention that requires sufficient relaxation of bureaucratic regulation to allow alternative ways of living and working to arise from the grass roots level of society. In due course, traditional institutions could yield to the new social forms that they have helped to create. Compared to industrial civilizations, activities in a revitalizing society would tend to be much more highly self-regulating, more uniquely adapted to local conditions, and consciously undertaken from a global perspective. (Additional attributes of a revitalizing civilization are discussed in Chapter 8 and in Appendices IV and V).

Two great paths lie before us. They overlap at present but will increasingly diverge as we move into the future. The manner in which we choose to conduct our individual lives will be of crucial importance in determining the civilizational path upon which we will make our journey into the future.

Civilizational Transition from a Planetary Perspective

We have been exploring the decline of Western industrial civilizations in relative isolation from the other nations of the world. Yet, our time of wrenching transition is not restricted to Western industrial nations. Although the reasons may vary, virtually all of the major civilizations of the world have, I think, entered a time of fundamental transition. The decline of Western developed nations is an integral part of this larger process of global evolution.

I think it is no accident that the very time when the human family finds itself shoulder to shoulder in an intensely interdependent and vulnerable world is also the time when traditional civilizations of both East and West are breaking down. This loosening is crucial. Our distress is a measure of the progress of birth—the labor pains of a global civilization are being felt. If we look beyond the despair of our immediate predicament, we can see that the process of disintegration we are now experiencing is a healthy one. The human family cannot open itself to the beginnings of a peaceful global society while we are doggedly fixed to a view of the world that no longer matches our situation.

Like it or not, we are moving toward some form of global

civilization at a breathtaking speed. Economically, culturally, environmentally, and in many other ways, members of the human family touch one another with growing frequency and intensity. Furthermore, the industrial era has generated problems that cannot be resolved by nation-states working in isolation from one another. Many of the critical problems (nuclear proliferation, environmental pollution, Third World poverty, etc.) that the human family now must deal with are part of a tightly intertwined network of global activity. To skillfully respond to these problems, we must embrace a perspective that is equal in scope to the problems that we face—and that is a perspective of global dimension. For many reasons, then, the human family is now obliged to begin to discover its shared common sense. We are being pushed by necessity and pulled by opportunity to find a shared human agenda that honors human unity while fostering human diversity.

Are we beginning to discover a new, global common sense? Is there a view of reality and human identity that is spacious enough to embrace human diversity and simultaneously compelling enough to genuinely encourage a sense of human unity? I think the skeletal outlines of a globally relevant common sense are already beginning to appear. I will not discuss this important but necessarily speculative topic here. Instead, I refer you to Chapter 10, where I explore the meeting of East and West (the principal civilizational parents of this emerging common sense).

It has not been my intention to unduly inflate the significance of this time of civilizational transition. We are forging but another link in a long chain of civilizational growth. In one sense, the present era is no more important than any other—failure to forge a strong link anywhere along the chain will weaken the entire structure of evolutionary unfolding. Yet, in another sense, the now emerging link in our civilizational chain—the link that leads toward some form of planetary civilization—seems particularly vital. If we can open to reciprocal learning with other cultures, and if through that learning we can find a shared sense of reality, human identity, and social purpose that draws out our wholehearted participation in life, then, I think, the evolution of the human family will lead in presently unanticipated directions and to unforeseen heights. On the other hand, if we are not open to the process of global social learning and we thereby fail to arrive at a widely shared common sense, then global integration may, by default, be achieved by force. If the threat of mass destruction is the principal glue that holds the global order together, then the civilizational form that will emerge will neither acknowledge our fundamental human unity nor celebrate our human diversity.

In the past, the notion of some form of peaceful global civilization (fostering both unity and diversity) was viewed as a utopian dream. Now it is a requirement for our survival. If we turn away from this challenge, we will surely unleash upon ourselves the most massive wave of suffering ever experienced in human history. Time has run out. The era of creative adaptation is already upon us. What happens in the next few decades will profoundly condition the future course of humankind's evolution. Just as the birth experience and first few years of life profoundly condition the development of a child, so too will the manner in which our global civilization is born condition the further evolution of the human species. As we shall discuss in Chapter 8, the emergence of voluntary simplicity as a widespread way of life seems crucial to the birth of some form of peaceful global civilization.

Conclusion

We have explored a number of themes in this chapter. I would like to summarize some of the more important conclusions here:

- The life cycle of growth for Western industrial nations can be usefully described as moving through four seasons or stages: Stage I: High Growth; Stage II: Fullest Blossoming of Potentials; Stage III: Initial Decline; and Stage IV: Civilizational Breakdown.

• Many Western developed nations have, I think, entered the Stage III region of Initial Decline.

• I think it is likely that the United States will move into the Stage IV region of Civilizational Breakdown no later than the 1990s.

• No particular group is to blame for this state of affairs as it is the natural outcome of our process of civilizational maturation. Although no one is to blame, we are all responsible for where we go from here.

• There are two likely outcomes from this time of Civilizational Breakdown: first, "stagnation"—a result that follows when we retreat from our time of civilizational challenge and seek security in a highly managed, pervasively bureaucratized social order; second, "revitalization"—a result that follows when we embrace this time of testing and challenge and begin a process of intense social innovation to develop more sustainable and satisfying ways of living and working.

• There is no necessity that we move into a condition of civilizational stagnation and arrested development. If we do, we bear the full responsibility.

• Among the more important factors that will determine whether we move toward stagnation or revitalization are how we respond psychologically to this time of transition and challenge; how we employ the mass media; whether we begin to consciously develop alternative institutions at the grass roots level; and whether we can achieve a new social consensus around a workable and meaningful social agenda that embraces the entire human family.

• The breakdown of civilization is not confined to the Western developed nations. All the major civilizations on the planet seem to be moving through a historic time of transition.

• A time of planetary-wide Civilizational Breakdown is also a time of freeing up. In the coming decades, there will be a genuine opportunity for a new common sense to emerge at a planetary level.

We have been examining the civilizational context within which voluntary simplicity is arising. The context is not one of social tranquillity and unending economic prosperity; rather, it is a context of wrenching and pervasive change occurring at many levels at once—from personal to planetary. How relevant is voluntary simplicity to these circumstances? Does this approach to living skillfully respond to the pushes of necessity and the pulls of opportunity? We turn to consider these and other issues in the following chapter.

CHAPTER 4

THE RELEVANCE
AND GROWTH OF
VOLUNTARY SIMPLICITY

The Relevance of Voluntary Simplicity

Is a life of voluntary simplicity relevant for coping with the stressful process of civilizational decline and breakdown? Given the massive forces and institutions involved in this process of transition, it may appear that the individual is helpless—powerless to make a difference. Yet, the opposite is more nearly true. In Stages III and IV, institutions become so locked into their historic roles and so paralyzed by the stranglehold of bureaucratic complexity that they have little freedom for creative action. Virtually all their creativity is being absorbed in an intense struggle to maintain themselves. Under these conditions, the power and responsibility for creative action is returned to the individual. Because the deliberate simplification of life fosters personal empowerment, self-determination, and self-organizing behavior, its relevance to this time of civilizational transition cannot be overestimated.

The conscious simplification of life could do much to promote the grass roots revitalization of our fragmenting civilizations. The attitudes and behaviors that accompany this way of living could contribute much needed flexibility, creativity, and coherence to our faltering civilization and thereby ease our transition into a more sustainable and satisfying society. Let's examine some additional ways in which voluntary simplicity is relevant to our time of transition:

- In a world where nearly 1 billion people live near the edge of physical survival, the relevance of intentional simplicity by the more affluent peoples of the world cannot be overestimated.

- Conscious simplicity, with its emphasis on living with frugality and balance, reduces wasteful consumption of precious, nonrenewable resources and also lessens damage to an already polluted environment.

- Because a life of intentional simplicity supports the pursuit of contributory livelihood, it encourages the growth of a more humane economy—an economy whose productivity and vitality result from workers' and managers' intending to be responsive to the real needs of people.

- In encouraging more human-sized living and working environments, there is enhanced the sense of community and meaningful participation with others in the affairs of daily life.

- In encouraging the acquisition of a broad range of work skills so as to increase self-reliance, the dependency upon specialists to handle the ordinary demands of everyday life is reduced.

- In favoring greater use of small-scale energy technologies (such as solar power), less reliance is placed on energy systems (such as nuclear power) that require exceedingly large and complex bureaucracies to manage and regulate them.

- With its emphasis on self-determination, higher levels of self-organizing activity are encouraged at the local level. In turn, this will tend to restore to the locality a higher level of responsibility for developing ways of living and working that are uniquely appropriate to local conditions.

• In embracing compassionate causes such as ending world hunger and halting the nuclear arms race, there is a conscious attempt to build a more workable and humane world.

More examples could be presented, but the pattern is clear. Voluntary simplicity responds to many of the critical problems of our era: environmental degradation, bureaucratic complexity, world hunger, a loss of social purpose and social cohesion, a dehumanizing economy, and many more. This way of life represents a creative and comprehensive response to a host of critical problems customarily considered to be separate. By coping simultaneously with scores of interrelated problems, this way of life provides a multifaceted approach that could not be achieved by addressing these problems on a one-by-one basis. This is not to say that a path of conscious simplicity is a cure-all for society's ills; rather, it represents a constructive beginning— an important first step toward their eventual resolution.

A life of voluntary simplicity also meshes with the eternal needs of individuals to grow both psychologically and spiritually. This conscious emphasis on including interior growth allows people to transfer some proportion of their growth potentials from strictly material concerns to the domain of psychological and spiritual maturation. Since we need all the maturity we can muster to cope with our mounting civilizational challenges, a greater emphasis on interior growth seems especially appropriate for our times and circumstances. Thus, the needs of the individual uniquely match the needs of society.

There is another important way in which voluntary simplicity is relevant to our time of civilizational transition; namely, this way of living is in harmony with our evolutionary agenda. What does this mean? A statement made by the feminist and philosopher Simone de Beauvoir provides us with a useful starting point. She said: "Life is occupied in both perpetuating itself and in surpassing itself; if all it does is maintain itself, then living is only not dying." In other words, a healthy individual or society must continuously balance two competing demands: We must both maintain ourselves (create a workable existence) and surpass ourselves (create a meaningful existence). On the one hand, if we, individually and collectively, seek *only* to maintain ourselves, then, no matter how grand that style of living might be, our living becomes "only not dying." On the other hand, if we strive *only* to secure a meaningful existence without assuring the material basis to support our lives, then physical life itself is threatened and the promise of surpassing ourselves is no more than a utopian dream. Clearly, we must skillfully maintain a continuous balance between these two central dimensions of life —we must create *both* a workable and a meaningful existence.

We can apply this compelling set of criteria to the growth of Western industrial civilizations. If Western civilizations are increasingly marked by the antithesis of simplicity (indirectness, complexity, dishonesty, ostentation, and secondary complications), it follows that virtually all available energy (psychological, economic, and political) will be consumed in just maintaining a wasteful, cluttered, confusing, and inefficient social order. With so much energy going into the maintenance aspects of life, very little is left for persons to surpass themselves —to forge a meaningful existence. It seems to me that many Western nations have reached just this condition—living has become little more than "only not dying." In this setting, a greater degree of conscious simplicity is of crucial relevance for revitalizing our disintegrating civilizations.

Let me be even more specific in suggesting the relevance of voluntary simplicity to the growth of our civilizations. The historian Arnold Toynbee traced the development of all the major civilizations throughout recorded history and concluded that civilizational growth could not be measured by increases in power over nature or in power over other people. "The conquest of the external environment, be it human or physical, does not by itself constitute the criterion of growth, attractive though this simple formula may appear at first sight." [1] What, then, is the criterion of growth? It is, he said, manifest in ". . . a progressive and cumulative increase in both outward mastery of the environment and in inward self-determination." [2] Growth is a twofold process that involves the balanced unfolding of both the outer world and the inner condition. Toynbee framed this principle of growth in what he termed the "Law of Progressive Simplification." [3] This law asserts that the progressive transfer of individual and social energy to increasingly more subtle and nonmaterial aspects of life is a key measure of the degree of civilizational growth. In other words, by learning how to handle the material requirements of life in a way that touches the earth and its inhabitants ever more lightly and gently, additional increments of energy and attention are released, which allow a culture to develop the social, psychological, and spiritual dimensions of existence.

Civilizational growth is thus characterized by: 1. the conscious refinement of the material side of life (greater simplicity); and 2. the simultaneous unfolding of the nonmaterial side of life (greater voluntariness or self-determination). Voluntary simplicity, then, is a way of life that is in alignment with civilizational evolution. Its relevance for our time of civilizational transition is enormous.

The Growth Potential of Voluntary Simplicity

If voluntary simplicity is so relevant to our time of civilizational transition, then it is reasonable to assume that it should already be emerging in response to our stressful circumstances. Is this happening? Indeed it is. For more than a decade, this way of life has been growing at the grass roots level of a number of developed Western nations. In the United States, Norway, Holland, Sweden, Canada, Australia, and other countries, a distinct change is occurring in the manner and intention with which a rapidly growing number of persons are living their lives. As we discussed in Chapter 2, people of all different backgrounds, ages, and living circumstances are, on their own initiatives and in their own unique ways, exploring alternative ways of living that contribute to a more workable and meaningful world.

Yet, what evidence is there to suggest that the general public in developed Western nations may be shifting its attitudes and behaviors in favor of the way of life exemplified by voluntary simplicity? The strength and pervasiveness of public sympathy for this orientation in living is revealed in a variety of national opinion surveys and social change movements, only a sampling of which is presented here.

First, there is considerable evidence that the attitudes of a small but intensely motivated minority during the 1960s had become rapidly diffused throughout the larger society by the mid-1970s. The survey researcher Daniel Yankelovich studied this forerunner group who held a new set of what he termed "post-affluent values." In surveying his group, he was struck by two motivations that seemed exceptionally strong: "One is private, directed at personal self-fulfillment, self-actualization, and creativity. The other is public, directed toward a vision of what a just and brotherly society might be." [4] In the late 1960s Yankelovich thought it would take "decades and perhaps generations" for some synthesis to occur between this subculture and the dominant culture. Then, in a 1974 study published in a book entitled *The New Morality*, he stated, "Our prediction that the process of diffusion might take decades and even generations to accomplish has been proven inaccurate by the present study. Indeed, we are amazed by the rapidity with which that process is now taking place . . ." [5]

Second, consider the findings from a 1975 Louis Harris poll of U.S. attitudes toward consumption. [6] Over two in every three people admitted they were highly wasteful and a much higher 90 percent thought they were going to have to find ways to cut back on the amount of things they consumed and wasted. Harris also reported that, ". . . when the alternative is posed between changing our life-style to have less consumption of physical goods, on the one hand, and enduring the risks of continuing inflation and unemployment due to raw material shortages, on the other, by 77% to 8%, the American people opt for a change in life-style."

Third, a 1977 Louis Harris poll further confirms this pattern.[7] Harris found that: "Significant majorities place a higher priority on improving human and social relationships and the quality of American life than on simply raising the standard of living." Here are some of the striking poll results that led to this conclusion:

> • By 79 percent to 17 percent, the public places greater emphasis on "teaching people how to live more with basic essentials" than on "reaching higher standards of living."

> • By 76 percent to 17 percent, a sizable majority opts for "learning to get our pleasures out of nonmaterial experiences," rather than on "satisfying our needs for more goods and services."

> • By 63 percent to 29 percent, a majority feels that the country would be better served if emphasis were put on "learning to appreciate human values more than material values," rather than on "finding ways to create more jobs for producing more goods."

> • By 66 percent to 22 percent, the public chooses "breaking up big things and getting back to more humanized living," over "developing bigger and more efficient ways of doing things."

> • By 59 percent to 26 percent, a majority feels that inflation can better be controlled by "buying much less of those products short in supply and high in price" than by "producing more goods to satisfy demand."

In summarizing these survey findings, Harris states: "Taken together, the majority views expressed . . . suggest that a quiet revolution may be taking place in our national values and aspirations." He concluded with the comment that ". . . there is no doubt that there has been a profound shift in many of the traditional assumptions which have governed the nation."

Other evidence to suggest the size of the group that may be pursuing an alternative way of life is found in research conducted by the Values and Lifestyles program at SRI International (formerly the Stanford Research Institute) in California.[8] Their research, based upon extensive national opinion surveys, describes three major groups of consumers:

- *Need-Driven Consumers*—These are persons living at or near the poverty level. Their lives are preoccupied with the struggle to make ends meet. Security considerations—adequate food, clothing, shelter, health care, etc.—are very important to this group that is estimated to constitute 11 percent of the adult population in the United States, or roughly 19 million persons as of 1980.

- *Outer-Directed Consumers*—These are members of the more affluent middle class. They tend to be pragmatic, materialistic, and traditional in their outlook on life. For the most part, they live according to the expectations of others. As a consequence, this group tends to consume with attention to appearance and prevailing fashion. As of 1980, outer-directed consumers were estimated to constitute 69 percent of the adult population, or approximately 110 million persons.

- *Inner-Directed Consumers*—These are often younger persons (members of the post-World War II baby boom generation), from middle-class backgrounds, who are relatively well educated. Inner-directed consumers tend to be idealistic, spiritually inclined, ecologically oriented, and experimental in their manner of living and consuming. This group consumes according to their inner sense of what is appropriate rather than relying upon prevailing fashion or the expectations of others as their primary guide. As of 1980, inner-directed consumers were estimated to constitute roughly 20 percent of the adult population, or around 33 million persons.

How can we relate this typology of consumer behavior to voluntary simplicity? If we assume that the majority of those who initially choose a life of conscious simplicity are likely to have an inner-directed orientation, this typology suggests that there exists a huge population segment (some 33 million adults in the United States as of 1980) that is already strongly oriented toward living and consuming in a way congruent with voluntary simplicity.

These opinion surveys, spread out over a half-dozen years, reveal an enormous receptivity within the U.S. population to a life of conscious simplicity. The United States is not alone in this dramatic shift in attitudes. If anything, there are other countries that are well in advance of the United States in the process of personal and social transformation.

In Norway, for example, a national opinion survey conducted in the mid-1970s found that 76 percent felt the standard of living was too high.[9] Moreover, 74 percent said they would prefer a simple life (with no more than essentials) to a high income (with many material benefits) if that higher income had to be obtained through increased stress. Two thirds said they would be willing to give up higher incomes and consumption to help solve the problems of the poorer countries.

Nor was this just a passing fad in Norwegian public opinion. In 1974 a popular movement was started called The Future in Our Hands campaign. This movement takes its name from the book with the same title written by the Norwegian, Erik Dammann.[10] This social movement is described as a "popular campaign for a new life-style and an equitable distribution of the world's resources." It is the intention of this campaign to nurture new attitudes and values that will be responsive to the needs of the world's poor. Within four years the movement attracted 20,000 members with seventy local chapters and it continues to grow rapidly. Expansion into other Scandinavian countries (Sweden and Denmark) is taking place through associated organizations arising at the grass roots level.

A related activity concerns the New Lifestyles Movement initiated in 1974 in Holland by the Dutch Council of Churches (which includes both Protestant Churches and the Catholic Church). At this council, a resolution was adopted that encouraged "all attempts to frame new life-styles in which a responsibility is expressed for present and future generations." [11] The resolution also stated that, ". . . in view of the very critical food situation in numerous parts of the world . . . a revision of the composition of our food consumption as well as a sparing use of minerals and energy is necessary." This is not viewed as an "austerity movement" but as a "quality of life movement." Since its formation, several hundred discussion groups have emerged, and the concerns of this movement seem to be making their way into the consciousness of the culture.

We cannot draw precise conclusions from this eclectic assortment of evidence. Whether the proportion of adults who sympathize with the values and attitudes consistent with voluntary simplicity is half or three quarters of a given nation is not at issue. The important point is that there is evidence of a substantial reservoir of support for this way of life—often as much as an absolute majority of the population. If the push of necessity meets this latent receptivity, as I think it increasingly will, then there are the makings for a profound and rapid change in the dominant way of life in many Western nations.

These striking changes in national attitudes are not the only evidence of social change toward attitudes and behaviors congruent with a life of deliberate simplicity. In the United States in the 1970s, a number of social-change movements blossomed that embodied attitudes highly compatible with a life of voluntary simplicity. These include feminism, environmentalism, consumerism, antinuclear protest, and the Greenpeace Movement.

When we turn from the outer dimension of social change to the inner dimension of personal change, we find further evidence of an awakening of new attitudes and perspectives that are highly compatible with voluntary simplicity. An awakening interest in the inner aspect of life is revealed by the rapid growth of the human potential movement (with its interest in authenticity in human encounters, encouraging human creativity, enhancing psychological integration and health, etc.); the emergence of "transpersonal psychology" (a psychology that looks beyond the ego and is thus a psychology of consciousness) coupled with a rapidly growing cultural interest in, and involvement with, various Eastern meditative traditions; developments in brain research that confirm there exists a biological basis for both the rational and the intuitive side of human potentials (so-called "split-brain" research); and a growing interest in sports as a form of meditation (for example, the "inner-game" of tennis, running, skiing, and more).

Overall, these value changes, attitude shifts, social-change movements, and inner-growth activities all suggest that a cultural context now prevails that is open to, and supportive of, the exploration of alternative ways of living, working, and consuming. Based upon evidence such as that presented above, I estimate that the number of persons in the United States who were wholeheartedly exploring a life of voluntary simplicity in 1980 to be roughly 6 percent of the adult population, or approximately 10 million persons.[12] Further, I estimate that at least one half of the adult population sympathizes with this way of life even though they may not be pursuing this alternative at present. Finally, I sense that from these modest origins, a life of conscious simplicity could well grow to become the dominant orientation for as much as a majority of the adult population of many Western developed nations by the year 2000.

This is an extraordinary rate of growth. Yet, we live in a time of extraordinary demands. This is apparent when we examine but a few of the many forces behind the emergence of voluntary simplicity and ask ourselves if they are enduring or temporary features of our national and global existence. For example, is the exhaustion of irreplaceable natural resources a fad? Is nuclear annihilation a fad? Is the starvation of millions of persons each year and the malnourishment of roughly a billion persons a fad? Is overwhelming bureaucratic complexity a fad? Each rhetorical question suggests the answer to the issue of whether voluntary simplicity is a "life-style" fad. This way of life will not soon lose its relevance. It has an enduring place in human evolution because it respects and usefully responds to awesome difficulties of the kind considered above.

Whether the rate of growth of this way of living will be sufficient to make an appreciable difference in the growth path of indhstrial civilization is impossible to predict. It could be argued that the numbers of persons choosing a life of deliberate simplicity are so few and the time to respond is so short that this way of living will not have any substantial impact on the direction of social evolution.

Yet, there are numerous examples in recent social history in which the coherent actions of a relatively small number of persons profoundly touched and transformed the lives of the many. The civil-rights movement, the environmentalist movement, the anti-Vietnam War movement, the feminist movement, the anti-nuclear movement, and the Greenpeace movement are all examples of potent social-change movements in which the creative leadership amounted to an exceedingly small fraction of the society. The point is not to equate voluntary simplicity with social protest movements; rather, it is to illustrate the ability of a relatively small fraction of the population to provide constructive guidance to the larger society. Surely, some critical mass of persons is essential to act as the catalyst for change. However, under conditions of growing social disarray (Stage IV conditions), the constructive actions of a relatively few persons could have a very positive influence in directing the course of social evolution toward a more workable and meaningful civilization.

In conclusion, both the relevance and growth potential of voluntary simplicity are, I think, enormous. What we must do to cope with physical necessity coincides with what we can do to meet evolutionary opportunity. We are being pushed and pulled in the same direction. What we must do in order to survive this time of planetary transition is the same as what we must do if we are to evolve as a species. We can choose to transform our apparent civilizational tragedy into the enormous creative opportunity that it truly is. We have the opportunity to engage in both personal and social revitalization, to bring new life to disintegrating cultures, and to become responsible members of the human family. If we fail to consciously meet our civilizational challenge, it is likely that we will be overwhelmed by the global problems that are already fast rushing in upon us.

The arrival of the future waits for no person or civilization. The examples are legion of civilizations that have not squarely met their time of challenge and, failing to mount a sufficient response, have disintegrated. Despite such apocalyptic-sounding warnings, I am hopeful as I look to the future. Make no mistake though—this is not an easy hopefulness, premised upon some magical transformation of people and institutions. I assume that the human family will have to respond to demands of a scope, persistence, and severity unlike anything yet experienced in human history. Still, I think we are equal to this challenge.

SECTION III

ROOTS

CHAPTER 5

APPRECIATING LIFE

Our discussion of voluntary simplicity has taken us across a wide-ranging field of subjects. At virtually every turn we have seen that this way of living is rooted in how each individual experiences life. Therefore, the purpose of this section is to examine these experiential roots of voluntary simplicity. We will explore in depth what it means to live more "voluntarily" and to live more "simply." It is clarifying to begin by renewing our appreciation of life. Why should an appreciation of life be so vital to our understanding of voluntary simplicity?

To live more voluntarily means to encounter life more consciously. To live more simply is to encounter life more directly. By its very nature, then, voluntary simplicity can be defined as living in a way that fosters our conscious and direct encounter with life itself. The "life" so encountered extends far beyond that typically acknowledged in the daily social routines of Western cultures. It is LIFE—in its vastness, subtlety, and preciousness—that is the context within which voluntary simplicity acquires its genuine significance. In turn, this suggests two vantage points from which the relevance of this way of life can become penetratingly apparent: first, when we view the universe as our home; and second, when we view death as our ally.

The Universe as Our Home

What is the nature of the universe of which we are an integral part? Our universe extends through reaches of space that are so vast, and through aeons of time that are so long, that it outstrips the capacity of the human intellect to comprehend. In the face of this, a natural tendency is to retreat into our socially constructed existence—a thin slice of reality that we can more readily comprehend because we are the architects of that reality. Yet, by ignoring the larger universe in which we are immersed —by concentrating our attention on an engaging and demanding social reality—we quickly forget that it is the universe that is our larger home.

It is important for us to remember where we live. As we encounter critical problems of global dimension, we must have a frame of reference for approaching those problems, and the world, as a whole. We can gain this perspective by looking beyond the bounds of the earth to the larger universe. It is within the context of our experience as beings inhabiting the universe that the earth can be perceived as whole. What, then, is the nature of the universe that serves as the vantage point for our much needed perspective?

The earth is part of a solar system that is millions of miles in diameter. Our solar system, in turn, is part of an enormous galaxy of some 100 billion stars arranged in a disc-shaped spiral some 100,000 light years in diameter (that is as far as light can travel at the speed of 186,000 miles per second over the course of 100,000 years!). Our own galaxy, despite its incomprehensible enormity, is, in turn, dwarfed by the larger known universe that is estimated to contain more than 100 billion galaxies beyond our own.

Additionally, modern physicists sound more and more like ancient mystics as they employ strange and paradoxical concepts to describe the nature of the universe: anti-matter, time flowing backwards, black holes in space, and so on. These concepts just begin to point to the awesome reality that we inhabit. Indeed, it was Einstein who said: "The most beautiful and most profound emotion we can experience is the sensation of the mystical. It is the sower of all true science. He to whom this emotion is a stranger, who can no longer wonder and stand rapt in awe, is as good as dead." [1]

In our "normal" daily existence we do not live with a direct and conscious appreciation of the universe. Instead, we live almost completely immersed in a socially constructed reality that so fully absorbs our energy and attention that virtually none remains to experience the wonder of our existence. The tragedy of modern industrial cultures is the superficiality that we accept and, indeed maintain, as the common denominator in human affairs. We unconsciously trivialize the human experiment with shallow pursuits of money and social status that mask rather than celebrate the magnificence of the human being.

All the while a miracle of creation surrounds us and intimately infuses every particle of our existence. American Indian lore speaks of our existence as a threefold miracle: "that things exist at all, that life came out of things, and finally, that life became conscious of itself." [2] The miracle of form. The miracle of living form. And the miracle of living form that is conscious of its life. We take these three amazing facts of our existence for granted. We become desensitized and behave as if these perpetual miracles were unimportant in the conduct of our everyday lives. Then, individually and culturally, we forget these miracles. Once forgotten by an entire culture, they are difficult to rediscover. Voluntary simplicity—encountering life more consciously and directly—facilitates that rediscovery.

Death as Our Ally

Death is an important ally for appreciating life. I am not referring to a morbid preoccupation with death. Rather, I mean the felt awareness of our finitude as physical beings—an honest recognition of the short time we have to love and to learn on this earth. The knowledge that we will inevitably die burns out our attachments to the dignified madness of our socially constructed existence. Death is an ally that helps us to release our clinging to social position, material accumulation, and superficial desires as a source of ultimate security. An awareness of death forces us to confront the reality of our existence, here and now. Gandhi once said: "Just as one must learn the art of killing in the training for violence, so one must learn the art of dying in the training for non-violence." [3] If we are to lead nonviolent and loving lives—lives that honor the preciousness of all life and thereby intend to touch the world gently—then we can begin by coming to terms with our own deaths. An appreciation that we must die awakens us from our social sleep and to the reality of our situation. Death is an unyielding partner in life—an unescapable certainty to push against as we sort out the significant from the trivial in our daily lives.

I would like to share with you three comments regarding death that reveal its relevance to a life of conscious simplicity. First, consider the words of Nadine Stair of Louisville, Kentucky, who was eighty-five years old when she wrote the following, entitled "If I Had My Life to Live Over":

> I'd like to make more mistakes next time. I'd relax. I would limber up. I would be sillier than I have been this trip. I would take fewer things seriously. I would take more chances. I would climb more mountains and swim more rivers. I would eat more ice cream and less beans. I would perhaps have more actual troubles, but I'd have fewer imaginary ones.

> You see, I'm one of those people who live sensibly and sanely hour after hour, day after day. Oh, I've had my moments, and if I had it to do over again, I'd have more of them. In fact, I'd try to have nothing else. Just moments, one after another, instead of living so many years ahead of each day. I've been one of those persons who never goes

anywhere without a thermometer, a hot water bottle, a raincoat, and a parachute. If I had to do it again, I would travel lighter than I have.

If I had my life to live over, I would start barefoot earlier in the spring and stay that way later in the fall. I would go to more dances. I would ride more merry-go-rounds. I would pick more daisies.[4]

Second, consider the wisdom from a now largely forgotten book, written in the United States over one hundred years ago. *The Royal Path of Life* describes in its closing pages a perspective on life that comes from an appreciation of death. Although written in a style of gracious eloquence that comes from an earlier era, it speaks plainly even today:

No sex is spared, no age exempt. The majestic and courtly roads which monarchs pass over, the way that the men of letters tread, the path the warrior traverses, the short and simple annals of the poor, all lead to the same place, all terminate, however varied their routes, in that one enormous house which is appointed for all living. . . . No matter what station of honor we hold, we are all subject to death. . . .

Ah, it is true that a few friends will go and bury us; affection will rear a stone and plant a few flowers over our grave; in a brief period the little hillock will be smoothed down, and the stone will fall, and neither friend nor stranger will be concerned to ask which one of the forgotten millions of the earth was buried there. Every vestige that we ever lived upon the earth will have vanished away. All the little memorials of our remembrance—the lock of hair encased in gold, or the portrait that hung in our dwelling —will cease to have the slightest interest to any living being.

We need but look into the cemetery and see the ten thousand upturned faces; ten thousand breathless bosoms. There was a time when fire flashed through those vacant orbs;

when warm ambitions, hopes, joys, and the loving life pushed in those bosoms. Dreams of fame and power once haunted those empty skulls. . . .

A proper view of death may be useful to abate most of the irregular passions. Thus, for instance, we may see what avarice comes to in the coffin of the miser; this is the man who could never be satisfied with riches; but see now a few boards enclose him, and a few square inches contain him. . . .

Approach the tomb of the proud man; see the haughty countenance dreadfully disfigured, and the tongue that spoke the most lofty things condemned to eternal silence. . . . Behold the consequences of intemperance in the tomb of the glutton; see his appetite now fully satiated, his senses destroyed and his bones scattered.[5]

A third suggestion of the relevance of death to voluntary simplicity is found in the following anonymous quote—a reminder that our lives are ever hastening to their rendezvous with death whether we are mindful of that fact or not:

On the plains of hesitation
Lie the bleached bones of countless millions
Who sat down to wait—
And while they waited, they died.
—ANONYMOUS

These three messages are clear. We cannot hide from death. Its embrace will consume our social existence entirely. Job titles, social position, material possessions, sexual roles and images— all must yield to death. Death, then, is an uncompromising friend that brings us back to the reality of life. This does not mean that we should abandon our material and social existence. Rather, it means that in consciously honoring the fact of our physical death, we are thereby empowered to penetrate through the social pretense, ostentation, and confusion that normally obscure our sense of what is truly significant. An awareness of death is an ally for infusing our lives with a sense of immediacy, perspective, and proportion. In acknowledging the reality of death, we can more fully appreciate our gift of life.

With the universe as our home and death as our ally, we turn to explore the two principal subjects of this section: first, the nature of living more voluntarily and, second, the nature of living more simply.

CHAPTER 6

LIVING MORE VOLUNTARILY

What does it mean to live more voluntarily? To act voluntarily requires not only that we be conscious of the choices before us (the outer world) but also that we be conscious of ourselves as we select among those choices (the inner world). We must be conscious of both choices and chooser if we are to act voluntarily. Put differently, to act voluntarily is to act in a self-determining manner. But who is the "self" making the determinations of behavior? If that "self" is both socially and psychologically conditioned into habitual patterns of thought and action, then behavior can hardly be considered voluntary. Therefore, self-realization—the process of realizing who the "self" really is—is crucial to self-determination and voluntary action.

The point is that the more precise and sustained is our conscious knowing of ourselves, the more voluntary or choiceful can be our participation in life. If we are inattentive in noticing ourselves going through life, then the choicefulness with which we live will be commensurately diminished. The more conscious we are of our passage through life, the more skillfully we can act, and the more harmonious can be the relationship between our inner experience and our outer expression.

Running on Automatic

Before we can fully appreciate what it means to act voluntarily, we must acknowledge to ourselves the extent to which we tend to act involuntarily. We tend to "run on automatic"—act in habitual and preprogrammed ways—to a much greater extent than we commonly acknowledge to ourselves.

Consider, for example, how we learned to walk as children. At first, walking was an enormous struggle that required all our energy and attention. Within a few months, the period of intense struggle passed. As the ability to walk became increasingly automated, we began to focus our attention on other things—reaching, touching, climbing. In the same manner, we have learned and largely automated virtually every facet of our daily lives: walking, driving, reading, working, relating to others, and so on. This habitual patterning of behavior extends into the most intimate details of our lives: from the knot we make in tying our shoes, to the manner in which we brush our teeth, to which leg we put first into a pair of pants, and so on. Not only do automatic patterns of behavior pervade every aspect of our physical existence (as in the examples just given), they also condition how we think and feel. To be sure, there is a degree of variety in our thinking, feeling, and behaving; yet, the variety tends to be predictable since it is derived largely from pre-programmed and habituated patterns of response to the world. If we do not become conscious of these automated patterns of thinking, feeling, and behaving, then we become by default human automatons who, in the language of behavioral psychology, exist "without freedom and dignity." If we are to act voluntarily, we are obliged to live more consciously.

We tend not to notice or appreciate the degree to which we run on automatic—largely because we live in an almost constant state of mental distraction. Our minds are constantly moving about at a lightning-fast pace, thinking about the future, replaying conversations from the past, engaging in inner role-playing, and so on. Without sustained attention, we cannot fully appreciate the extent to which we live ensnared in an automated, reflexive, and dreamlike reality that is a subtle and continuously changing blend of fantasy, inner dialogue, memory, planning, and so on. The fact that we spend years acquiring vast amounts of *mental content* does not mean that we are thereby either substantially aware of, or in control of, our *mental process*. This fact is clearly described by Roger Walsh—a physician, psychiatrist, and brain researcher. His vivid description of the nature of thought processes (as revealed in the early stages of meditative practice) is so useful to our discussion that I quote his comments at length:

> I was forced to recognize that what I had formerly believed to be my rational mind preoccupied with cognition, planning, problem solving, etc., actually comprised a frantic torrent of forceful, demanding, loud, and often unrelated thoughts and fantasies which filled an unbelievable proportion of consciousness even during purposive behavior. The incredible proportion of consciousness which this fantasy world occupied, my powerlessness to remove it for more than a few seconds, and my former state of mindlessness or ignorance of its existence, staggered me. . . . Foremost among the implicit beliefs of orthodox Western psychology is the assumption that man spends most of his time reasoning and problem solving, and that only neurotics and other abnormals spend much time, outside of leisure, in fantasy. However, it is my impression that prolonged self-observation will show that at most times we are living almost in a dream world in which we skillfully and automatically yet unknowingly blend inputs from reality and fantasy in accordance with our needs and defenses. . . . The subtlety, complexity, infinite range and number, and entrapping power of the fantasies which the mind creates seem impossible to comprehend, to differentiate from reality

while in them, and even more so to describe to one who has not experienced them . . .[1]

The crucial importance of penetrating behind our continuous stream of thought (as largely unconscious and lightning-fast flows of inner fantasy-dialogue) is stressed by every major consciousness tradition in the world: Buddhist, Taoist, Hindu, Sufi, Zen, etc. Western cultures, however, have fostered the understanding that a state of continual mental distraction is in the natural order of things. Consequently, by virtue of a largely unconscious social agreement about the nature of our inner thought processes, we live individually and collectively almost totally embedded within our mentally constructed reality. We are so busy creating ever more appealing images or social facades for others to see, and so distracted from the simplicity of our spontaneously arising self, that we do not truly encounter either ourselves or one another. In the process, we lose a large measure of our innate capacity for voluntary, deliberate, intentional action. We forfeit that capacity in favor of the illusory security of a mentally constructed self-image.

Our thoughts, then, are expressed as both words and behaviors. As we identify who "we" are with those words and behaviors, they develop into characteristic patterns of personality. Repeated over many years, these characteristic patterns harden into our social facade, which is comprised of habitual and largely unconscious patterns of intellectual and emotional response, physical tension, and posture. It is important, then, to watch our thoughts carefully and to attend to their expression in ourselves and our behavior in the world.

Bringing more conscious attention to our thought processes and behavior has profound social as well as personal implications. The late E. F. Schumacher expressed this forthrightly in his book, *A Guide for the Perplexed*:

> . . . it is a grave error to accuse a man who pursues self-knowledge of "turning his back on society." The opposite would be more nearly true: that a man who fails to pursue

self-knowledge is and remains a danger to society, for
he will tend to misunderstand everything that other people
say or do, and remain blissfully unaware of the significance
of many of the things he does himself.[2]

How are we to penetrate behind our automated and habitual
patterns of thinking and behaving (and thereby be enabled to
live more voluntarily)? The remedy is to live more consciously.
But what does this mean?

Living More Consciously

The word "consciousness" literally means "that with which
we know." It has also been termed the "knowing faculty." To
live more consciously means to be more consciously aware, moment by moment, that we are present in all that we do. When
we stand and talk, we know that we are standing and talking.
When we sit and eat, we know that we are sitting and eating.
When we do the countless things that make up our daily lives,
we remember the being that is involved in those activities. We
remember ourselves (and to "re-member" is to make whole; it
is the opposite of dis-memberment). To live consciously is to
move through life with conscious self-remembering.

We are not bound to habitual and preprogrammed ways of
perceiving and responding when we are consciously watchful
of ourselves in the process of living. Let's look at several examples. It is difficult to relate to another person solely as the
embodiment of a social position or job title when moment by
moment we are consciously aware of the utter humanness that
we both possess—a humanness whose magnificence and mystery
dwarfs the seeming importance of status and titles as a basis of
relationship. It is difficult to deceive another person when moment by moment we are consciously aware of our unfolding
experience of deception. It is difficult to sustain the experience
of sexual desire by projecting a sexual fantasy when moment by

moment we are conscious that we are creating and relating to a fantasy rather than the authentic individual we are with. In short, when we begin to consciously watch ourselves in the activities of daily life, we begin to cut through confining self-images, social pretenses, and psychological barriers. We begin to live more voluntarily.

We all have the ability to consciously know ourselves as we move through life. The capacity to "witness" the unfolding of our lives is not an ability that is remote or hidden from us. To the contrary, this is an experience that is so close, so intimate, and so ordinary, that we easily overlook its presence and significance. An old adage states: "It's a rare fish that knows it swims in water." Analogously, the challenge of living voluntarily is not in gaining access to the conscious experiencing of ourselves but rather in consciously recognizing the presence of this experience, and then learning the skills of sustaining our opening to that experience.

To further clarify the nature of conscious watchfulness, I would like to ask you several questions. Have you been conscious of the fact that you have been sitting here reading this book? Have you been conscious of changes in your bodily sensations, frame of mind, and emotions? Were you totally absorbed in the book until I asked? Or had you unintentionally allowed your thoughts to wander to other concerns? Did you just experience a slight shock of self-recognition when I inquired? What does it feel like to notice yourself reading while you read; to observe yourself eating while you eat; to see yourself watching television while you watch television; to notice yourself driving while you drive; to experience yourself talking while you talk?

Despite the utter simplicity of being consciously watchful of our lives, this is a demanding activity. At first, it is a struggle to just occasionally remember ourselves moving through the daily routine. A brief moment of self-remembering is followed by an extended period where we are lost in the flow of thought and the demands of the exterior world. Yet with practice, we find that we can more easily remember ourselves—while walking down the street, or while we are at home, at work, at play. We come to recognize, as direct experience, the nature of "knowing that we know." We become conscious of what it feels like to be conscious. As our familiarity with this mode of perception increases, we get lost in thought and worldly activities less and less frequently. In turn, we experience our behavior in the world as more and more choiceful, or voluntary.

The conscious knowing of ourselves as we live our lives affords us insight into the workings of the ego. We are increasingly liberated from habitual and automated patterns of behavior, thought and feeling. Bringing conscious attention into our daily lives may lack the mystery of searching for enlightenment with an Indian sorcerer and the spiritual glamour of sitting for long months in an Eastern monastic setting, but consciously attending to our daily-life activities is an eminently useful, readily accessible, and powerful tool for enhancing our capacity for voluntary action (and all that it implies for more wholeheartedly participating in life).

Embedded and Self-reflective Consciousness

We have been discussing two different modes of consciousness. Each has profound implications for either enhancing or diminishing our capacity for voluntary action. Because these two modes of consciousness are so crucial to our discussion, I want to define them more carefully. What follows is not an original distinction but an ancient one that has been variously labeled but similarly described by many others.[3]

The first mode of consciousness I will call "embedded consciousness." Embedded consciousness is our so-called "normal" or waking consciousness and it is characterized by our being so embedded within the stream of inner-fantasy dialogue that little conscious attention can be given to the moment-to-moment experiencing of ourselves. In forgetting ourselves, we tend to run on automatic and thereby forfeit our capacity for voluntary action. In the distracted state of embedded consciousness, we tend to identify who we are with habitual patterns of behavior, thought, and feeling. We assume this social mask is the sum total of who we really are. Consequently, we feel the need to protect and defend our social facade. Having identified ourselves with this limited and shallow rendering of who we are, we find it difficult to pull away from our masks and freshly experience our identity. We find life is unsatisfactory—we can neither fully give nor fully receive as both giver and receiver are but a social facade, and the real "self" remains hidden within.

The next step beyond embedded consciousness I will term "self-reflective consciousness." Where the distinctive quality of embedded consciousness is self-forgetting (running on automatic), the distinctive quality of self-reflective consciousness is self-remembering (acting in the world intentionally, consciously, voluntarily). It is as though self-reflective consciousness provides us with a mirror that reveals or reflects who we are as we move through our daily lives. This is not a mechanical watchfulness but a living awareness that changes moment by moment. It means that to varying degrees we are continuously and consciously "tasting" our experience of ourselves. Overall, the opening to self-reflective consciousness is marked by the progressive and balanced development of the ability to be simultaneously concentrated (with a precise and delicate attention to the details of life) and mindful (with a panoramic appreciation of the totality of life). Nothing is left out of our experience as both the minute details and larger life circumstances are simultaneously embraced in our awareness.

To make friends with ourselves in this way requires that we be willing to accept the totality of ourselves—including our sensual desires, self-doubts, anger, laziness, restlessness, fears, and so on. We cannot move beyond the habitual pushes and pulls of these forces until we are conscious of their presence in our lives. In turn, to see ourselves in this manner calls for much patience, gentleness, and self-forgiveness as we will notice ourselves thinking and acting in ways that we would like to think we are above or beyond. Thus, self-reflective consciousness gives us access to a trustworthy observer or watcher from which we can view the workings of our ego and its habitual patterns of thought and behavior. To the extent that we are able to see or know our automated patterns, we are then no longer bound by them. We are enabled to act and live voluntarily.

Beyond Self-reflective Consciousness

The conscious evolution of consciousness does not end with becoming knowingly attentive to our ordinary life experience. This is but a beginning on a much larger journey. Self-reflective consciousness or self-remembering is the immediately accessible doorway that gradually opens into the further reaches of conscious knowing. It is through this next and readily approachable step—by being knowingly attentive to the "self" moving through the ordinary, day-to-day life experience—that the entire spectrum of conscious evolution unfolds. Just as a giant tree grows from the smallest seedling, so too does the seed experience of self-reflective consciousness contain within it the furthest reaches of conscious evolution.

What is the nature of experiencing that lies beyond self-remembering? When we simply tune into our moment-to-moment experiencing with persistence and patience, our experience of "self" is gradually though profoundly transformed. The boundaries between the "self-in-here" and the "world-out-there" begin to dissolve as we refine the precision with which we watch ourselves moving through life. The inner and outer person gradually merge into one continuous flow of experience. In other words, in the next stage beyond self-reflective consciousness, the duality of "watcher and watched" merges into the unity of an integrated flow of conscious experiencing.

The capacity to ultimately experience the totality of existence as an unbounded and unbroken whole is not confined to any particular culture, race, or religion. This experience of ineffable unity is sometimes referred to as the "Perennial Philosophy" because it appears throughout recorded history in the writings of every major spiritual tradition in the world: Christianity, Buddhism, Hinduism, Taoism, Judaism, Islam, and more.[4] Each tradition records that if we gently though persistently look into our own experience, we will ultimately discover that who "we" are is not different or separate from that which we call God, Cosmic Consciousness, Unbounded Wholeness, the Tao, Nirvana, and countless other names (for this ultimately unnameable experience). The common thread of experience found at the core of every major spiritual tradition is suggested in the following statements:

The Kingdom of Heaven is within you.
—Words of Jesus

Look within, thou are the Buddha.
—Words of the Buddha

Atman (the essence of the individual) and Brahman (the ultimate reality) are one.
—Words from the Hindu tradition

He who knows himself knows his Lord.
—Words of the Muhammed

The experience of unity or wholeness or love lies at the core of every major spiritual tradition. This does not mean there exists a universal theology; rather, it means that we are all human beings and there are common experiences we share. For example, the capacity to experience love is not confined to any particular culture, race, or religion. It is a universal human experience. And what is the ultimate nature of love? The theologian, Paul Tillich, described love as the experience of life in its actual unity.[5] If the experience of love is the experience of life in its actual unity, then consciousness is the vehicle whereby that experience is known. When we become fully conscious of life, we find that it is an unbroken whole and, in turn, we may describe this experience of wholeness as "love." Love or unity is our most fundamental nature that is known through the vehicle of consciousness.

The Trappist monk Thomas Merton wrote of the experience of unity in a way that clarifies the drive toward a way of life of voluntary simplicity:

> And so I stand among you as one who offers a small message of hope, that first, there are always people who dare to seek on the margin of society, who are not dependent on social acceptance, not dependent on social routine, and prefer a kind of free-floating existence under a state of risk. And among these people, if they are faithful to their own calling, to their own vocation, and to their own message from God, communication on the deepest level is possible. And the deepest level of communication is not communication, but communion. It is wordless. It is beyond words, and it is beyond speech, and it is beyond concept. Not that we discover a new unity. We discover an older unity. My dear brothers, we are already one. But we imagine that we are not. And what we have to recover is our original unity. What we have to be is what we are.[6]

We have briefly examined the nondualistic experience of identity that accompanies movement beyond self-reflective consciousness. Yet, these difficult times call for useful and practical approaches to developing the "knowing faculty" or consciousness. Rather than emphasize the fascinating but remote regions of conscious experiencing (the nondualistic or "mystical" sense of self), I want to concentrate on the next step in the evolution and ecology of consciousness. Therefore, in the remainder of this chapter, I will restrict the discussion to that realm of human experience—self-reflective consciousness—that is immediately, usefully, and widely accessible.

Enabling Qualities of Living More Consciously

To more concretely describe the worldly relevance of living more consciously, I would like to briefly explore four ways in which this is an empowering and enabling process. First, being more consciously attentive to our moment-to-moment experience enhances our capacity to see "what is." Given the obscuring and distracting power of our lightning-fast movements of fantasy-dialogue, it is no small task to clearly and accurately see things as they really are. When we do see life more clearly and immediately, the quality and workability of our lives are greatly enhanced. For example, if in everyday life we do not pay much attention to what we are doing—if we are distracted and preoccupied much of the time—then we will find that our path through life is rougher, more stressful, and that things don't seem to mesh as well as they might. Why? Being inattentive, we will tend to have more accidents, misunderstand others more often, overlook many things, bump into things more often, and so on. On the other hand, if we are living more consciously— being attentive to ourselves moving through the countless small happenings that comprise our daily lives—then life will tend to go more smoothly. We will tend to be more productive in what we do since we are more concentrated or focused; we will tend to listen more carefully and understand more fully, we will have fewer accidents along the way, and we will be more present and available in our relationships with others. This example illustrates the utterly straightforward and practical nature of living more consciously. Just as this example applies to the conduct of our lives as individuals, so too does it apply to our lives as citizens, as members of a culture in a period of stressful transition.

As we develop the perceptual skill of living more consciously, we can bring the same degree of discernment to our social circumstances that we bring to our individual lives. In other words, in moving from embedded to self-reflective consciousness, we are enabled to not only examine the underpinnings of our personally constructed reality (as habitual patterns of thought and behavior), but additionally, we are enabled to examine our socially constructed reality (as equally habitual patterns of thought and behavior that characterize entire cultures). In being more consciously attentive to our social as well as our personal lives, we are provided with the means to penetrate through the political posturings, glib advertisements, and cultural myths that sustain the status quo. Seeing more clearly "what is," we can bring greater integrity and balance into our manner of living. Overall, in an era dominated by hideously complex problems of global dimension, the capacity to see more clearly the reality of our situation is essential to the well-being and, indeed, the survival of the human family.

Second, living more consciously enables us to respond more quickly to subtle feedback that something is amiss. In other words, in being more attentive to the reality of our situation, we enhance our capacity to respond with greater speed toward self-corrective action. If we were more attentive to our situation as a society, we would not have to be shocked or bludgeoned into remedial action by, for example, massive famines or catastrophic nuclear accidents. Instead, more subtle signals would suffice to indicate that corrective actions are warranted. In the context of an increasingly interdependent world—where the strength of the whole web of social, political, and economic relations is increasingly at the mercy of the weakest links—the capacity to respond quickly to subtle warnings that we are getting off a healthy track in our social evolution is indispensable to our long-run survival. This seems particularly relevant as we note the growing sluggishness of response of our massive bureaucracies in business and in government.

Third, living more consciously expands our domain of choice and allows us to respond to our situation with greater flexibility and creativity. In becoming more consciously attentive to our daily lives, we can see our habitual patterns of thought and behavior more clearly. We then have greater choice as to how we will respond. We are not bound by those patterns when we are conscious of them. To say that we have greater choice if we are conscious of ourselves acting in the world does not mean that we will always make the "right" choices. Rather, with conscious attention, our actions and their consequences become much more visible to us and thereby become a potent source of learning. With learning can come increasing skillfulness of action. This implies a self-forgiving and self-correcting process whereby we gradually refine our capacity to be consciously attentive to our life experience, and then accept that experience as a basis for learning ever more skillful action in the world. To consciously select among, and then learn from, an ever widening spectrum of choices seems crucial to our future evolution and our survival.

Fourth, living more consciously promotes an ecological orientation toward all of life. With conscious attention to our moment-to-moment experience, we begin to directly sense the subtle though profound connectedness of all life. We begin to see that who "we" are is not exclusively confined to our social personality and physical body. As we learn to focus and expand simultaneously our watchfulness, we begin to sense the entirety of existence as an unbroken whole. This awareness of intimate relationship with the rest of life generates a sense of compassion and caring for all humankind. Our vision is expanded outward and this brings with it a strong sense of social responsibility and worldly involvement. In approaching critical problems of global scope, we begin to move from an "us and them" approach to a "we together" approach. Overall, a nonviolent orientation toward social change is encouraged by living more consciously. Since we live in a time when the weapons of destruction are proliferating and the potential for conflict is enormous, the ecological orientation that accompanies living more consciously seems indispensable to our long-run survival.

These four enabling qualities only begin to suggest the down-to-earth, practical relevance of living more consciously. * These are not trivial enhancements of human capacity. Each enabling factor was described as essential to both our further evolution and to our survival. Our civilizational crisis has emerged in no small part from the gross disparity that exists between our relatively underdeveloped "inner faculties" and the extremely powerful external technologies now at our disposal. When we had limited mastery of our environment, we could not do much harm. Now, with our power enormously magnified through our technologies, we can do irreparable damage. The reach of our technological power exceeds the grasp of our inner learning. Unless we expand our interior learning to match our technological learning, we are destined, I think, to act to the detriment of both ourselves and the rest of life on this planet.

We must right the imbalance by supporting a degree of interior growth and maturation that is at least commensurate with the enormous exterior technological growth that has occurred over the last several centuries. For this reason, the transition from embedded to self-reflective consciousness (and beyond) can no longer be considered a spiritual luxury for the few; rather, it is increasingly a social necessity for the many. Just as the faculty of the human intellect had to be developed by entire cultures in order to support the emergence of the industrial revolution, so too, I think, must we now begin to cultivate the widespread development of the "knowing faculty," or consciousness, if we are to support the emergence of a revitalizing civilization. This is not to say how this learning should take place. There are countless paths among which to select on this "journey of awakening" (the list of readings in the first Appendix suggests a few of these paths). My point is that in one way or another, we must begin to live more consciously if the

---

* Appendix IV describes the crucial role of self-regulating behavior arising from self-reflective consciousness for effectively coping with the problems of social complexity and a faltering political-economy.

human species is to survive the coming decades and make a successful transition to some form of peaceful global civilization.

The Nature of Human Nature

To some, the suggestion that some substantial change in human consciousness could actually occur is nothing more than unwarranted idealism since "you can't change human nature." An entire attitude toward life is neatly contained in that small phrase. The phrase, if believed, is self-fulfilling and thereby wraps up and tightly binds people's beliefs about their realizable potentials. What, then, is the nature of our human nature?

What do people mean when they say that human nature cannot change? I suspect they mean something like: "I am powerless to change the experience of myself and my life circumstances in any significant way." In short, the philosophy of life contained in this phrase seems to assert that the only rational thing to do is to acquiesce to the status quo—to enjoy life as much as possible and forget the futile process of intentional change. Thus, the notion that human nature cannot change is a convenient catch-all rationalization for apathy, passivity, helplessness, and cynicism. Let's look more carefully at our human nature before accepting so defeatist an approach to life.

What is human "nature"? The dictionary defines the term "nature" as the "inherent character or basic constitution of a person or thing, its essence." The question arises, does human nature or the "inherent character, basic constitution, or essence" of a person ever change? To answer this question we can ask an analogous question: Does the essence or nature of a seed change when it grows into a flower? Not at all. The potential for becoming a flower was always resident within the seed. For the seed to grow into a flower does not constitute a change in the nature of the seed; rather, it represents a change in the degree to which the potential, always inherent in its original nature, is realized. Similarly, we can say that "no, human nature does not change." Yet, like the seed with the potential of becoming a flower, *human nature is not a static "thing" but a spectrum of potentials.* Just as a seed can grow into a flower without that process representing a change in its fundamental nature, so too can the human being grow from a "primitive" to an "enlightened" entity without that progression representing a change in basic human nature.[7]

There is, however, a crucial difference between the manner in which the flower and the person realize their potentials. For the seed to realize the full expression of its basic nature as a flower it only had to find the fertile soil for its growth and the organic cycle of growth would happen automatically. However, the human being cannot fully realize his or her potentials in an equally automatic manner. For we humans to actualize our potentials, at some point there must be a shift from embedded to self-reflective consciousness (and beyond) if maturation is to continue.

Our culture provides the soil—either moist and fertile or dry and barren—within which we grow. However, the ultimate responsibility for growth, irrespective of cultural setting, remains with the individual. Only by free choice and conscious intention does the evolution of consciousness occur. Thus, a person who says that human nature cannot change perhaps really is saying, "My culture does not support and guide me in the realization of my fuller human potentials and, without that support, I choose not to make the attempt to grow." A person may be unwilling to suffer the discomfort of moving beyond the culturally defined character of realizable human potentials and may then rationalize his or her predicament by saying that people never change, so why bother. At that point, living truly becomes little more than "only not dying."

In summary, human nature is not a static thing but a spectrum of potentials. We can move along that spectrum of potentials without that movement constituting a change in basic human nature. That we do progress along a spectrum of potentials is vividly illustrated by the fact that the human species has moved from primitive nomad to the verge of global civilization in an instant of geological time. Despite the enormity and speed of our evolution of culture and consciousness, we are far from being fully evolved. We are, I think, still in the adolescence of our species and have not yet begun to collectively imagine where our journey could lead in the future.

Conclusion

We began this chapter by considering the nature of voluntary action. We saw that unless we are conscious of our passage through daily life, we tend to run on automatic. When we run on automatic we act in habitual and preprogrammed ways and our behavior can then hardly be considered voluntary. Thus, our capacity to act voluntarily—freely, choicefully, intentionally, deliberately—is inextricably bound up with our capacity to be consciously attentive to ourselves as we move through life. This is a realizable capacity that already exists within our spectrum of human potentials. If anything, we are overendowed with capacities we do not use and too often do not realize we have. No small part of our contemporary civilizational challenge is to acknowledge, and then begin to consciously develop, these vitally important potentials.

CHAPTER 7

LIVING MORE SIMPLY

In the last chapter we discussed the nature of living more voluntarily. Now we turn our attention to the nature of living more simply. Although living voluntarily and living simply are considered as separate topics, they are inextricably intertwined. It makes an enormous difference whether greater simplicity is voluntarily chosen or involuntarily imposed.

For example, consider two persons, both of whom ride a bicycle to work in order to save gasoline.[1] The first person voluntarily chooses to ride a bicycle and derives great satisfaction from the physical exercise, the contact with the outdoors, and the knowledge that he or she is conserving energy. The second person bikes to work because of the force of circumstances—this may be financial necessity or stringent gasoline rationing. Instead of delighting in the ride, the second individual is filled with resentment with each push of the pedals. This person yearns for the comfort and speed of an automobile and is indifferent to the social benefit derived from the energy savings.

In outward appearances, both persons are engaged in identical activities. Yet the attitudes and experiences of each are quite different. These differences are crucial in determining whether or not bicycling would prove to be a workable and satisfying response to energy shortages. For the first person it would. For the second person, this is clearly not a satisfying solution and perhaps not even a workable one (to the extent that he or she, along with many others, tries to circumvent the laws and secure his or her own personal advantage). This example illustrates how important it is whether our simplicity is consciously chosen or externally imposed. *Voluntary* simplicity, then, involves not only what we do (the outer world), but also the intention with which we do it (the inner world).

The nature of simplicity that I will focus on in this chapter is that of a consciously chosen simplicity. This is not to ignore a majority of the human family that lives in involuntary material simplicity—poverty. Rather, it is to acknowledge that much of the solution to that poverty lies in the voluntary actions of those who live in relative abundance and thereby have the real opportunity to consciously simplify their lives and to consciously assist others.

The Nature of Simplicity

What does it mean to live more simply? The dictionary defines "simplicity" as being "direct, clear; free of pretense or dishonesty; free of vanity, ostentation, and undue display; free of secondary complications and distractions." In living with simplicity, we encounter life more directly—in a firsthand and immediate manner. To live more simply, then, means to encounter life more directly, fully, and wholeheartedly. The value of bringing conscious simplicity into our lives thus seems directly proportional to the value we place upon living.

We need little when we are directly in touch with life. It is when we remove ourselves from direct and wholehearted participation in life that emptiness and boredom creep in. It is then that we begin our search for something or someone that will alleviate our gnawing dissatisfaction. Yet, the search is endless to the extent that we are continually led away from ourselves and our experience in the moment. If we fully appreciate the learning and love that life offers to us in each moment, then we feel less desire for material luxuries that contribute little to our well-being and that deprive those in genuine need of scarce resources. When we live with simplicity, we give ourselves and others a gift of life. To live simply does not mean we should abandon all of our worldly possessions. Rather, it means that if we truly seek a sense of immediacy and authenticity in our lives, we can begin by living with greater balance, with greater simplicity.

We both seek and fear immediacy of contact with life. We search for aliveness, and yet we mask our magnificence in a shell of material ostentation and display. We seek genuineness in our encounters with others and yet allow pretense and dishonesty to infuse our relationships. We look for authenticity in the world about us and find that we have covered our miraculous existence with layer upon layer of fashions, cosmetics, fads, trivial technological conveniences, throwaway products, bureaucratic red tape, and stylish junk. How are we to penetrate through these obscuring layers?

If you were to choose death as an ally (as a reminder of the preciousness of each moment), and if you were to choose the universe as your home (as a reminder of the awesome dimensions of our existence), then, would a quality of aliveness, immediacy, and poignancy naturally infuse your moment-to-moment living? If you knew that you would die within several hours or days, would the simplest things acquire a luminous and penetrating significance? Would each moment become precious beyond all previous measure? Would each flower, each person, each crack in the sidewalk, each tree become a wonder? Would each experience become a fleeting and never-to-be-repeated miracle? Simplicity of living helps to bring this kind of clarity and appreciation into our lives.

An old Eastern saying states: "Simplicity reveals the master." As we gradually master the art of living, a consciously chosen simplicity emerges as an expression of that mastery. Simplicity allows the true character of our lives to show forth—like stripping, sanding, and waxing a fine piece of wood that had long been painted over. To further suggest the broad relevance of the factor of simplicity, let's turn to examine its worldly expression in three diverse areas: consumption, communications, and work.

Simplicity and Consumption

To bring the quality of simplicity into our levels and patterns of consumption, we must learn to live between the extremes of poverty and excess. Simplicity is a double-edged sword in this regard: living with either too little or with too much will diminish our capacity to realize our human potentials. Bringing simplicity into our lives thus requires that we understand the ways in which our consumption either supports or entangles our existence. We must learn the difference between those material circumstances that support our lives and those that constrict our lives. Simplicity requires living with balance.

Balance occurs when there is sufficiency—when there is neither excess nor deficit. To find such balance in our daily lives requires that we understand the difference between our personal "needs" and our "wants." Needs are those things that are essential to our survival and our growth. Wants are those things that are extra—that gratify our psychological desires. For example, we *need* shelter in order to survive. We may *want* a huge house with many extra rooms that are seldom used. We *need* basic medical care. We may *want* cosmetic plastic surgery to disguise the fact that we are getting older. We *need* functional clothing. We may *want* frequent changes in clothing style to reflect the latest fashion. We *need* a nutritious and well-balanced diet. We may *want* to eat at expensive restaurants. We *need* transportation. We may *want* a new Mercedes.

Only when we are clear about what we need and what we want can we begin to pare away the excess and find a middle path between extremes. No one else can find this balance for us. This is a task that we each must do for ourselves.

The hallmark of balanced simplicity is that our lives become clearer, more direct, less pretentious, and less complicated. We are then empowered by our material circumstances rather than enfeebled or distracted. Excess in either direction—too much or too little—is complicating. If we are totally absorbed in the struggle for subsistence or, conversely, if we are totally absorbed in the struggle to accumulate, then our capacity to participate wholeheartedly and enthusiastically in life is diminished.

The Simple Living Collective of San Francisco, long a leader in exploring a life of conscious simplicity, has suggested four consumption criteria that touch at the very heart of the issue of balanced consumption: [2]

- Does what I own or buy promote activity, self-reliance, and involvement, or does it induce passivity and dependence?

- Are my consumption patterns basically satisfying, or do I buy much that serves no real need?

- How tied is my present job and life-style to installment payments, maintenance and repair costs, and the expectations of others?

- Do I consider the impact of my consumption patterns on other people and on the earth?

This compassionate approach to consumption stands in stark contrast to the traditional Western view, which assumes that if each of us seeks to maximize his or her personal consumption, we automatically maximize our well-being and happiness. This approach to consumption severely limits the realization of our larger human potentials—individual and collective. How is this the case?

When we equate our identity with that which we consume—when we engage in "identity consumption"—we become possessed by our possessions. We are consumed by that which we consume. Our identity becomes, not a free-standing, authentic expression in the moment, but a material mask that we have constructed so as to present a more appealing image for others to see. The vastness of who we are is then compressed into an ill-fitting shell that obscures our uniqueness and natural beauty. When we believe the advertiser's fiction that "you are what you consume," we begin a misdirected search for a satisfying experience of identity. We look desperately beyond ourselves for the next thing that will make us happy: a new car, a new wardrobe, a new job, a new hairstyle, a new house, and so on. Instead of lasting satisfaction, we find only temporary gratification. After the initial gratification subsides, we must begin again— looking for the next thing that, this time, we hope will bring some measure of enduring satisfaction. Yet, the search is both endless and hopeless because it is continually directed away from the "self" that is doing the searching. If we were to pause in our search and begin to discover that our true identity is much larger than any that can be fashioned through even the most opulent levels of material consumption, then the entire driving force behind our attempts at "identity consumption" would be fundamentally transformed.

It is a radical simplicity when we voluntarily withdraw from the preoccupations with the material rat race of accumulation and instead accept our natural experience—unadorned by superfluous and suffocating goods—as sufficient unto itself. It is a radical simplicity when we affirm that our happiness cannot be purchased, no matter how desperately the advertiser may want us to believe the fiction that we will never be happy or adequate without his or her product. It is a radical simplicity when we accept our bodies as they are—when we affirm that each of us is endowed with a dignity, beauty, and character whose natural expression is infinitely more interesting and engaging than any imagined identity we might construct with layers of stylish clothes and cosmetics.

A conscious simplicity, then, is not self-denying but life-affirming. Voluntary simplicity is not an "ascetic simplicity" (of strict austerity). Rather, it is an "aesthetic simplicity" (where each person considers whether his or her level and pattern of consumption fits with grace and integrity into the practical art of daily living on this planet).

In considering the relevance of simplicity for consumption, it is imperative that we include an appreciation of the material circumstances of life for all people on this planet. To reiterate a staggering statistic—nearly 1 billion members of the human family live in absolute poverty. Furthermore, each year millions of children die from starvation. Millions more die from diseases that find easy prey in bodies weakened by years of severe malnutrition. Many who do survive will be physically and mentally impaired by the effects of prolonged malnutrition.

In stark contrast, Western industrial nations are islands of relative affluence in an ocean of global poverty and human suffering. Many Western industrial nations have an overabundance of food. Surplus grain rots in storage waiting for higher prices, crash diets for losing weight abound, and many pets are fed better than the children of Third World nations. This is insane. How can a more harmonious balance be achieved?

Since the gap between rich and poor nations is widening rather than narrowing, balance requires a much more equitable distribution of consumption-capacity among the members of the human family. Given the rapid growth of global interdependence in every facet of life—economic, environmental, political, cultural—it is inconceivable that this condition of growing imbalance can persist for long. The mounting disparities between rich and poor people on this planet are so great that if they are not voluntarily brought into balance, they are very likely to be remedied by violent means. If violence is the primary vehicle for achieving a more equitable distribution of the world's critically needed resources, then the probable outcome will be even more widespread human suffering, global economic collapse, and political chaos. The relevance of greater material simplicity for people in the affluent nations is both compelling and obvious.

Balance also requires that we find new forms of material growth that are sustainable at a global scale. The abundance of the industrial era has been realized by making unsustainable demands upon the world's resources and environment. We do not have sufficient energy, mineral resources, and environmental carrying capacity to allow all of the people in the world to consume at the levels, and in the forms, that have characterized industrial growth in the West. In particular, we need much more efficient forms of growth—forms that are marked by simplicity, lightness, ecological integrity, recyclability, and durability. Food production, health care, housing, transportation, appliances, energy production, and many more areas of our lives will have to be diversely and creatively adapted if we are to sustain the process of global development into the next century. Overall, we must begin to develop levels and patterns of consumption that are globally appropriate—that wisely use the world's resources and that do not unduly upset the world's fragile, and already greatly stressed, ecology. In such an endeavor, simplicity of living has enormous relevance—particularly for the industrial nations of the West.

Simplicity and Interpersonal Communications

Simplicity has relevance beyond consumption; it enhances the quality of our interpersonal communications. The ability to communicate is at the very heart of human life and human civilization. If we cannot communicate clearly and directly, then civilization itself is threatened. In this era, when the ability to effectively communicate is being challenged at every level, from interpersonal to global, it is vital that we enhance the quality of our exchanges by introducing the factor of simplicity. How can we do this?

Recall the definition of simplicity as meaning direct, clear, and unpretentious. If we were to consciously simplify our communications, then they would, by definition, tend to become more clear, direct, and honest. To illustrate, let's look at five areas in which simplicity can enhance the quality of interpersonal communications.

First, to communicate more simply means fundamentally to communicate more honestly. Dishonesty is the source of much confusion and complexity in our exchanges with others. Honest communications tend to be straightforward, direct, and precise. When we bring honesty into our lives, we are connecting our inner experiencing with our outer expressions. Integrity, authenticity, and personal responsibility are at the heart of truthful communication. In turn, honesty encourages the development of trust. With trust there is a basis for cooperation, even when there remain disagreements. With cooperation there is a foundation created for mutually helpful living. Simplicity of communication—as greater honesty—is thus a vital ingredient to the civilizing process.

Second, simplicity is evident in our communications when we begin to let go of idle gossip and wasteful speech. Wasteful speech can assume many forms: distracted chattering about people and places that have little relevance to what is happening in the moment; name dropping and building social status by association; using unnecessarily complex language or overly coarse language, and so on. When we simplify our communications by eliminating the irrelevant, we infuse what we do communicate with greater dignity and intention. Further, given that we are daily inundated with thousands of messages (through television, radio, newspapers, billboards, etc.), it is a gift of consideration to others to communicate with as little excess as possible.

Third, simplicity is also manifest in communication by consciously respecting the value of silence. The revered Indian sage Ramana Maharshi once said that silence speaks with "unceasing eloquence." [3] When we appreciate the power and eloquence of silence as a backdrop for our communication, our exchanges with others come into much sharper focus. Yet, we tend to feel uneasy with silence. Extended pauses in conversation are often considered painful lapses to be filled as quickly as possible. Perhaps we fear that the penetrating quality of silence will too starkly reveal the presence of our collective social facades—

masks that are held in comfortable position by a continuous flow of conversation. The sometimes painful or awkward quality that silence in social settings may bring is, I think, a measure of the mismatch between our social masks and our more authentic sense of self. Once we are comfortable in allowing silence its place in our communication, we find there is space for our more authentic experience of "self" to be present. As a heightened appreciation of silence, simplicity fosters dignity, depth, and directness in communication.

Fourth, simplicity is also expressed in communication as greater eye contact with others. The eyes have been called the seat of the soul. Not surprisingly, more direct eye contact with others tends to cultivate more "soulful" communication. The quality of our communication is thus enhanced, and the task of communication simplified, when we are willing to see, and be seen by, another. This does not mean that we should approach everyone with a tight, hard, and demanding gaze. Rather, we can open to gentle eye contact with loving acceptance of self and other. As it is, Western cultural taboos against direct and sustained eye contact are so pervasive that we seldom notice how infrequently we actually look into another's eyes. Yet, when we do directly "see" another, there is a mutual flash of recognition. The source of that mutual recognition or shared knowingness resides not in the pigmented portion of the eyes, but within the darkness of the interior center—therein is the place that yields the spark of conscious recognition. It is the dancing and brilliant darkness of the interior eye that reveals that the essence of "self" and "other" share the same source. Emerson spoke eloquently of how poverty, riches, status, power, and sex are all forms whose veil yields to our knowing eyes. What is seen goes beyond all these forms and labels to mutually reveal the essence of who we are. In sum, the simplicity of our communication— its directness, clarity, and unpretentiousness—is enormously enhanced by gentle eye contact with others.

Fifth, simplicity can also be manifested in our communications as greater openness to nonsexual, physical contact.

Hugging and touching that is free from disguised sexual manipulation is a powerful way of more fully and directly communicating with another. Yet, the simple act of touching another is relatively uncommon in many Western cultures. In turn, learning the skills of physical touching is vital to our present era. Studies have shown that a strong correlation exists between acceptance of physical touching and a tendency toward gentleness.[4] If we are to learn to live together as a global family, then we must learn to touch one another with less physical and psychological violence. In doing so we enhance the simplicity, directness, and clarity of our communication.

Overall, it is apparent that the quality of simplicity—as greater directness and clarity—has a relevance that is not confined to our material consumption. It is also of enormous importance to our interpersonal communications.

Simplicity and Work

The breadth of relevance that the factor of simplicity has for the conduct of our lives is suggested further by a third area—that of work. Let's consider how our work can be touched by this orientation in living. Simplicity (as greater directness, clarity, and unpretentiousness) can transform our approach to work in a variety of ways, only three of which I will mention here.

First, our relationship with our work is enormously simplified when our livelihood makes a genuine contribution both to ourselves and to the human family. It is through our work that we find opportunity to develop our skills, relate with others in shared tasks, and contribute to the larger society. If our work is directly contributory, it can be a source of great satisfaction and great learning. It was Thomas Aquinas, I think, who said: "There can be no joy of life without joy of work." Our relationship with our work is enormously simplified when we move from an intention of "making a killing for myself" to that of "earning a living in a way that contributes to the well-being of all." This shift represents a profound clarification of intention that is enormously simplifying. Once our intention is clear, we can cut through pretense, self-interest, status seeking, and conflicting personal objectives to realize more appropriate action in the world. Without the clarifying frame of reference provided by sensing the contribution of our work to the well-being of the world, it is immensely more difficult to find satisfaction and fulfillment in our work. In sensing the needs of the world, our work acquires a natural focus and intention. This focus helps us to bring clarity into our work and simplicity into our lives.

Second, the quality of simplicity—as greater clarity and directness of involvement with work—is often enhanced by more human-sized places of work. How is this the case? In Western nations, many persons work within massive bureaucracies: huge corporations, vast government agencies, enormous educational institutions, sprawling medical complexes, and so on. These workplaces have grown so large and so complex that they are virtually incomprehensible, both to those who work within them and to those who are served by them. Not surprisingly, the work that emerges from these massive organizations tends to be routine, intensely specialized, boring, stifling of creativity, and stress producing. Simplicity in this setting implies that the imbalance toward gigantic scale would change in favor of more human-sized workplaces. This does not mean abandonment of the institutions that have arisen during the industrial era. Instead, it means that we might undertake a grass roots revitalization of our institutions by redesigning them in such a way that they are of more comprehensible size and manageable complexity. Such a change would promote our more wholehearted involvement with our work. By consciously creating our workplaces of such size that they encourage meaningful involvement and personal responsibility, the rampant alienation, boredom, and emptiness of work would be greatly reduced.

Third, the quality of simplicity is also manifest in more direct and meaningful participation in decisions about our work. For example: direct worker participation in decision making about what to produce; direct worker involvement in the ongoing process of deciding how to best organize work; direct worker participation in deciding the structure of working arrangements such as flexible hours, job sharing, job swapping, team assembly, and other innovations.

We have looked at three very different areas—consumption, communications, and work—and have barely touched upon the pervasive relevance of the factor of simplicity. Overall, we have seen that simplicity is a vital ingredient if we are to create more satisfying and sustainable lives in our work, consumption, and communications. In earlier chapters we also noted how the progressive simplification of life is at the very heart of the process of civilizational growth (the progressive refinement of the material side of life allows the simultaneous unfolding of the emotional and spiritual side of life). Furthermore, greater material simplicity is essential if we are to cope with the severe imbalances between rich and poor members of the human family, as well as cope with growing resource shortages and mounting pollution of the environment. Clearly, greater simplicity has a wide-ranging relevance that touches every facet of our lives.

Voluntary Simplicity: An Integrated Path for Living

In this section we have been examining the roots of the notion of "voluntary simplicity." Given this overview, what can we say about voluntary simplicity as an integrated path for living?

To live more voluntarily is to live more consciously. To live more consciously is to live in a "life-sensing" manner. It is to directly "taste" our experience of life as we move through the world. It is to consciously open—as fully, patiently, and lovingly as we are able—to the unceasing miracle of our "ordinary" existence.

To live more simply is to live in harmony with the vast ecology of all life. It is to live with balance—taking no more than we require and at the same time giving fully of ourselves. To live with simplicity is by its very nature a "life-serving" intention. Yet, in serving life, we serve ourselves as well. We are each an inseparable part of the life whose well-being we are serving. In participating in life in this manner, we do not disperse our energy frivolously, but employ our unique capacities in ways that are helpful to the rest of life.

Voluntary simplicity, as a life-sensing and life-serving path, is neither remote nor unapproachable. This way of life is always available to the fortunate minority of the world who live in relative affluence. All that is required is our conscious choosing. This path is no farther from us than we are from ourselves. To discover our unique understanding and expression of this path does not require us to start from anywhere other than where we already are. This path is not the completion of a journey but its continual beginning anew. Our task is to freshly open to the reality of our situation as it already is, and then to wholeheartedly respond to that which we experience. The learning that unfolds along the path of our life-sensing and life-serving participation in the world is itself the journey. The path itself is the goal. Ends and means are inseparable.

A self-reinforcing spiral of growth begins to unfold for those who choose to participate in the world in a life-sensing and life-serving manner. As we live more voluntarily—more consciously —we feel less identified with our material possessions and thereby are enabled to live more simply. As we live more simply, our lives become less filled with unnecessary distractions, we find it easier to bring our undivided attention into our passage through life, and thereby we are enabled to live more consciously.

Each aspect—living voluntarily and living simply—builds

upon the other and promotes the progressive refinement of each. We pull ourselves up by our own bootstraps. Gradually, the experience of being infuses the process of doing. Life-sensing and life-serving action become one integrated flow of experience. We become whole. Nothing is left out. Nothing is denied. All faculties, all experience, all potentials are available in the moment. And the path ceaselessly unfolds.

SECTION IV

REVITALIZATION

CHAPTER 8

VOLUNTARY SIMPLICITY AND CIVILIZATIONAL REVITALIZATION

Thus far we have explored the notion of voluntary simplicity primarily as a personal path for living. In this chapter we turn to examine the relevance of simplicity of living as a social pathway leading to civilizational revitalization. To provide a context for our discussion, it is useful to briefly recall the conclusions from Chapter 3 in which we examined the nature of the civilizational challenge that we now confront.

We encounter a wide array of critical problems including rapid depletion of cheaply available petroleum and natural gas, severe environmental degradation, a burgeoning global population, a widening gap between rich and poor peoples of the world, the proliferation of weapons of war (chemical, biological, nuclear, and conventional), widespread malnutrition and outright starvation of millions in Third World nations, overwhelming bureaucratic complexity, a loss of cultural cohesion and compelling social purpose, and many more. Overall, these problems are of enormous scope, complexity, and severity. The meshing of these problems into a larger and intensely intertwined pattern of problems constitutes a "macro-problem" or "world-problem" that will yield to only our most inventive and compassionate solutions.

179

Because of forces related to the emergence of these critical national and global problems, a number of Western developed nations, such as the United States, seem to have moved beyond their golden summer of growth. The era of fullest blossoming of the potentials of the industrial era has ended. We have already entered a stage of initial decline. This stage seems likely to be soon followed by a time of civilizational breakdown unless a whole constellation of fundamental adjustments is made in our manner of living, working, and consuming.

We face an unyielding future. We are, I think, in a three-way race between oblivion (massive physical destruction), stagnation (paralysis in the web of an authoritarian bureaucracy that attempts to forcefully manage the rapidly deteriorating situation), and revitalization (in which a new burst of life and creativity infuses our unraveling civilization as a result of the enthusiastic participation of millions of persons working cooperatively toward the realization of a shared human agenda). The latter alternative is the subject of this chapter.

If necessity is the mother of invention, then we had best become skilled midwives to aid in the birth of the social, economic, political, and cultural inventions that must emerge from our time of growing necessity. For the first time in centuries, entire cultures are being forced to consider the nature and purpose of the human experiment. We are being challenged to imagine entirely new directions and dimensions of both personal and social evolution. One promising evolutionary direction is exemplified, I think, by the path of conscious simplicity, with its emphasis on balanced growth involving both inner and outer dimensions of life. This way of life, if voluntarily chosen and enthusiastically explored, could serve to energize and revitalize our nearly exhausted industrial civilizations.

It would represent a profound change if a majority of persons in countries such as the United States were to shift their patterns of living, working, and consuming in the direction of a consciously chosen simplicity. Enormous demands would be made upon everyone. The transition to this social path would require patience, commitment, compassion, and the wholehearted participation of millions upon millions of persons. We would be challenged to work together with a level of social maturity never before demanded in human history. Although the demands would be great, the satisfactions that would accompany this social journey seem even greater. The satisfactions are those that come from enthusiastic participation in life: of doing work that we know is contributing to the well-being of others, of learning with others as we collectively undertake tasks that are of shared value, and of having many opportunities to express our unique talents in the world.

If, during the decades of the 1980s and 1990s, a majority of people in nations such as the United States were to move toward a life of deliberate simplicity, then how might this become manifest in everyday life? Clearly, there are so many possibilities for change that might be considered that it is impossible to do more than suggest the skeletal outlines of a revitalizing civilization. I leave it to you to put more flesh on these few conceptual bones and thereby translate this into a personal, living possibility.

Characteristics of a Revitalizing Civilization

As a first step in describing the nature of a revitalizing industrial civilization, I would like to briefly note some of the more tangible changes that I think would accompany the emergence of voluntary simplicity as the dominant way of life. It is an eclectic assortment of changes but it usefully suggests the quality of life and character of civilization that would begin to emerge. These changes include:

- Moderation in the overall levels of consumption in developed nations, and a change in the patterns of consumption (consuming products that tend to be more functional, durable, energy efficient, nonpolluting, easily repairable, healthy, and produced by "ethical firms").

• Widespread efforts at energy conservation ranging from the development of much more fuel-efficient autos and airplanes, to the insulation and redesign of homes to allow maximum use of passive solar heating, to the small-scale use of wind power, to the use of biomass and photo-voltaic sources, etc. Overall, the society would begin to turn away from the "hard energy path" of reliance upon imported petroleum, coal, and nuclear power and instead move toward a "soft energy path" that emphasizes conservation, solar power, and the use of renewable energy resources.

• Much more extensive and intensive use of electronic modes of communication as a substitute for increasingly expensive physical travel.

• Greater localization of markets—buying from nearby producers so as to minimize the costs of distribution in an energy-scarce society.

• A rebirth of entrepreneurial activity at the local level. Small businesses that are well adapted to local conditions and local needs would flourish.

• Greater use of more energy-efficient modes of transportation: bicycles, mopeds, motorcycles, car pools, buses, trains, etc.

• Continued population migration as people search for geographic areas more favored with resources such as fresh water and a warm climate.

• Selective economic growth or differentiated growth—some sectors of the economy would be contracting (especially those that are energy wasteful and oriented toward items of conspicuous consumption), while other sectors of the economy would be expanding (for example, information processing, communications, intermediate technologies, service industries, and agriculture).

• A mounting consumerist revolution as more and more

people boycott goods and services sold by firms whose policies are considered "unethical" or "unsound" with regard to the environment, worker participation, reinvestment policy, etc.

• A decline in agribusiness (with its heavy reliance upon petrochemicals) coupled with a rebirth of family farming (using more labor-intensive and organic modes of food production).

• Widespread recycling of materials—glass, metal, paper, clothing, etc.

• Job sharing, multiple work roles, and democratization of the economy through much higher levels of worker participation in management.

• New types of markets and marketplaces—flea markets, community markets, and extensive bartering networks would likely proliferate (a potential greatly enhanced by the new generations of computers that can assist in matching goods and services with potential consumers).

• Massive investments in cleaning up the environment— land, air, and water. A concerted effort to remove toxic wastes allowed to build up over the preceding decades. Much emphasis would be placed on designing new generations of industrial processes that are nonpolluting and that recycle wastes.

• Rapid growth in the number of classes, publications, video-cassettes, etc., dealing with do-it-yourself activities ranging from home construction and repair to cooking and gardening. Overall, a rebirth in the sense of personal competence and craftsmanship.

• An expanded approach to health care. There likely would be greater emphasis on preventive medicine, the healing powers of the mind in conjunction with traditional medicine, neighborhood clinics run by paramedical staffs, the role of nutrition in maintaining good health, the reduction of environmental stressors that contribute to the activation of disease, etc.

• A rebirth in the importance of local community with a strong emphasis on the neighborhood as an area of work, play, sharing, recreation, and mutually helpful living. There likely would be a growing number of "urban villages" or intentional neighborhood communities that contain a diverse range of activities (for example, neighborhood workplaces, community gardens, health-care facilities, child-care centers, recycling centers, food cooperatives, neighborhood schools, neighborhood banks, etc.). These urban villages would tend to have the flavor and cohesiveness of a small town and the sophistication of a larger city (as they would be nested within a communications-rich urban setting).

• A gradual transformation in the use of urban space: fewer roads and more community commons. Additionally, urban land formerly used for lawns and flower gardens would be increasingly used for supplemental food sources (for example, vegetable gardens, nut and fruit trees).

• Redesign of homes to allow more intensive use of housing. New building forms and designs would promote energy conservation and efficiency of space utilization. Each house would tend to become a more integrated living unit that would provide a supplementary energy source (such as solar heating), a supplementary food source (through intensive gardening), and a supplementary workplace (through the use, for example, of the new generation of computer and communications technologies). This would be a time of economic, legal, architectural, and technical innovation in housing. To support this innovation, there would be accompanying changes in financing methods, ownership arrangements, building codes, and zoning laws.

• A redefinition of the "good life"—an overall lowering of material expectations and a countervailing increase in learning how to get more satisfaction from the nonmaterial aspects of life through psychological and spiritual learning in community with others.

• A renaissance in new forms of music, art, drama, literature, entertainment, and learning that expresses the emerging way of life and view of reality.

• A more unified social order that is able to honor human diversity. Widespread agreement would exist around such fundamentals as the need to conserve resources, the importance of a planetary perspective in understanding how to cope skillfully with our situation, an ecological orientation, a reverence for life, and affirmation of the importance of the inner dimension.

• In democratic societies, central governments would have less material power over people's lives and instead would tend to exercise power by encouraging public consensus around shared goals and assumptions. A primary function of the nation-state would be to bring the diverse parts of this highly differentiated society into a cohesive whole. National leaders would also provide a source of perspective and creative vision that bridges between the local level and the planetary sphere of human relations.

• In terms of social organization, a twofold process would be at work that may be described roughly as simultaneous decentralization and globalization (Appendix V discusses this process in more precise terms). Decentralization would manifest as a systematic attempt to reduce the scale and complexity of living and working environments. Many institutions, workplaces, neighborhoods, schools, hospitals, etc. would be redesigned and rebuilt so as to be of more approachable size, graspable scope, and manageable complexity. Globalization would manifest as a concerted effort to find democratic means for the human family to cope with critical planetary problems (such as nuclear proliferation, environmental deterioration, resource depletion, population growth, and poverty).

• New political parties and coalitions would emerge around a new political perspective: The traditional perspective (egoistic-materialistic-nationalistic) would be replaced gradually by a transpersonal-material/spiritual-planetary perspective.

• Inflation would be moderated by extensive innovation in areas that have contributed much to escalating prices; for example, emphasizing energy conservation and use of renewable resources (solar, biomass, wind, and hydro power); encouraging alternatives to traditional, high-technology medical care (preventive medicine, the use of paraprofessionals, and other "holistic" health-care approaches); promoting the development of alternative forms of housing (owner-built homes, smaller and more efficient homes, urban homesteading, etc.); encouraging dietary changes (shifting away from expensive meat, sugar, and highly processed foods); and so on. Innovations such as these would begin to cope with the structural roots of inflation.

• Rapid growth of global communications networks would allow a quantum increase in the levels of cross-cultural sharing and learning. It would also allow intense debates by all members of the human family around issues of global concern. Aided by the creative use of communications technologies, we would begin to move toward a clearer sense of global community, species identity, and shared human agenda.

This illustrative sampling of changes reveals that movement toward greater simplicity of living does not mean the return to a more primitive past, but movement ahead into a more sustainable, compassionate, and cooperative future. This list only begins to suggest the practical, down-to-earth adaptations that likely would characterize a revitalizing civilization (Appendix V discusses the structure and dynamics of such a society at greater length).

In addition to these more tangible changes, there are more intangible, but no less important, changes that also would occur. In particular, there are three additional adaptations that, I think, must begin to emerge over the next several decades if a revitalizing civilization, premised on the conscious simplification of life, is to have a skillful birth at this time. These changes are: 1. movement toward a life-sensing and life-serving cultural orientation, 2. the transformation of television to allow active social learning and creative visualization of social alternatives, and 3. the acknowledgment of love or compassion as a necessary foundation for evolving toward some form of peaceful planetary civilization. Each of these is discussed below.

A Life-Sensing and Life-Serving Cultural Orientation

What does it mean to become a "revitalizing" civilization? The dictionary defines "vitality" as the quality of having life, vigor, and an animated character. We cannot become a revitalizing civilization when we are out of touch with the source of our vitality—when we are disconnected from life itself. To become a revitalizing civilization we are obliged to re-establish our contact with life. This profoundly simple notion is of utmost importance because the industrial world view has encouraged us to think of ourselves as apart from life—as above and/or separate from the rest of nature. We cannot renew either ourselves or our civilizations when we maintain a posture of aloofness from life. Yet, this is exactly our predicament as the industrial view of reality is fundamentally life-denying and self-serving in its orientation. How is this the case?

First, let's examine how the industrial revolution has been

built upon a life-denying view of reality. In the industrial era, the universe has been conceived as being fundamentally material—composed of elemental particles of lifeless matter. Furthermore, consciousness has not been viewed as a subtle life-essence infusing the universe; instead, consciousness has been viewed as little more than a by-product of biochemical and electrical activity in the brain. Our universe, then, has been seen as a largely lifeless, though exceedingly complex, machine. Consistent with this mechanistic description of reality, the intellect was deemed the highest faculty that humankind might develop. Why? The rational-logical mind could discern the lawful patterns of behavior of the complex machine-universe, thereby allowing us to acquire growing mastery over the material universe and, in turn, insure continuing material progress. With a universe composed of lifeless particles, and with the knowing faculty, or consciousness, largely ignored, and with the emotional and bodily dimensions of experience relegated to a secondary position behind the functioning of the intellect, it is not surprising that we now find ourselves in a sterile middle ground that is cut off from the sources of our vitality.

The narrow focus of the industrial view of reality has acted as a reducing valve that diminishes our capacity to experience directly and consciously the essence of life. Thus, to restore vitality to our lives and to our civilizations, we must learn the skills of moving beyond the limits of the industrial view. We must freshly engage life. We must relearn ancient truths forgotten in the rush to industrial development. We must move from an unconsciously life-denying orientation to that of a consciously life-affirming and life-sensing orientation.

There is a second and complementary dimension of our traditional view of reality that must also be transformed if we are to revitalize our faltering industrial civilizations. That is, we must move from a self-serving orientation to that of a life-serving orientation. To see the relevance of this we need to first note how the industrial view has promoted self-serving rather than life-serving behavior.

In the industrial view of reality that arose more than two centuries ago, the overriding goal in life was for each person to pursue his or her personal material gain to the utmost of his or her ability. Greed was thus elevated to the position of a social virtue. The ethicality of this posture toward living and working was rationalized through the so-called "natural law of the marketplace." In accord with this law, people were assured that if each person were to pursue *only* his or her own personal gain, then a process would ensue, which, as if "led by an invisible hand," would result in the promotion of the overall welfare of society. With the welfare of the whole society automatically assured by the unrestrained pursuit of material gain, the industrial revolution began in earnest. Now, two centuries later, it is not surprising to find that with the pursuit of personal gain as a fundamental organizing premise for human relations, we have created an alienating society—one that fosters wasteful extravagance and spiritual impoverishment.

For a revitalizing society to emerge we must move beyond the industrial view of reality and human identity—we must move from greed to creative altruism, from cutthroat competition to cooperation, from "making a killing" to "earning a living," from narrow self-serving behavior to broad life-serving behavior. Instead of encouraging obliviousness to the needs of the larger world under the guise of a "natural law of the marketplace," we must encourage each individual to be more conscious of, and responsive to, the impact of his or her actions upon the rest of the world.

How are we to move toward a life-sensing and life-serving orientation? How can we empower ourselves to act in ways that are equal to the challenges we face? We can clarify the nature of the "life-sensing" process by considering one of the most severe global problems that we confront—that of starvation. Instead of *thinking about* the incomprehensible statistics of millions of persons dying of starvation each year, we can choose to *sense directly* the more intensely vivid reality of what this means for one or two persons. By focusing on the experience of the individual rather than the masses of people, we are given a different perspective. In an instant of time we can sense the extent to which our lives are in alignment with the needs of the larger human family.

Such an instant occurred for me as I was reading a news story concerning the plight of starving refugees in Southeast Asia. One sentence in particular burned into the very core of my being: ". . . a feverish young mother collapses as she staggers toward a pesthole of a refugee camp; her skeletal 6-year-old daughter tries in vain to pick her up while other starving refugees stream past unseeing." [1] Upon encountering that single sentence I suddenly found myself thrust into the unyielding reality of that brief episode played out on a dusty road on a hot afternoon in Cambodia. First there washed through my body a sense of empathy—for a few moments, I was the mother of that child. It was I lying on the rough dirt road—my body devastated by years of malarial fever and starvation, the other members of my family either dead or missing—feeling a sense of profound despair as my life slowly ebbed away and knowing that I was soon to leave my only remaining child to die alone and unattended. In the next instant, my sensing shifted to this small child. It was I who was pulled by starvation to leave and search for food, and pulled by the bond of parental kinship to stay with the last known remnant of security in a world gone insane.

It is when we move behind the numbing statistics of starvation, disease, environmental deterioration, and related sorrows of our world that we begin to change our lives. It is when we taste, chew, swallow, and then digest into the bowels of our being the distress and suffering of life on this planet that we begin to change of our own accord. It is when we have a direct, felt understanding of the conditions of life for the larger human family that we are empowered to act in ways that are equal to the challenges we confront. It is then that the reasonableness of E. F. Schumacher's statement, "We must live simply that others may simply live," strikes home.

It is difficult to allow these life-sensing experiences into our lives. Yet, until we can allow the direct experience of the world into our beings, we are cut off from the reality of our situation. It is only when we can feel our connection with, and our love for, the other members of the human family that we are able to respond fully to their needs. The despair that we feel is not debilitating; to the contrary, it is the gateway to finding the creativity, energy, and love with which to respond to our situation. When we open to the plight of the world, the world reaches into our lives and draws from us the potentials that we must realize in order to be of skillful service in healing (making whole) the world.

The world is our teacher. In making our encounter with the world firsthand and direct, we are empowered to act, and we are guided in our actions by what we experience. When we actually experience the suffering of this world, we naturally recognize appropriate action. We then act, not from the push of guilt, but from the pull of compassion. Our individual lives begin to come into alignment with the needs of the larger human family. We become an integral part of the larger organism of life. Our unique capacities can then contribute to the well-being of the whole. Our inner experience and outer expression are reconnected and can work toward creating a more harmonious balance in the world.

By moving from a life-denying and self-serving orientation to that of a life-sensing and life-serving orientation, we reconnect with the source of our vitality and we create a channel for that vitality to flow into the world. In acting in the service of life itself, we find that our inner experience has a clear channel for expression into the outer world.

Acting in a life-sensing and life-serving manner, either as individuals or as an entire nation, does not merit special praise nor does it mean that we are embarking on a path of sacrifice. Inasmuch as we are an integral part of the life that we are serving, we are acting on our own behalf as well when we act in a life-serving manner. To act in a life-sensing and life-serving way is its own justification, its own reward.

Acting in a life-sensing and life-serving manner is not a spiritual platitude divorced from the hard realities of life. To the contrary, living in this way is a crucial necessity if we are to move beyond the stage of civilizational stagnation and paralysis. There is no amount of bureaucracy and regulation that can substitute for the effectiveness of self-determining individuals who are acting on their own initiative on behalf of all life. If one corporate officer were to move from a life-denying and self-serving intention to that of a life-sensing and life-serving intention, that change could contribute more to meeting corporate social responsibilities than a whole new maze of government red tape and regulation. If one engineer were to make it a heartfelt intention to place the long-run well-being of the consumer and the environment above the short-run profit pursuits of the firm, that change in intention could have more impact on the design of products than, for example, a multimillion-dollar safety study funded by the federal government. If one media executive were to view his or her task as that of wholeheartedly promoting the active social learning of a culture rather than maximizing short-run profits from deadening programming, that change could have more impact than a thousand petitions from despairing viewers.

The point is that we all have our unique work to do—our unique contributions to make to life. If we each were to begin to act in a consciously life-sensing and life-serving manner, no matter how imperfect or partial or tentative our actions, the cumulative result for the entire society would be enormous. Bit by bit, many small changes would accumulate into a tidal wave of revitalizing change.

A revitalizing civilization, premised on life-sensing and life-serving behavior, cannot emerge through manipulation, coercion, or regulation; it must be freely and voluntarily chosen by each person. If this change in intention were to become widely acknowledged by the culture as a legitimate and workable basis for worldly action, a new foundation for cultural relations and a new cultural agenda would be set into motion. Our life-sensing and life-serving actions may be imperfect, awkward, and halting. Nonetheless, a genuinely vitalizing process will have been set in motion. Since this is a process that, by its very nature, is conscious of, and responsive to, the hard realities that we now face, its utter realism would serve to carry it forward.

To act in a life-sensing and life-serving manner is not a utopian ideal. To the contrary, it is the unadorned, unpretentious, and unsentimental sensing of life as it is, and then acting in a way that responds to the totality of what is perceived. Acting in this way brings one into a more accurate or precise relationship with life as it is.

One practical area in which a life-sensing and life-serving orientation would become visibly manifest in everyday life is that of consumption. This shift in orientation would alter the whole purpose and meaning of consumption. The possessions that were strived after in an earlier era of high industrial growth —a large home with luxurious furnishings, a high-horsepower car, the latest in fashions—would gradually lose the intensity of their appeal. Instead of an emphasis on amassing much that was not genuinely needed, there would be a cultural premium placed upon learning how to live ever more lightly, skillfully, aesthetically. The individual who in the past was admired for a large and luxurious home would find that the mainstream culture increasingly admired those who had learned how to combine functional simplicity and beauty in a smaller home. The individual who was previously envied for his or her expensive car would find that a growing number of people were uninterested in his or her displays of conspicuous consumption. The person who was previously admired for always wearing the latest in fashions would find that more and more persons viewed "high fashion" as tasteless ostentation that was inappropriate in a world of great human need. This does not mean that people would completely turn away from the material things in life. Rather, it means that people would increasingly sense that the totality of life is not well served by the endless accumulation of luxuries and nonessentials. As more and more persons began to simplify their lives in a life-sensing and life-serving manner, the cumulative effect, when summed across entire societies, would be staggering.

Transformation of the Mass Media

Civilizational revitalization begins with personal revitalization and accumulates—person by person, bit by bit—into a pervasive wave of change. One accompanying change that I think is crucial to the revitalizing process is the transformation of our use of the mass media, particularly television. Why?

The ability to communicate is at the very heart of civilization. If we are to cope with our time of wrenching transition democratically, then the ability to communicate with one another is absolutely essential. Television is the most potent medium that we as a whole society have for the communication of our shared hopes, fears, and changing social goals. Television has become even more powerful than our schools, churches, and workplaces in its ability to create a common frame of reference or a shared view of the world. Given the power of television to dominate the consciousness of entire cultures, we must ask ourselves whether television is being used to negotiate skillfully our time of civilizational transition and challenge. My sense is that it is not.

There are three key shortcomings in our use of the mass media that are of great relevance here. First, instead of encouraging greater frugality of consumption, the mass media are being used to promote aggressively conspicuous consumption. Second, instead of providing images of real people who are empowered to cope creatively with the problems that touch us all, the mass media produce role models who tend to be exploitive, shallow, and manipulative. And third, instead of being a source of information about our critical national and global problems, television either ignores these vital concerns, or treats them in such a superficial manner that we, as a citizenry, are not empowered to participate effectively in decisions about these problems. These are strong assertions and I would like to explore them more carefully.

First, let's examine how television is far from neutral with regard to the patterns of living and consuming that it promotes. Although in theory this industry is supposed to act with balanced regard for the public interest (since it uses the public air waves), in practice the overriding goal of the television industry has been profit making. This is not surprising since the television industry (in its present form) is a creature born of the values and motivations of the industrial era. The economics of the profit-making process are straightforward.

Television networks make their profits primarily by delivering the largest possible audience of potential consumers to view the commercials of the huge corporate advertisers. The more people watching, the higher the charge to corporate advertisers and, in turn, the higher the revenue to the television networks. A self-fulfilling process is thereby set into motion: Mass entertainment is used to capture a mass audience that is appealed to by mass advertising which, in turn, promotes the psychology of mass consumption. The average consumer relies upon the mass entertainment that television provides in order to escape the pain and alienation of a social existence largely devoid of any greater expressed purpose than ever more mass consumption.

Not surprisingly, more frugal patterns of living and consuming do not appear on television. These themes would threaten the legitimacy of the television-induced cultural hypnosis generated by a self-perpetuating cycle of mass entertainment, mass advertising, and mass consumption. By default, our culture is left with programming and advertising that selectively portray and powerfully reinforce a materialistic orientation toward life. As a result, we are becoming a civilization divided against itself: Television advertising exhorts us to consume more while our instincts for human survival and human growth tell us that we need to learn how to live with less.

The enormous mismatch between television programming

and changing public needs is suggested by the opinion surveys discussed in Chapter 4. Recall, for example, changing U.S. attitudes toward consumption. When asked what emphasis they would place on living, over three quarters of the national sample said they would place greater emphasis on "teaching people how to live more with basic essentials" than on "reaching higher standards of living." Additionally, more than three quarters also said they would opt for "learning to get our pleasures out of nonmaterial experiences" rather than opt for "satisfying our needs for more goods and services."

Does the current use of television reflect these dramatically changing attitudes and values in its advertising and programming? To the contrary, television continues to promote a one-sided, materialistic, and consumeristic orientation toward life. The values and perspectives of people who have little to spend (the poor) and people who want little (the frugal consumer who is more concerned with the quality of being rather than the quantity of having) are unrepresented in today's uses of television. As a consequence, we are building a profound bias into our cultural consciousness. We program the media and then the media program us! To reiterate, television is being used to unrelentingly urge us to consume ever more when we intuitively know that we must learn to live with less. Rather than serving as a helpful tool in our social evolution, television is diverting the flow of social adaptation away from more satisfying and sustainable ways of living and consuming.

A second area in which the mass media inhibit civilizational revitalization is in their distorted portrayal of what it means to be a responsible member of the human family. Television programming fills our collective consciousness—hour after hour, week after week, years after year—with images of people who tend to be superficial, sexually exploitive, dishonest, greedy, and violent. Seldom do more elevated images of human behavior appear. At a time when we require excellence of ourselves, we are inundated with the lowest common denominator of human behavior in order to feed the profits of a few corporations. Instead of depicting competent and compassionate individuals who might provide a diversity of role models for alternative ways of living and consuming, television portrays the average individual as largely incompetent and oblivious to the world in which we live. The hard realities of life—the sharp edges and painful struggles of real people—are replaced by a fantasy world inhabited by plastic characters moving through predictable conflicts that are told through mind-numbing dialogue and supported by machine-produced laughter. Given this situation, it seems little wonder that the cultural self-image of many in the United States today is that of an increasingly cynical, alienated, incapacitated, and powerless people. For the revitalization of our faltering civilizations, it seems imperative that we expand our use of the mass media to portray people who are capable of learning about, and experimenting with, alternative ways of living, working, and consuming that are more appropriate to to our era of growing scarcity and mounting human needs.

A third way in which our current use of television dampens the vitality of civilizational growth concerns our failure to employ this powerful tool for our active social learning. Why is this so important? A democracy cannot function without an informed citizenry. Therefore, in a democracy, there exists a fundamental need and right to be informed about matters that affect the society. If as a society we want a democracy in fact as well as in name, then the process of active social learning (the lifeblood of any democracy) must continuously evolve to fit our changing circumstances. Television has become a vital instrument of social learning and communication. Therefore, it is essential that television be consciously employed in assisting the citizenry in acquiring the social learning we need in order to take an active and effective part in the affairs of society. At present, we are using television frivolously and thereby trivializing and demeaning our experiment in democratic freedoms in the process. We must rapidly learn to use television in ways that bring greater understanding to our participation in the precious experiment in human freedom that is our democracy. If we do not creatively expand our uses of this medium, we will not have the necessary social learning with which to mount effective responses to our time of mounting civilizational challenge.

One important reason why we require a quantum increase in our social learning was touched upon in Chapter 3 (and is discussed more fully in Appendices III and IV). Briefly stated, our pace of social learning is now much slower than the pace at which our society and its problems are becoming complex. We are losing the dynamic race with growing social complexity. We are being overwhelmed by an avalanche of complexity in every sector of society. Our entire social apparatus is becoming increasingly unmanageable and out of control. There is a real and mounting concern whether many of our basic institutions can survive this time of testing and challenge.

To retain our democratic freedoms in the context of escalating levels of social complexity will require a vast increase in our pace of social learning. Yet, as it is, the most potent tool of social learning that we have—television—is an electronic wasteland filled with immature and demeaning programming and advertising that are utterly out of touch with the reality of life on this planet. We are being lulled into oblivion instead of awakened to our desperate plight. Television advertising, for example, takes exceedingly trivial considerations (such as which deodorant, shampoo, or denture adhesive to use) and blows them up into issues of seemingly enormous importance for the conduct of our lives. Concerns that are utterly insignificant, relative to the larger task of just living through a time of profound social transition, are given vastly inflated significance and then force-fed into our collective consciousness through incessant programming and advertising.

This manner of using television is more than a minor inconvenience or an offense to "good taste." It is crippling our capacity to comprehend and respond to our situation as a civilization. We are unconsciously prostituting the most precious resource that we have as a culture—our shared consciousness. We are selling access to our cultural consciousness to the highest corporate bidders—the conglomerate advertisers. We are literally putting our minds, values, and attitudes up for sale. We are deadening ourselves at the same time that we desperately need to experience our aliveness and vitality. We are obscuring the reality of our situation at the same time that we have a critical need to understand clearly the nature of our disintegrating world.

We inadvertently have handed over a substantial portion of our cultural consciousness to an electronic dictatorship that promotes extravagant consumption, social passivity, and personal impotence. For a revitalizing society to emerge, we require an alternative approach: an electronic democracy that encourages material frugality, active social learning, and personal empowerment. We must step back from our current use of television and fundamentally rechoose how we want it to be employed. If we allow the use of television to continue along its present track, I think this will do much to insure our movement into a time of civilizational stagnation and arrested growth.

The responsibility for change lies not so much with the television networks (as massive corporate bureaucracies) but with ourselves as individuals. Television networks are huge corporations that are acting on what the prevailing ground rules (profit making above all else) dictate as rational behavior. If there is to be a change, then it is we, the general public (including those who work within the television industry), who must first redefine the nature of the public interest that television is in theory obliged to serve. Once we have a clearer sense of our changing public interest, we can then legitimately request that the institutions that run this medium be vastly more responsive to the public interest or else forfeit their right to access to the public airwaves.

What is the changing nature of the public interest? It is, I think, in the public interest to use television for in-depth and continuing learning about critical national and international problems (energy, ecology, global equity, the arms race, Third World problems, etc.); visualizing alternative ways of living, working, and consuming as manifest in the lives of real people; communicating with our elected representatives via interactive television about our shared hopes, fears, and changing goals; learning more about the cultural heritage, living circumstances, and points of view of the other members of the human famliy with whom we share this planet; and many more.

I do not think there are any magical solutions that will remedy our situation overnight. The reason is that we require not minor improvements but a vast increase in the skillfulness with which we use this enormously powerful medium. We are being challenged to create a level and a scope of communication, culture, and collective imagination that have never before existed in human affairs. This is such an important task, and it is so integral to the process of civilizational revitalization, that the *entire* use of this medium must become a major social issue worthy of sustained and searching debate by all members of society.

Love as a Foundation for Planetary Revitalization

For civilizational revitalization to occur, we must respond to a gentle but insistent imperative; namely, that we begin to consciously infuse our international relations with a sense of love, or compassion. In saying this, I assume that unless we return to some form of Dark Ages in the aftermath of massive nuclear war or pervasive environmental disruption, the world will continue along its path toward rapid integration into some form of global community. Economically, environmentally, culturally, electronically, and in many other ways the nations of the world increasingly impinge upon one another. The fact that we are rapidly becoming a global civilization seems inescapable. Yet, the form that this emerging global social order will eventually assume is by no means clear. Our fast arriving planetary civilization could be governed by a harsh military dictatorship, imposed by one or more superpowers, or it might be governed by a gentle democracy collectively chosen by a majority of the human family. The form that the emerging planetary social order takes will profoundly affect the potential for civilizational revitalization, both globally and within individual nation-states. Therefore, I want to consider the three basic foundations upon which some form of global social order might arise: force, law, and love.

A first foundation for a global social order is force. Already there are enough nuclear weapons to destroy every person on this planet many times over. Still, more and more nations seek to possess these awesome weapons. Trillions of dollars worth of resources and millions of hours of precious human time are being diverted from desperate human needs to build ever more terrifying and destructive weapons. As the complexity and sophistication of weapons mount exponentially, the costs mount exponentially as well. Thus, the short-run search for security in superior armaments is leading rapidly to either bankruptcy of the superpowers or to a massively destructive confrontation.

Clearly, it is essential that we not ignore the arms race—a solar-heated home, frugality of consumption, a natural diet, and so on will mean nothing if the planet on which we all depend is devastated by nuclear war. Dr. Helen Caldicott, a compassionate activist who is devoting her life energies to halting the nuclear arms race, has described the terrifying consequences of an all-out nuclear war—a tragedy that would likely be completed within the space of one or two hours:

> If you live in a targeted area and you do manage to get into a fallout shelter, you won't survive because the firestorms will be so huge. One 20 megaton bomb (20 million tons of TNT equivalent) will create a firestorm of 3000 square miles. The fire will use up all the oxygen in the air, so if you're in a shelter, you'll asphyxiate. . . . If you're in a rural area and you do hear the sirens and you get into a shelter in time, you can't come up for two weeks because short-lived radioactive isotopes are so intensely radioactive that you'd die. When you do come up in two weeks, from

a psychiatric point of view, you'll be numb with grief, possibly psychotic. Certainly there will be no doctors left, or hospitals, because they're targeted. There will be no food. The water will be intensely radioactive. It's possible that the destruction of the ozone layer will be so intense that you won't be able to stay out in the sun for more than three minutes before you'd develop third-degree sunburn. That means the earth will be a parched, scorched planet. If you survive you must live underground to escape the fallout. And you'd probably get leukemia in five years. . . . We'd see plagues of typhoid, polio, dysentery—things we've cured. They'd all come back. . . . You can let your imagination wander a little bit and envision, generations later, the earth inhabited by bands of roving humanoids, unrecognizable as human beings. It will be the end of civilization . . .[2]

Even if global nuclear war is avoided, some form of global social order could still arise through the threat that nuclear weapons will be used. This foundation for planetary civilization would likely give rise to a monolithic military-political order of global proportions. Such a system would neither honor our deeper human unity nor tolerate much in the way of human diversity; as such, it would greatly inhibit the human freedom and creativity that are essential to vigorous renewal of our faltering civilizations. With a global social order premised upon the psychology of terror, and with the vast diversion of resources into armies and armaments to make that terror credible, the result would be that for many, living would truly be little more than "only not dying."

Gandhi often spoke about the wasteful detour in human evolution that results when we depend upon violence to solve our difficulties as nations.[3] He said this "law of the jungle" behavior was fitting for the consciousness of animals, but for we humans to conduct our lives in this manner was to reverse the course of evolution. It was, he said, to turn away from our higher potentials, which include the capacity for brotherly love and forgiveness.

If force is the foundation upon which we build a global social order, then we will be retreating from our evolutionary journey and instead will be moving back into the darkness of human conflict and suffering from which we have struggled so mightily to free ourselves. As we see the magnitude of unnecessary suffering that we are now inflicting upon ourselves, it seems apparent that the human family, as a whole, has yet to consciously learn the ancient lesson that "As you sow, so shall you reap." Again, Gandhi spoke clearly about this. He said: "All of us are one. When you inflict suffering on others, you are bringing suffering on yourself. When you weaken others, you are weakening yourself . . ." [4] Such statements are consistent with the teachings and example of Jesus who encouraged us to unceasingly work toward the transformation of our relationships with our enemies through the healing power of love. East and West thus converge in agreeing that force does not further human evolution. Force does not foster the development of a sense of human community that is essential to widespread revitalization.

A second foundation for global civilization is that of law. Assuming that the human family turns away from massive violence and/or widespread military domination, then a legalistic basis for human community could emerge as a practical alternative. By this I mean that the human family could establish agreements and rules of conduct at a global level that would allow people and nations to relate with a minimum of forceful coercion and with a maximum degree of freedom for voluntary association. For a legalistic foundation for global community to be effective, some democratically constituted body (such as the United Nations) would have to assume a much more prominent role in the conduct of global affairs. The responsibilities for such a global body would likely range from a peace-keeping function to insuring at least minimal well-being of persons and the planet with regard to food, health, energy, and the environment. With an effective legal apparatus for governing global relations, the process of global disarmament could begin in earnest.

This does not mean that the world would be free from tension and conflict. Instead, it means that the most destructive forms of warfare between nations would be removed. Conflict would still exist but would be more localized and less threatening to the totality of life on the planet. With widespread and substantial disarmament, massive amounts of human and physical resources would be liberated for productive work in coping with the enormous problems of the human family.

While a legalistic foundation for global community seems a necessary condition for civilizational revitalization, it is not, I think, a sufficient foundation for the longer run. The reason is that a legalistic foundation is primarily a bureaucratic foundation. I think it is apropriate that we have a healthy mistrust of a solely bureaucratic basis for maintaning a global community. Many developed nations have already had a taste, although on a smaller scale, of a social order where a parental bureaucracy manages many facets of life. When we consider the size and diversity of the human family and then visualize the level and form of bureaucracy that would likely emerge in an attempt to regulate that diversity, it seems quite plausible that the eventual outcome could be that of a suffocating bureaucracy of planetary scope.

Furthermore, if a legalistic foundation is the primary basis for creating a global social order, then a "law and order" orientation would likely become the prevailing norm. If what is "lawful" is the then prevailing social order, and if any attempt to change that social order quickly or substantially is considered to be creating disorder, then a "law and order" orientation would strongly incline toward maintaining the status quo. As a consequence, the fluidity and dynamism that is intrinsic to all evolution would be inhibited by a predominantly legalistic, and therefore bureaucratic, basis for global community.

The foregoing comments are not made to diminish the role or importance of law in global affairs. Rather, it is to see that at the same time that law may liberate humanity from the threat of physical devastation, it could begin to suffocate our creativity in a vast web of bureaucracy. As admirable and rational as it might seem, a legalistic and thereby bureaucratic foundation for global community would, over the long run, greatly dampen the vitality, vigor, and creativity of civilizational growth.

A third foundation for global community is that of love. Although love is a commonly recognized human experience—every bit as much as greed and fear—it is seldom seriously considered as a practical basis for governing our planetary relationships. Although love may seem an impractical and utopian basis for establishing a global community, I assure you that I think it is highly realistic and workable. Let me put the matter in different terms to clarify why I think this is the case.

Compassion could provide a powerful basis for establishing a cohesive global social order. But what does this mean? The word "passion" literally means "to suffer." Thus, the word "compassion" literally means "to be with suffering." Obviously, there is much suffering in the world. Therefore, if we open ourselves to the unadorned experience of just being in the world, we will naturally encounter the world's suffering. As we allow that experience to enter into our beings, we are relating to the world with compassion. To experience the world compassionately does not require that we manufacture any feelings. The only thing we must do is open to the world as it already is. The very act of experiencing the world as it already is—without sentiment or pretense—is to experience the world compassionately.

Importantly, in relating to the world compassionately, we are relating to the world more accurately. This is to have fewer delusions about what is going on. This is to be clear—in our immediate, direct, visceral experience—about what the situation really is. To relate to the world compassionately means that we are not perceiving the world primarily through the filters of nationalistic image or pride, we are just taking the world as it is—straight, unadulterated.

To relate to the world compassionately is a powerfully enabling experience. Recall the four enabling qualities that accompany living more consciously (discussed in Chapter 6). In living more consciously we are empowered: 1. to see more clearly what is happening within and about us, 2. to respond more quickly to subtle warning signals that corrective actions are needed, 3. to respond more creatively (we are not locked in to habitual patterns of thinking and acting), and 4. to respond more compassionately (we have a clearer sense of how our actions contribute to the well-being of the whole).

Love or compassion is a highly practical basis for human relations. With compassion as the foundation for relationship, we will tend to touch the world more lightly and gently. With compassion we will tend to honor human unity while tolerating, even encouraging, human diversity. Therefore, with compassion or love as the cohesive force for global community, a legalistic approach to global integration could touch people and nations more lightly and more gently. The more compassion infuses our global relations, the more lightly will bureaucracy touch our lives. Love or compassion thus provides the most fruitful basis for a revitalizing global civilization.

Is there a realistic possibility that the human family could even begin to come together from a place of love or compassion? Do we, as a human family, recognize compassion as integral to our shared "common sense"? Indeed, I think that compassion is already a commonly recognized, though largely ignored, basis for human affairs. The following quotes illustrate how, although this common sense may be variously stated, it is widely recognized:

Christianity:
As you wish that men would do to you, do so to them.
Luke 6:31

Buddhism:
Hurt not others in ways that you yourself would find hurtful.
Udanavarga

Judaism:

That which is hateful unto you, do not impose on others.

Talmud, Shabbat 31a

Hinduism:

Do naught unto others which would cause you pain if done to you.

Mahabharata 5:1517

Islam:

No one of you is a believer until he desires for his brother that which he desires for himself.

Sunan

Confucianism:

Do not unto others what you would not have them do unto you.

Analects 15:23

These statements are like different facets of a single jewel or like different branches of a single tree. At some level the human family already recognizes the immense practical value of compassion as a basis for human affairs. How might a compassionate intention become manifest in global human relations if it were more consciously and widely acknowledged?

If people and nations were to bring a compassionate intention into global relations, the result would be transformative. It would be to recognize that in weakening others we are weakening ourselves. It would be to recognize that the human family needs *all* of its strength if it is to skillfully manage this time of planetary transition.

Consider, for example, how aid to developing nations would be transformed by a compassionate intention. As of 1980, the United States devotes less than $2/10$ of 1 percent of its GNP to aid developing nations. This is a minuscule fraction of its available resources. A compassionate intention implies that instead of giving the least that is required, we would do all that we could to promote self-reliance and self-determination of people in the

Third World. Instead of giving a slight amount from the excess of normal production, we could begin to voluntarily restructure economic activity in such a way as to become fully participating partners in the process of global development. Instead of producing large quantities of nonessential luxuries for the conspicuous consumption of the few, we could voluntarily choose to produce functional necessities that will sustain the lives of the many, both domestically and internationally. Instead of the traditional intention in foreign assistance (to give little, ask much, and foster dependency), we could voluntarily give much, ask little in return, and encourage self-reliance and self-determination. A compassionate intention would thus infuse international relations with a spirit of mutually helpful living where, in the past, a spirit of competition and exploitation has prevailed.

We have briefly explored three foundations for global relationship: force, law, and love. We may imagine love to be quite utopian, but consider the alternatives. In not choosing love we are left with law and the prospect of global bureaucratic stagnation. In not choosing law we are left with force and the prospect of either global devastation or global domination. If we value our freedom and vitality as a species, we are obliged to do no less than learn to love one another as a human family or else destroy ourselves in the learning.

What is required to move from force to love in global relations? The pacifist A. J. Muste stated the process well. He said: "There is no way to peace. Peace is the way." We must work with a nonviolent intention and a compassionate belief in the possibility of abolishing devastating war between nation-states. Furthermore, we must see that the world's transition is not apart from our own. The world's transition is our own, written large. We cannot expect there to be peace within the human family if we are at war within ourselves. The outer world reflects our inner condition. External crises reveal equally profound internal crises. The inner and outer worlds are intensely interconnected. Both must change in concert with each other.

To move toward a peaceful intention in global relations represents a significant departure from the traditional premises of mistrust and competition that have historically governed the foreign policy of the superpowers. As a consequence, change is not likely to occur without the strong support, and indeed the initiative, of ordinary persons like ourselves. Our governments are best at muddling along. Seldom do they lead the way in making major changes. The civil rights movement, the feminist movement, the environmentalist movement, and many more reveal that the activism of ordinary persons is crucial to any social movement that would affirm the dignity of people or the preciousness of life. Just as these movements arose from individual initiatives at the grass roots level, so too must a change toward a peaceful intention in global relations follow a similar pattern of birth.

Yet, how are we to succeed in building a peaceful global civilization in the face of a massive, worldwide arms buildup? As Daniel Berrigan, a leading figure in the attempt to bring love into our global relations, has expressed both in words and in actions, we cannot wage peace halfheartedly when the waging of war is total. To move toward a peaceful global society will require a total commitment of our energy and resources. Peace is not simply a condition that is allowed. It is a dynamic process that must be continuously chosen, and the circumstances that support it must be continuously created. In turn, we must make major adjustments in our manner of living, working, and consuming if we are to be able to create the conditions of life that will sustain a peaceful global civilization. For example, the global imbalances between rich and poor nations are so great that if we want to eliminate war, we must take responsibility for helping to create the material conditions in life in poorer nations that will support peace. As a different kind of example, the United States cannot be viewed as a nation that is in earnest in helping the world move toward peace when it continues to be the world's largest supplier of weapons of war. Yet, if the United States were to halt arms sales abroad, it would put a severe short-run strain on the balance of payments (as weapons sales are a major source of revenue to offset the costs of imported oil). What we see, then, is that our manner of living and consuming is intimately connected with whether we are involved with a "peace system" or a "war system" in global relations.

If we are to create the conditions of life that will sustain a peaceful global civilization, then we must become educated and involved. In this regard, recall the crucial role of television for the process of active social learning. As the technologies of violence proliferate, there must be a countervailing spread of technologies that encourage grass roots communication among all members of the human family. If we can creatively and enthusiastically use our many tools of communication (such as satellite-assisted television) to aid the various members of the human family in understanding the plight of their counterparts around the world, then there will begin to emerge in the consciousness of our planetary culture a foundation for realistically moving toward a peaceful global civilization. If we choose instead to invest our scarce resources exclusively in weapons of destruction, we will create a self-fulfilling condition, the only outcome of which can be violence.

There is no place to hide. There is no safe enclave that is remote from the levels of violence that humankind can now unleash upon itself. Our way of life can either encourage the use of that violence or it can encourage mutually helpful living. The way of conscious simplicity—with its altered approach to living, working, and consuming—is a path that fosters a compassionate basis for global human relations.

Conclusion

Every facet of life would be touched if, as entire cultures, we were to choose a path of conscious simplicity with its life-sensing and life-serving orientation. Patterns and levels of consumption would be voluntarily altered. Living and working environments would tend to become much more self-regulating and self-organizing. Television would become a medium of active social learning and creative visualization of alternative pathways into the future. At a global level, we would begin to acknowledge the practical importance of love (and law) for building a peaceful global civilization. There would be many other changes only hinted at here: in the structure of economic activity, in the role of technology, in the nature of education, and in the character of domestic politics. (Additional changes characterizing the structure and dynamics of a revitalizing civilization are discussed in Appendix V.) This brief overview of a revitalizing civilization raises more questions than it answers—and this seems appropriate as we truly encounter multiple new frontiers with virtually unexplored potentials.

The renewed sense of vigor and purpose that would characterize a revitalizing civilization does not mean that it would be without problems. To the contrary, a massive tangle of difficulties would accompany the building of the human, social, technological, and economic infrastructure. Many of the problems would concern issues of equity. For example, when one area is more favored than another in terms of availability of natural resources (such as sun and water), would there be an obligation to share those benefits with others? What rights would people have to migrate freely into a more favored area when that area is threatened with the overloading of its ecological holding capacity? What rights would more wealthy persons have to live in affluent enclaves of resource-favored areas? What maximum and minimums of income would be legally mandated and socially tolerated under these circumstances? To what extent would the federal government or other political body have the right and/or obligation to interfere with the workings of an intentional community that was experimenting with alternative social, economic, and political forms?

The point is that a revitalizing society based on the widespread choosing of a life of conscious simplicity offers no magic cure-all. At the same time that this social pathway would moderate problems that are technical and bureaucratic in nature, it likely would intensify other problems that are social and political in nature. A revitalizing civilization would not erase the accumulated problems of two centuries of industrial development. Instead, it would have to build upon and transform that heritage in a turbulent process of social invention that would require enormous compassion, ingenuity, and tolerance for human diversity.

Despite the magnitude and diversity of change implied by a revitalizing civilization, there is one overriding principle that is useful to recall. Just as the individual expression of voluntary simplicity is to be found in the intention of living with balance, so too with its social expression. Therefore, the social expression of this way of life will be manifest as greater balance between material excess and material impoverishment; between huge cities and small communities; between massive corporations and smaller entrepreneurial activities; between highly specialized work roles and more generalized work roles, and so on. To bring greater balance into our social existence, we may in the short run have to move toward one end of these polarities; for example, toward greater material frugality and toward greater localization of economic and political activities. Yet, the requirements for bringing greater balance in the short run should not obscure the long-run dynamic at work—that of finding a middle path through life.

The magnitude of these changes may seem so great as to be overwhelming. Yet, we are not required to make these transformations overnight. We are challenged to *begin* the process of revitalizing our faltering industrial civilizations. It is the many, small actions that we take in the short run that will determine the outcome over the longer run. Our situation seems similar to that which occurs in driving a car—a small change in the steering direction can result over the space of several miles in a very considerable change in the ultimate location of the car. Analogously, we can begin to make small changes in our lives and thereby steer our social evolution over the long run along a more workable and satisfying course. Otherwise, like the driver who fails to acknowledge and respond to an already sweeping bend in the road, we will imperil many passengers and may ultimately forfeit the right to steer our own course.

The United States and many other Western developed nations have entered a transitional era. We have traveled an enormous social, psychological, technical, and political distance over the past several hundred years. In doing so we have entered a fundamentally different era in human affairs. We are akin to adolescents who face the irreversible fact of aging and the unavoidable necessity of assuming the difficult responsibilities of adulthood. We are faced with the challenge of moving beyond our cultural adolescence and into a new stage of maturity. As we experience the waning of the industrial era, we may feel a great longing for an earlier innocence. We may also experience great uncertainty at the prospect of having to make our way in a world that seems barely comprehensible. Yet, it is our responsibility and opportunity to re-establish our relationship with the world in a manner that holds the long-run prospect of a more workable and meaningful existence. Whole new dimensions of human possibility await us if we will but assume the responsibilities of mature citizenship in our rapidly changing world.

CHAPTER 9

CHOOSING OUR FUTURE

The dimensions of change that are now occurring are awesome. Like giant icebergs breaking loose from ancient moorings and beginning to float free for the first time in hundreds, perhaps thousands, of years, entire civilizations are melting, moving, and reforming. We have begun a process of transition that extends from the individual to the global scale.

We are not alone in this time of change. Everyone we meet is in some way involved with his or her own personal struggle to respond to this time of challenge. Whatever our other differences may be, we are all participants in this historical rite of passage. The human family is creating a shared history as we work through this time of planetary transition.

We are not powerless in the face of this change. Opportunities for meaningful and important action are everywhere: the food that we choose to eat, the work that we choose to do, the transportation we choose to use, the manner in which we choose to relate to others, the clothing that we choose to wear, the learning that we choose to acquire, the compassionate causes that we choose to support, the level of attention that we choose to give to our moment-to-moment passage through life, and on and on. The list is endless since the stuff of social transformation is identical with the stuff from which our daily lives are made.

We are each responsible for the conduct of our lives. Additionally, we are each unique. Thus, we are each uniquely responsible for our response to this time of transition and challenge. There is no one who can take our place. Each of us weaves a strand in the web of creation. There is no one else who can weave that strand for us. What we have to contribute is both unique and irreplaceable. What we withhold from life is lost from life. The entire world depends upon our individual choices as much as we depend upon everyone else's choices for the fate of our world.

More than anything else, then, the outcome of this time of planetary transition will depend upon the choices that we make as individuals. There are no preconditions to our choosing a revitalizing path. There is nothing lacking. Nothing more is needed than what we already have. We require no remarkable, undiscovered technologies as a prerequisite for revitalization. There is no need to wait for heroic, larger-than-life leadership. The *only* requirement is that we, as individuals, choose a revitalizing path and then work in community with others to bring it to fruition. By our conscious choices we can move from alienation to community, from despair to creativity, from passivity to participation, from stagnation to learning, from cynicism to caring. We tend to think that we are powerless, helpless, impotent. Yet, the reality is that only we—as individuals working in cooperation with one another—have the power to transform our situation. Far from being helpless, we are the only source from which the necessary creativity, compassion, and will can arise. The time of civilizational challenge is already upon us. Our civilizational autumn is deepening into winter. It is time for us to begin the next stage in our human journey.

SECTION V

EPILOGUE

CHAPTER 10

EAST-WEST SYNTHESIS: THE SOURCE OF AN EMERGING COMMON SENSE

The purpose of this epilogue is to explore the connections between voluntary simplicity and the larger dynamics of planetary evolution. Voluntary simplicity has global relevance because it has deep roots in the traditions of both East and West. In this chapter I want to explore these roots and suggest how voluntary simplicity represents a practical, down-to-earth integration of the historic learnings of both East (the Orient) and West (the Occident).

How East and West could mesh into a new view of reality, and accompanying way of life, is a sparsely charted area of inquiry.[1] Therefore, this exploration is necessarily speculative, relying substantially on personal interpretation. Furthermore, to discuss a topic as immense as the synthesis of East and West in the space of a single chapter, I must bleach out the historical richness of these two traditions and work with only the most simplified and stereotypical rendering of each: This extreme simplification serves one highly relevant purpose: It reveals that East and West are not competing views of reality, but instead are intensely complementary.

What does this have to do with voluntary simplicity? As we shall discuss, voluntary simplicity is a way of living that honors both the Eastern orientation (with its emphasis on self-mastery and more conscious living) as well as the Western orientation (with its emphasis on worldly mastery and full participation in the social and material affairs of life). Voluntary simplicity is, I think, one of the first worldly glimmerings of a down-to-earth and practical integration of East and West.

An Overview of East-West Integration

One of the central themes of this book has been that as we move with growing speed toward some form of global social order, it is imperative that we, the human family, find a shared "common sense" around which to align ourselves. A common sense does not refer to a common logic, ideology, or dogma; rather, it means what it says—a common *sense*. To "sense" something is to have a felt appreciation for it. Words and concepts are not themselves a common sense. Words and concepts are only pointers that invite us to look in a particular domain of our own experience for a felt sense that may be held in common with others. A "common sense" is thus utterly ordinary. It is so ordinary that it becomes a common frame of reference for entire societies. It is a shared knowing that does not need to be explained as it is already a part of the common sensing of how things are. So, although many diverse concepts are discussed in this chapter, what we are really searching for is an utterly ordinary "sense" of reality, human identity, and social purpose held in common with many others.

The historical common sense in the West has for the most part assumed that only a fragment of the earth was our home, and that only a fragment of humanity was a member of our family. Yet, fragmentation is true only in our imagination. The inescapable reality is that the earth is whole and there is only one human species in which all must claim our membership. We are being pushed by unyielding necessity and pulled by extraordinary opportunity to recognize our wholeness with the earth and our oneness with the human family. If we succeed in establishing this new common sense among ourselves, then a new foundation will have been formed from which the human adventure can further unfold.

In order to get our bearings on this exploration of a new, planetary common sense, let's jump ahead and examine the great complementarity of the views of East and West. The traditional emphasis of the East has been on inner growth and rising above an unchanging social and material existence. The Eastern perspective thus places self-mastery above worldly-mastery. In contrast, the emphasis of the West (particularly during the industrial era) has been on outer growth and progressing along the social and material dimensions of existence. The Western view thus places worldly-mastery above self-mastery.

Now, after thousands of years of development, these two streams of human growth and learning seem to have exhausted their evolutionary potentials. This is not surprising since each is a relatively one-sided and unbalanced view of human development. The West has tended to overlook the role of self-mastery (evolving human consciousness) in its excessively materialistic orientation. The East has tended to overlook the role of worldly-mastery (evolving the social and material forms that support human existence) in its excessively transcendental orientation. Both perspectives badly need each other if each is to evolve further. The West desperately requires the learning of the East, and the East desperately requires the learning of the West. Furthermore, neither has the luxury of several thousand years in which to add the required learning to its cultural repertoire.

Thus, as a human family, we are being pushed by necessity to begin an intense process of shared global learning. In order to learn actively as a human family we each must honor the diversity of the human family and respect the value of that diversity for contributing to the process of global revitalization. Stagnation or devastation are the alternatives to this learning.

With this as background, let's examine more carefully the views of East and West and note the limitations, as well as the contributions, of each to the evolution of the human family. We will then explore a view of evolution that begins to integrate these two traditions into a coherent and mutually supportive whole. Finally, we will note the intimate connection between the integration of East and West and a life of conscious simplicity.

Traditional Western View of Reality

By "Western" view of reality I am referring to a perspective that historically has developed in Western European nations and is exemplified by the Greek philosophical traditions and the Judaeo-Christian religious traditions. There are several key features of this view that serve to distinguish it clearly from its Eastern counterpart.

First, the Western scientific view of the universe is profoundly materialistic. The fundamental stuff of the universe is conceived to be elementary particles of matter that interact with one another in a predictable fashion. Not surprisingly, this has sometimes been described as a "billiard ball" model of the universe.

Second, the Western view of reality is profoundly dualistic. The Judaeo-Christian religious tradition sets "God" apart from this reality. God is viewed as the force that created this complex machine-universe; having created it and set it into motion, God could then be viewed as apart from "his" creation.

Third, the West tends to view the universe as being largely lifeless. Since the stuff of the universe is seen as consisting of elementary particles of matter, the foundations of the universe are viewed as essentially nonliving. The universe is seen as an inanimate machine wherein humankind occupies a unique and elevated position among the sparse life-forms that do exist. Assuming a relatively barren universe, it seemed only rational that humankind exploit the lifeless material universe (and the lesser life-forms of nature) on behalf of the most intensely living—humankind itself.

Fourth, the Western view places the intellect and rationality at the pinnacle of human faculties. The faculty of the intellect is viewed as the primary instrument of worldly-mastery. With rational thought and the power of reason, it was felt that humankind could discover the natural laws governing the vast machine-universe and thereby acquire growing mastery over nature.

Fifth, the Western view affirms the potential for material change and progress. The material world is viewed as an arena or field of action where the interplay between God and humankind could manifest as an unfolding drama. The ancient Jewish tradition, in particular, injects this sense of spiritual involvement in the course of worldy evolution. The result is that the material world is viewed as "going somewhere." There is a sense of real potential for social and material progress.

Sixth, in a materialistic and largely lifeless universe, who "we" are has been defined by the perimeter of the physical body. In other words, our individuality has been viewed as synonymous with our physical existence. The individual, then, is both unique and alone—apart from others and apart from the Divine. The knowing faculty, or consciousness, is viewed as little more than the product of biochemical activity in the brain. Thus, consciousness is not viewed as a bridge beyond physical separateness.

The foregoing greatly simplifies the Western view of reality and by no means exhausts the pattern of thought and assumption that characterize the Western world view. Yet, it is sufficient to allow us to note important contributions and limitations of this view.

The Western view of reality has been enormously successful in realizing its overriding goal: that of material and social development. This includes not only more goods and services, but also the development of highly efficient modes of organization— economic, legal, political—designed to promote and support the material development of society. In realizing this goal, Western cultures have also cultivated the development of autonomous individuals capable of relatively high levels of self-regulating behavior. Although personal material gain has often been the motivating force for self-regulation, the Western setting has pushed the individual to learn to take charge of his or her own life, particularly with regard to material and social concerns. Thus, the principal contributions of the Western world view are, I think, twofold: sociomaterial growth and psychological maturation.

Yet, the unparalleled achievements in these two areas have not been without their costs. Material growth without a larger sense of purpose makes living little more than "only not dying." Institutional development without the simultaneous growth of life-serving social purposes results in those institutions' being run on behalf of the narrow concerns of special interest groups. Psychological maturation without a balanced integration of the spiritual or consciousness dimensions of life yields autonomous individuals who tend to be alienated from self, society, and the cosmos.

The overriding limitation of the traditional Western scientific view of reality is, I think, that it tends to encourage a socially and materially oriented existence that lacks depth of meaning, connection, and purpose. To acknowledge the superficiality of the Western view of reality—to say that it touches only a very thin veneer of life—does not mean that the learning of the West should be discarded. Rather, it points to the importance of recognizing the partiality and incompleteness of the Western view of reality. In sensing the very real limitations of the Western view of things, we are naturally invited to explore other perspectives that may fill out dimensions of life we have overlooked in our rush toward material development.

Traditional Eastern View of Reality

By "Eastern" view of reality I am referring to a perspective that historically has emerged in countries such as India, Tibet, Japan, China, Southeast Asia, and is exemplified by spiritual traditions such as Buddhism, Hinduism, Taoism, and Zen. There are several key features of this view that serve to clearly distinguish it from its Western counterpart.

First, where the Western scientific view of reality is profoundly material, the Eastern view is profoundly spiritual. According to the Eastern view of things, all that exists is a manifestation of a Divine Life-Force. Beneath the surface appearance of things, an Ultimate Reality is continuously creating, sustaining, and infusing our worldly existence. The Life-Force that instant by instant creates and sustains our manifest universe is seen as the fundamental reality (and physicality, or materiality, is viewed as a more superficial quality that breaks down upon close inspection—for example, with sustained meditation).

Second, where the Western view is dualistic (viewing mind and body as separate, as well as God and humankind as separate), the Eastern view is profoundly nondualistic, or holistic. The all-sustaining Life-Force is not viewed as apart from ourselves or our worldly existence. Rather, this subtle and immensely powerful Life-Force is viewed as continuously creating and intimately infusing every aspect of the cosmos—from its most minute details to its most grand-scale features. Because the totality of the universe is viewed as being continuously drawn from, and residing within, a more embracing Life-Process, everything that exists is viewed as arising from a common source. The Eastern view thus places much attention on the common Source out of which all things arise, while the Western view places much attention on learning to master what is visibly here and present to us. Not surprisingly, the West tends to see the world as comprised of separate pieces to be manipulated, while the

East tends to see the world as an undivided totality to be appreciated. Ultimately, these are not competing but complementary views of reality—each is "correct" from its own perspective, and a complete view of reality requires them both.

Third, where the Western view tends to portray the universe as mechanistic and inanimate, the Eastern view tends to portray the universe as organic and living* From the Eastern perspective the entirety of the universe can be viewed as a vast, multi-dimensional, living organism that is intensely conscious and engaged in a continuous dance of creation. In this sense, the very foundations of the material universe are "alive" with the all-pervading, all-infusing Life-Force. And because all manifest things arise from this Life-Force, all things are fundamentally alive. Because all that exists is to some degree alive, all things are viewed as sacred and worthy of great respect.

Fourth, where the Western view tends to place the intellect and rationality at a pinnacle, the Eastern view tends to place the "knowing faculty," or consciousness, at a pinnacle. The knowing faculty is the vehicle through which the undivided wholeness of the universe can be known as direct experience. Since the Eastern view of reality focuses on the underlying wholeness of all things, it is not surprising that primary attention would be given to developing the faculty that allows us to know directly the oneness and intense aliveness of all that exists.

Fifth, where the Western view expresses its drive for growth in material progress and social change, the Eastern view ex-

* In emphasizing the useful polarity of East and West, I do not want to leave the impression that the views of the East, for example, were confined to the geographic Orient. The American Indians also had a strong appreciation for the intense aliveness of all things. Here is how the Cheyenne chief, Old Lodge Skins, speaks of the difference between "white people" and "human beings" in the novel, *Little Big Man*: "The Human Beings believe that everything is alive: not only men and animals but also water and earth and stones. . . . But white people believe that everything is dead: stones, earth, animals, and people . . ."[2] As this example suggests, the views of "East" and "West" are more a varied geographic mosaic than a clear-cut polarity.

presses its drive for growth in spiritual attainment. It seems only natural (given a spiritual view of the universe) that growth potentials would be expressed through the conscious evolution of consciousness. This attention to consciousness rather than the intellect is powerfully reinforced by the traditional Eastern perspective, which sees genuine material progress for masses of people as virtually impossible. Historically, the East has tended to view material existence as cyclical and has often characterized worldly existence with the metaphor of a wheel. The "wheel of existence" turns round and round but is not seen as going anywhere. Although some actors in the worldly drama might experience a rise or fall in their personal fortunes, the lot of the whole is felt to be fundamentally unchanging. Because worldly time is not experienced as going anywhere and in spiritual time there is nowhere to go but the eternity within the now, or the moment, the future is expected to be virtually the same as the past. Therefore, the goal of life is to get off the wheel of an unchanging worldly existence by transcending or rising above it all. And the vehicle of transcendence (getting off the wheel of worldly existence) is spiritual attainment. The evolution of consciousness is thus viewed more as a way out of the suffering of worldly existence than it is as an instrument of worldly transformation.

Sixth, where the Western view fosters the development of relatively autonomous individuals with relatively strong ego identification, the Eastern view selectively reinforces a different pattern of identity. In particular, a twofold sense of identity is, I think, cultivated by the Eastern view of reality. First, the Eastern view asserts that who "we" are is not limited to our physical existence. Consciousness is viewed as the bridge between the finite (our sense of uniqueness) and the infinite (the experience of wholeness). With sufficient perceptual training, each person can discover that who "we" are and what the "Divine" is are one and the same. "We" are not other than the Tao, the Ultimate Reality, the Divine Life-Force, Nirvana, God.

There is also a second view of identity that is cultivated by the Eastern view of reality. In the historical Eastern context of an unchanging agrarian-based existence, worldly identity was experienced as being embedded within an immutable social order. In other words, people tended to acquire their sense of identity from an affiliation with, and participation in, a virtually unchanging social order. The sense of "self" that emerged from this social context was not the strongly differentiated and dynamic "existential ego" of the West, but a more weakly differentiated and unchanging "social ego" (that accompanies participation in a largely static, tradition-bound social order of limited scope).

The foregoing greatly simplifies the Eastern view of reality, and by no means exhausts the pattern of thought and experience that characterize this view. Yet, it is sufficient to allow us to note several important contributions and limitations of the Eastern orientation. The Eastern view of reality has been enormously successful in promoting the development of a wide variety of paths and techniques helpful in the development of human consciousness while simultaneously maintaining a stable social order. The relatively unchanging social and material circumstances have allowed generation after generation to pursue a virtually unbroken stream of learning about the process of human awakening. As a consequence, the East has, I think, explored the interior human potentials for evolving human consciousness as fully as the West has explored the exterior potentials for technological change and material growth. Overall, the primary contributions of the Eastern view of reality are twofold: spiritual attainment (developing techniques for the conscious evolution of consciousness), and ego transcendence (seeing that who "we" are is not limited to our physical body and social identity).

Just as the Western view of reality has major limitations, so too does the Eastern view. The Eastern view of the world does not promote material and social development. It does not encourage worldly activism nor does it promote the empowerment of individuals to change fundamentally the social and material circumstances of life. Furthermore, instead of building greater ego strength and the capacity for more self-determining behavior, the Eastern view tends to work toward either ego extinction (transcendence) or toward ego dependency and passivity (as people conceive of themselves as being locked into an unchanging social order). By turning away from the potential for material and social development that is realized through self-determining and psychologically mature individuals, the Eastern orientation perpetuates a more rudimentary and fragmented social order—one that is oriented of necessity around subsistence concerns.

Although this is a greatly oversimplified assessment, it makes the useful point that the Eastern view is also unbalanced and one-sided. This does not mean that the learning of the East is to be discarded; rather, it points to the importance of recognizing the incompleteness and partiality of the Eastern perspective. The East has as much to learn from the West as the West has to learn from the East.

Reciprocal Contributions of East and West

It seems appropriate that the very time when the human family is moving rapidly toward some form of global civilization is also the time when both East and West are finding they have largely depleted the evolutionary potentials of their respective views of reality. When viewed from a global perspective, this planetary-wide process of civilizational breakdown can be seen as a constructive process. A time of "breaking down" is also a time of loosening—a time of "freeing up." No civilization can be receptive to a larger common sense when it is rigidly attached to the "rightness" of its historical perspective. If only a few civilizations were freeing up while most others remained locked in to their traditional patterns of thinking and acting, there would be little opportunity for a genuine global synthesis of civilizational perspectives to occur. We cannot attain a higher level common sense unless most members of the human family are open to that possibility to some degree. We are being pushed by planetary problems and pulled by planetary communications to a level of receptivity to global integration that would have been unthinkable just a few decades earlier. Assuming this essential receptivity, what might East and West learn from each other?

First, what might the East learn from the West? The West brings, as its primary contribution to furthering the evolution of the human family, a practical appreciation for the process of wordly growth and change. The crux of the Western perspective of change is found in its view of time. Particularly with the industrial revolution, the "wheel of time" was transformed into a hard, linear arrow of machinelike dynamism. It became pervasively and inescapably apparent that everything could change. No longer need the human being passively accept an unchanging social order or political order or material order. Even the psychological order was seen as changeable. The message of the West, then, is that we are not locked in—we are free, within ecological limits, to create our worldly reality as we want.

The West thus reveals to the East the very real possibility for masses of people to move beyond a subsistence-level existence and an unchanging sociocultural order. Such a view encourages worldly activism, psychological maturation, and personal empowerment. In opening to the insights of the West, the East can begin to moderate the tendency toward escape—rising above it all—transcending. Instead, there can be an enhanced opportunity for people to participate in the world as self-determining individuals who are empowered to create the social and material circumstances of life that support the evolution of consciousness.

In emphasizing the Western contributions of worldly dynamism, psychological maturation, and sociomaterial development, I am not suggesting that the East has been devoid of learning in these areas. Rather, I think the range and sophistication of Western contributions to the material side of life far exceed the historical learning of Eastern cultures. This does *not* mean that the values, behaviors, and institutions of the West should be substituted for their Eastern counterparts. The East should no more adopt wholesale the values and institutions of the West than the West should adopt wholesale the values and religions of the East. Our task is not to trade one view for another (and thereby repeat the excesses of the other). Our task is to integrate, not substitute. The purpose of evolution is not to create a homogeneous mass, but to continuously unfold an ever more diverse and yet organic whole. Our task is not to move toward some lukewarm planetary amalgam; rather, it is to find our human unity and simultaneously to express increasingly our magnificent diversity. The power and purpose of evolution is to do both at the same time.

We have examined what the East may learn from the West. Now, let's look at the other side of the coin; namely, what the West can learn from the East. One significant contribution that the East brings to the West is an enormous amount of practical learning regarding the "journey of awakening"—techniques that facilitate opening to our capacity to experience life with both focus and spacious awareness. To affirm the importance of Eastern insights regarding the evolving of human consciousness is not to suggest that the West has been devoid of such learning. Rather, it is to acknowledge that the range and sophistication of Eastern contributions to our understanding of the spectrum of human consciousness far exceed the historical learning of Western cultures. Western cultures, with their materialistic and rationalistic orientation, tend to diminish the value of the subtle learnings of the East. Just as the East does not yet in general possess the sociocultural setting necessary in order to use many of the technological advances of the West, the West does not yet possess the sociocultural maturity necessary to fully appreciate and begin to make use of the advances in the "interior technologies" of Eastern consciousness traditions.

A second quality that the East would bring to the West is that of an expanded appreciation of time. With an infusion of the Eastern view of reality, the West would reacquire an appreciation for the rhythms of nature—the seasons, the cycles of birth and decay, biological rhythms, and many more. Further, the Eastern understanding of the "Eternal Now"—the "timeless moment" that is embedded within the precise center of each moment of historical time—would become a more consciously acknowledged part of our experience of time. With the addition of these two temporal qualities, the time experience of the West would be expanded to then include the circular rhythms of nature, the spiral of worldly progression, and the vast openness of the Eternal Now.

A third quality that the Eastern view would bring to the West is a heightened appreciation of the aliveness of the universe we inhabit. In the Eastern view, the universe is engaged in a continuous dance of creation at each instant of time. Everything that exists is viewed as intensely alive—humming, brimming with a silent, clear energy that creates, sustains, and infuses all that exists. If we even occasionally experience our immersion within a universe that is a vast, multidimensional living organism, that experience will naturally foster a profoundly ethical posture toward the totality of life. If we experience that we are life-forms that live within a living entity—the universe—this experience, however fleeting or subtle, will transform our existence. In sensing that life is nested within life—we will tend to act in ways that honor the aliveness of the whole.

Fourth, in stretching our perspectives to include the Eastern view of reality, we also expand our sense of identity. In the Eastern view, who "we" are is not limited to our physical body and social identity. Because we have the capacity for self-reflective consciousness and beyond, our knowing is not limited to our physical existence but reaches out to include the essence of the entire universe. With consciousness as the bridge, our sense of identity can expand to that of beings who are both finite *and* infinite, unique *and* whole, material *and* spiritual.

We have briefly explored some of the more significant contributions that East and West might make to each other. Now

I would like to consider an integrative view of reality that begins to combine them both and note the overlap between this integrative view and voluntary simplicity.

East-West Integration and Voluntary Simplicity

We have seen that when the historic views of East and West are considered in isolation, each appears partial and unbalanced. The West has pursued material and social growth without a balanced regard for the development of interior human potentials. The result has been the emergence of a life-denying and self-serving social order that has exhausted both its vitality and its sense of direction. The East has pursued spiritual attainment without a balanced regard for the development of the exterior potentials of social and material growth. The result has been to render the development of human consciousness a spiritual luxury for the few while making the lives of the many a stultifying struggle for subsistence.

If the views of East and West were to merge into a fruitful synthesis, then what would be the nature of this integrative approach to living? Instead of an emphasis on material and social growth that excludes the evolution of human consciousness (the Western orientation), and instead of an emphasis on spiritual transcendence that excludes worldly growth and development (the Eastern orientation), there would emerge a path that moves beyond them both. The whole is greater than the sum of the parts. With an integration of the historic streams of human growth represented by East and West, a greater and more powerful flow of evolutionary potential would be released. The goal of life would be to bring both inner and outer aspects together and give them their fullest integrative expression in the here and now. The resulting orientation toward life would move beyond the worldly passivity characteristic of the East, and beyond the all-consuming involvement in the material affairs of life characteristic of the West. With integration there would emerge a balanced regard for both the finite and infinite, material and spiritual, form and essence.

When integrated, the learnings of East and West are mutually supportive of each other. How? First, material growth can create the physical circumstances of life that support the widespread realization of our higher human potentials—including the conscious evolution of consciousness. Second, non-material or interior growth can increase our capacity for compassionate self-regulation which, in turn, lessens the need to rely upon paternalistic bureaucracies to manage the affairs of everyday life. This, in turn, encourages human freedom and creativity—two essential ingredients for the continuing refinement of the material side of life.

Thus, the orientation of evolution seems that of simultaneously evolving both the material and the consciousness aspects of life in balance with each other—allowing each aspect to infuse and inform the other synergistically. Overall, evolution seems to be moving toward ever greater integration and balance of these two fundamental aspects of life:

• A progressive refinement of the social and material aspects of life—learning to touch the earth ever more lightly with our material demands; learning to touch others ever more gently and responsively with our social institutions; learning to live our daily lives with ever less complexity and clutter; and so on.

• A progressive refinement of the spiritual or consciousness aspects of life—learning the skills of touching life ever more lightly by progressively releasing habitual patterns of thinking and behaving that make our passage through life weighty and cloudy rather than light and spacious; learning how to "touch and go"—to not hold on—but to allow each moment to arise with newness and freshness; learning to be in the world with a quiet mind and an open heart; and so on

However described, the human agenda would shift to a process whereby we would begin to consciously pull ourselves up by our own bootstraps in a co-evolving spiral of simultaneous refinement of both the material and the consciousness dimensions of existence. This twofold refinement of the material and the spiritual aspects of life seems akin to the double helix of the DNA spiral. These two strands spiral around each other and support each other in their mutual ascent toward an ever wider scope of integration and differentiation, unity and diversity. Each time the spiral returns to its former position (although at a "higher," or more refined, level), the world is known and realized more fully.

How does this integrative view of reality connect with voluntary simplicity? A life of conscious simplicity embodies this integrative view. Recall that in Chapter 4 we discussed this same pattern of growth as being at the heart of both voluntary simplicity and civilizational evolution. Growth was described as a twofold process involving 1. the conscious refinement of the material side of life (progressive simplification), and 2. the simultaneous refinement of the nonmaterial side of life (living more consciously or voluntarily). Thus, a path of conscious simplicity is at the heart of the integration of East and West.

The path of voluntary simplicity integrates both Eastern and Western orientations into a worldly relevant way of living. Voluntary simplicity is a middle way that draws equally from East and West, inner and outer. In simultaneously attending to both aspects of life, each tends to serve as a corrective against the misapplications and excesses of the other.

It is, I think, a very hopeful sign that a life of conscious simplicity is now emerging at the grass roots level of a number of developed Western nations. This suggests that a worldly relevant integration of East and West—as a commonly understood, though diversely expressed, way of life—is beginning to establish itself on our planet.

If the human family is able to consciously bring these two, long-separated streams of human learning together into a synergistic whole, we can then embark on an evolutionary journey that would not have been possible, and could not have been imagined, by either East or West working in isolation. The creativity and innovation that will be generated by this historic integration is far greater than we can presently envision. The convergence of East and West (as symbolic of the meeting of the potentials of the entire human family) is not simply additive in its consequences; it is multiplicative, it is synergistic. Who we are as an entire human family is much greater than who we are as the sum of isolated cultures.

Voluntary simplicity represents the practical convergence of two major flows of human growth and learning that are thousands of years in the making, and that find their crossroad at this juncture in human history. The grass roots blossoming of the way of life termed "voluntary simplicity" thus reflects much larger evolutionary forces at work. Voluntary simplicity is not a fad, soon to go away. This way of life is a microcosm of the global convergence of the human family. In this living experiment are the seeds of new human frontiers that we have only scarcely begun to imagine and explore.

APPENDICES

APPENDIX I

SUGGESTED READINGS

There is no cookbook approach to voluntary simplicity. There are no rules or checklists against which we can (or should) evaluate our lives and try to measure the degree of aesthetic simplicity contained therein. We all must do our own learning and find our own way of living, working, consuming, etc. Still, there are resources that can be helpful to us along the way.

In this appendix, I have not tried to provide a comprehensive listing of all the books, magazines, journals, and catalogues that are relevant to voluntary simplicity. Instead, I have selected a few that provide a useful entry into different facets of this approach to living. The reading list is divided into four major sections: 1. simple living, 2. social transformation, 3. the inner journey, and 4. helpful sources.

I. Simple Living

Listed below is a wide-ranging array of books that deal with various facets of simplicity of living. Some are highly practical while others are more philosophical.

Simple Living Collective, *Taking Charge*, New York: Bantam Books, 1977. This book was written by members of the Simple Living Collective of San Francisco. It is filled with practical suggestions for change in our daily lives.

239

Topics include food, clothing, health care, personal growth, work, and more.

Ernest Callenbach, *The Ecotopian Encyclopedia for the Eighties*, Berkeley, California: And/Or Press, 1981. This is an updated version of Callenbach's book, *Living Poor With Style*, that was published in 1972. It is a practical guide to simple living and has an encyclopedic coverage of topics such as housing, food, clothing, work, relationships, and more.

Michael Clossen, et al., *Work Is for People: Innovative Workplaces of the San Francisco Bay Area*, published by New Ways to Work, 457 Kingsley Ave., Palo Alto, CA 94301, 1978. This book was written by a group that is involved in helping unemployed persons find new ways of work. They believe that work should be organized to benefit people (i.e., allow them to work creatively, cooperatively, and responsibly). In this book they explore practical and humanizing innovations that have already been made in dozens of workplaces in the San Francisco Bay area. They describe innovations in the creating, financing, owning, organizing, etc., of many kinds of workplaces (for example, small businesses, alternative schools, media groups, private health care service agencies, and more).

Briarpatch Community, *The Briarpatch Book,* San Francisco: New Glide Publications, 1978. The "Briarpatch" describes itself as ". . . a network of small-business people who have three values in common: we are in business because we love it; we find our reward in serving people rather than in amassing large sums of money; and we share our resources with each other as much as we can, especially our knowledge of business." People who have been practicing this business philosophy describe their experiences and offer advice in simple living and "right livelihood."

David Morris and Karl Hess, *Neighborhood Power*, Boston: Beacon Press, 1975. Simplicity seems to lead naturally to the search for community with others who are exploring a similar path. This book is related to that search. Morris and Hess provide a working tool for bringing political and economic power down to a human scale—the neighborhood. Topics include neighborhood awareness, neighborhood economy, local housing, local government, and more.

The Farallones Institute Staff, *The Integral Urban House*, San Francisco: Sierra Club Books, 1979. This book explores the redesign of our urban homes in ways that support more self-reliant and ecologically sound living. It is filled with information, diagrams, and plans that show how they redesigned and rebuilt a city dwelling. Topics include intensive gardening, composting, recycling, energy conservation, and more.

Laurel Robertson, et al., *Laurel's Kitchen*, New York: Bantam Books, 1978. This is a first-rate handbook for vegetarian cooking and nutrition. A warm, well-crafted, and interesting book that provides a useful guide to whole foods and whole living, with over 400 recipes.

Alternative Celebrations Catalog, now in its 4th edition, published by Alternatives, 1924 East Third Street, Bloomington, IN 47401. This book describes compassionate alternatives to the excessive commercialization of occasions such as Christmas, Thanksgiving, weddings, and many more. It also offers information about projects intended to assist persons in Third World countries.

Philip Slater, *Wealth Addiction*, New York: E. P. Dutton, 1980. This book explores the psychology of the single-minded pursuit of wealth. An insightful look into the underpinnings of a consumer society. Slater concludes with suggestions for a more integrated approach to living and a discussion of voluntary simplicity.

Arthur Gish, *Beyond the Rat Race*, Scottdale, Pennsylvania: Herald Press, 1973. Gish examines the nature and relevance of simplicity of living from a Christian perspective. Topics include spending less and enjoying it more, simplicity as a life-style, the costs of affluence, arguments against simplicity along with counterarguments, and many more.

II. Social Transformation

Included in this section is a sampling of books and reports that are highly relevant to the process of social transformation.

Eknath Easwaran, *Gandhi the Man*, published by Nilgiri Press, Box 477, Petaluma, CA 94952, Second edition, 1978. A highly readable and engaging introduction to the life, work, and thinking of Gandhi. If we want to see how the spiritual path can be integrated into a life of worldly action, this book provides a compelling example.

Tom Hayden, *The American Future: New Visions Beyond Old Frontiers*, published by the South End Press, Box 68, Astor Station, Boston, MA 02123, 1980. In this book, Tom explores a number of the pressing issues of our time and offers explicit policy alternatives to meet them head on. This is both a philosophical and a practical book that examines a changing American identity and responses to issues ranging from inflation, energy, health, excessive corporate power, and global relations.

Erik Dammann, *The Future in Our Hands*, New York: Pergamon Press, 1979. This is the English translation of the book that inspired the launching of the Norwegian popular campaign of the same name. Dammann examines the exploitation of many Third World nations that occurred during the industrial revolution and proposes radical adjustments in our manner of living and consuming as essential to bringing greater equity and balance into our global relations.

Marilyn Ferguson, *The Aquarian Conspiracy: Personal and Social Transformation in the 1980s*, New York: St. Martin's Press, 1980. This is an encyclopedic exploration of personal and social transformation. The "conspiracy" she talks about is a network of love and mutual support. The major theme of the book is that a leaderless but powerful network of persons from all walks of life is working to bring about transformative changes in health care, education, politics, and many other areas.

Gerald Barney, Study Director, *The Global 2000 Report to the President*. This is a report prepared for President Carter in 1980 and is available from Superintendent of Documents, U.S. Government Printing Office, Washington, D.C. 20402. This report was prepared by the Department of State and the Council on Environmental Quality. It pulls together for the first time all the various government projections on population growth, income growth, environmental quality, etc., to suggest what the world will look like in the year 2000. The picture that emerges is a grim one and it underscores the urgency of concerted action of global scope if we are to avert disaster.

Robert Johansen, *Toward a Dependable Peace*, working paper Number 8 of the World Order Models Project, Institute for World Order, 777 United Nations Plaza, New York, NY 10017. In this brief report, Johansen provides a rational and compelling description of one route to a peaceful global civilization. Other publications by the Institute also provide valuable insights for alternatives to nuclear proliferation and a "war system."

Theodore Roszak, *Person/Planet*, New York: Anchor Press /Doubleday, 1978. A passionate exploration of the needs of the person and the needs of the planet and how they coincide. Roszak is one of the pioneers in exploring the process of cultural renewal through an integration of the inner and outer aspects of life.

III. Inner Growth

With the growth of the communications era, we are seeing the "democratization of consciousness traditions." Spiritual teachings that historically were available to only a select few have now become accessible to the many. There is such a large number of insightful books from such a wide diversity of consciousness traditions that it is impossible to do more than hint at what is available. Listed below is a sampling of a few of these books.

Ram Dass, *Journey of Awakening: A Meditator's Guidebook*, New York: Bantam Books, 1978. Ram Dass is a spiritual teacher who has studied and practiced a wide range of meditative traditions over the years. In this book he shares his understanding of various practices and offers advice on how to find a meditative path suitable for oneself. Topics include getting your bearings, picking a path, finding your way, losing your way, and many more. Also included is an extensive listing of groups that teach meditation in the United States and Canada.

Tarthang Tulku, *Openness Mind*, and *Skillful Means*. Both books are available from Dharma Publishing, 2425 Hillside Ave., Berkeley, CA 94704, and both were published in 1978. Tarthang Tulku is a Tibetan Buddhist who has been teaching in the West for over a decade. His teaching and writing provide a simple and clear introduction to Buddhist thought for the Westerner. The book *Openness Mind* is an excellent introduction to meditation, and the book *Skillful Means* describes how we can reawaken the joy of work and cultivate inner awareness in all that we do. Both are written in a nontechnical fashion.

Robert Bly, *The Kabir Book*, Boston: Beacon Press, 1977. This is a small book that contains forty-four of the ecstatic poems of the fifteenth-century Sufi master Kabir. His poetry (masterfully translated by Robert Bly), is irreverent, insightful, and intensely alive.

Gerald Jampolsky, *Love Is Letting Go of Fear*, published by Celestial Arts, 231 Adrian Road, Millbrae, CA 94030, in 1979. Jerry is a psychiatrist who has worked extensively with dying children. This book is based on material from "A Course in Miracles" (a self-study course in Christian mysticism). His book provides an easy-to-read and straightforward approach to encountering our basic nature—which is love.

Satprem, *Sri Aurobindo or The Adventure of Consciousness*, New York: Harper and Row, 1968. Aurobindo is one of India's better known sages who in his early years was also a political activist. Aurobindo taught an integral yoga—involving the union of both material and spiritual aspects of life in a process of mutual transformation. This is an excellent summary and overview of Aurobindo's extensive writing. It is an immensely rich but very demanding book. I pick it up from time to time to read a few pages and then reflect on what was said.

Leo Buscaglia, *Love*, New York: Fawcett Crest Books, 1972. Leo is an enthusiastic lover—a being whose life is an expression and exploration of love. This book is drawn from various talks that he has given.

Joseph Goldstein, *The Experience of Insight*, Santa Cruz, California: Unity Press, 1976. Joseph is a Westerner who has studied Buddhist meditative practices in the East for a number of years. This book is a record of the instructions, commentary, questions, and answers of a month-long meditation course. An insider's view of a direct, no-frills approach to becoming more attentive to our "ordinary" life experience.

Huston Smith, *The Religions of Man*, New York: Harper and Row, 1958. This is a classic and masterful exploration of a number of the major spiritual traditions of the world: Hinduism, Buddhism, Christianity, Taoism, Islam, Judaism, and Confucianism. With penetrating insight and heartfelt appreciation, Smith explores the core qualities of each of these traditions. An excellent source for acquiring an overview of these major religions.

Nancy Ross, *The World of Zen*, New York: Random House, 1960. This book contains a wide-ranging collection of articles, poetry, art, drama, and quotations—with many that invite the reader to directly encounter the world of Zen. An excellent introduction.

Roger Walsh and Frances Vaughn, *Beyond Ego: Transpersonal Dimensions in Psychology*, Los Angeles: J. P. Tarcher, Inc., 1980. A scholarly overview of the field of "transpersonal psychology"—a psychology that looks beyond the ego to explore extremes of psychological health and well-being. Topics include the nature of consciousness, psychological well-being in the East and West, transpersonal psychotherapy, implications for other sciences, and more.

IV. Helpful Sources

Listed below is a sampling of magazines, journals, and catalogues that provide access to a broad range of ideas, activities, tools, and human networks relevant to alternative approaches to living. In some ways, these sources are more useful than the books mentioned previously since these magazines and catalogues provide relatively up-to-date access to a rapidly evolving field.

New Age Journal. (New Age, Subscription Department, Box 1200, Allston, MA 02134). Monthly news about the "new age" culture. Articles and regular features cover a wide range of topics: holistic health, food and diet, nuclear disarmament, consciousness traditions, new age politics, alternative energy sources, reviews of books, films, and music, and more. An alive, interesting, and balanced publication. Because much of the subject matter is not quickly dated, it's worth looking through the back issues to see if there are topics of interest.

The Next Whole Earth Catalog, Stewart Brand, editor, New York: Random House, 1980. This catalogue provides access to books, tools, people, and activities that support individuals who want ". . . to conduct their own education, find their own inspiration, shape their own environment, and share the adventure with whoever is interested." The catalogue lists thousands of items ranging across topics such as owner-built housing, solar heating, wood-working tools, living cheaply, medical self-care, video, film, computers, feminism, parenting, Buddhism, and many more. This is the "Sears Catalog" of the new age culture. An excellent source.

Co-Evolution Quarterly, Box 428, Sausalito, CA 94966. This journal is also edited by Stewart Brand and features the same type of material found in the Whole Earth Catalog. Although eclectic and idiosyncratic, it provides valuable access to ideas, books, magazines, activities, films, etc., that are relevant to alternative ways of living.

Inner Development: The Yes! Bookshop Guide, published by the Yes! Bookshop, 1035 31st Street, N.W., Washington, D.C. 20007. This is a massive catalogue of books pertaining to inner growth. It contains bibliographic information and a thoughtful review of more than 10,000 books, plus an author index and publishers' names and addresses. A useful resource that covers topics ranging from American Indian religion to Buddhism, Christianity, comparative religion, children's books, and many more.

Leading Edge: A Bulletin of Social Transformation, Marilyn Ferguson, editor, P.O. Box 42247, Los Angeles, CA 90042. A concise, triweekly report on many facets of social transformation: a review of new books, advances in communications technologies, upcoming seminars and workshops on personal/social transformation, research findings in the social sciences that have a bearing on social revitalization, and more. A useful source for those who want to connect with networks of people and activities relevant to social transformation.

The Futurist, Edward Cornish, editor, World Future Society, P.O. Box 30369, Bethesda Branch, Washington, D.C. 20014. *The Futurist* is a journal of forecasts, trends, and ideas about the future that is published six times a year. Although it is not focused on the notion of alternative ways of living, this is a subject that has been increasingly addressed in more recent years. Topics often covered include ecology, economics, Third World problems, technology, religion, alternative life-styles, and more. A readable and important source of information about alternative views of the future.

APPENDIX II

VOLUNTARY SIMPLICITY QUESTIONNAIRE

The material developed in Chapter 2 was drawn from responses to a questionnaire that appeared in the summer, 1977, issue of the *Co-Evolution Quarterly*. This questionnaire, shown below, accompanied the article entitled "Voluntary Simplicity" that was co-authored by Arnold Mitchell.

Name (optional) _____

Address (optional) _____

1. Age: ___2. Sex: Male ☐ Female ☐

3. Married ☐ Single ☐
   or Living Together ☐

4. Race: White ☐ Black ☐ Brown ☐
   Other _____

5. Personal Annual Income:
   Under $3,000 ☐
   $3,000-$5,000 ☐
   $5,000-$8,000 ☐
   $8,000-$12,000 ☐
   $12,000-$16,000 ☐
   $16,000-$25,000 ☐
   Over $25,000 ☐

6. Education:
   No high school diploma ☐
   High school graduate ☐
   Some college ☐
   College graduate ☐
   Some post graduate schooling ☐

MA or MS or equivalent ☐
Ph.D., LLD, MD or equivalent ☐

7. Politics:
   Democrat ☐ Republican ☐
   Independent ☐
   Other _____

8. Place of Residence:
   ☐ Rural (country)
   ☐ Small rural town (under 10,000)
   ☐ Suburban town (under 100,000)
   ☐ Small city (100,000-500,000)
   ☐ Big City (over 500,000)

9. Would you characterize your family during your childhood and adolescent years as being:
   ☐ low   ☐ middle, or
   ☐ high income?
   (High would be today's equivalent of $25,000, or more; low would be today's equivalent of $5,000 or less).

10. Are you now practicing or actively involved with a particular

inner growth process? (Check those that apply).

- ☐ Traditional religion (e.g., Catholicism, Judaism, Christianity)
- ☐ Meditative discipline (e.g., TM, Zen, Yoga)
- ☐ Psychotherapy (e.g., Freudian, Jungian, Behaviorist)
- ☐ Human Potential (e.g., encounter, gestalt, psychosynthesis, rolfing)
- ☐ Other (e.g., biofeedback, hypnosis, mind expanding drugs, etc.)

11. To what extent do you feel supported by friends and larger community in pursuit of your inner growth processes?
- ☐ Discouraged
- ☐ Tolerated (neither encouraged nor discouraged)
- ☐ Some support
- ☐ A great deal of support

12. Would you describe yourself today as living a life of:
- ☐ "full" voluntary simplicity
- ☐ "partial" voluntary simplicity
- ☐ sympathetic only
- ☐ indifferent to it
- ☐ opposed to it
- ☐ unaware of it

13. If you are fully living the VS style, could you please help us understand what this means by commenting on the questions below:
  - a. At what age and under what circumstances did you consciously start to live simply?
  - b. Why did you take up voluntary simplicity?
  - c. What are the major changes in living arrangements you made as a result?
  - d. Please comment on the satisfactions and dissatisfactions associated with this way of life.
  - e. Do you see it as a movement that is likely to spread rapidly? Why or why not?

14. If you rate yourself as a "partial" adherent to voluntary simplicity:
  - a. In what ways are you acting in VS style?
  - b. In what ways are you not acting in VS style?
  - c. Do you expect to become ☐ more so, ☐ less so, or ☐ remain the same for the foreseeable future? Why?
  - d. What kinds of things would prompt you to embrace more fully a life-style of voluntary simplicity?

15. If you are sympathetic to VS but not acting substantially on your sympathy, could you say why you are not and what might trigger you to change your life-style in the direction of VS?

16. If you are opposed to voluntary simplicity, could you give us your main reasons why?

17. Did you disagree with parts of this article? If so, what parts?

18. Do you think we omitted important points?

Thanks tremendously for your help.

Duane S. Elgin
Arnold Mitchell

APPENDIX III

AN OVERVIEW OF THE RACE WITH COMPLEXITY AND STAGES OF GROWTH

The purpose of this appendix is twofold: first, to explore the origins of the stages of growth model used to characterize the growth dynamics of industrial civilizations (Chapter 3); and second, to explore one of the most persistent and perplexing problems of our era—that of mounting social systems complexity. These are intimately interwoven topics. We can approach them both by examining a model of social systems growth that is derived from personal research on the limits to managing the large, complex bureaucracies that dominate life in industrial societies. Given the extensive nature of this research, I will present here only an overview of this model of growth (for a more complete discussion, see the report from which this material is drawn).*

* See the report "Limits to the Management of Large, Complex Systems" that was prepared as part of a larger study, *Assessment of Future National and International Problem Areas* (Project #4676, February, 1977). This study was prepared for the Presidential Science Advisor and was funded by the National Science Foundation. The study was conducted by the Center for the Study of Social Policy, Stanford Research Institute, Menlo Park, CA 94025. (The conclusions summarized in this appendix rely upon a diverse body of literature. References to these sources are not listed here but may be found in the technical paper on which this appendix is based.)

The bureaucracies, whose functioning is our concern, are of many different kinds: They may be federal (such as the U.S. Department of Energy or the U.S. Congress), local (such as the huge bureaucracies that run major cities), corporate (such as massive multinational corporations), educational (such as enormous university complexes), and so on. The common characteristics of these bureaucracies are that they are all very large, exceedingly complex, highly interdependent, and involve very high levels of human interaction.

The Race with Complexity

Before we develop the four-stage description of growth, we should examine the process whereby we can rapidly become information-rich and knowledge-poor—and thereby lose the race with mounting bureaucratic complexity. To understand the complexity problem we need to approach the issue in dynamic rather than static terms. In other words, to manage a bureaucracy successfully, decision-makers must acquire knowledge at a rate at least equal to the pace at which decisions are becoming more complex, more numerous, and more wide-ranging in their impacts. If the size, complexity, and span of bureaucracy mounts more rapidly than the rate at which the knowledge to comprehend it can be acquired, then, despite *absolute* increases in knowledge by decision-makers, the managers' *relative* capacity to comprehend the system will be declining. In other words, we confront a continuous race between "knowledge demand" (the growth of complexity) and "knowledge supply" (the growth of learning). If complexity outraces our learning, we will be knowledge-poor and our capacity to make skillful decisions will be commensurately diminished. Before we explore this crucial relationship more fully, we should distinguish between "information" and "knowledge."

Information is potential knowledge—it is knowledge that is at least one step removed from the decision-maker. Information can take the form of libraries of books and reports, huge quantities of computer-generated data, staffs of experts, etc. When information such as this has been internalized by the decision-maker (and thereby can be usefully brought to bear in the decision-making process), then it may be considered knowledge. Knowledge is what we possess within—it is information that has been absorbed and is thereby accessible to us when we make decisions. Knowledge is firsthand, visceral, and digested whereas information is secondhand, abstract, and yet to be internalized.

This distinction reveals how we can be information-rich and knowledge-poor. Just because huge quantities of information are available does not mean that knowledge is growing commensurately. To the contrary, there are substantial limits on the human capacity to absorb the huge quantities of information available to us.

With this as background, let's define and then examine the relationships between knowledge demand and knowledge supply. First, the rate at which knowledge can be acquired (information absorbed) I will term the "learning curve," or knowledge-supply curve.[1] The rate at which the supply of knowledge can grow is subject to biological, mechanical, and time limitations. For example, there are only so many hours in a day that a decision-maker can spend in acquiring the knowledge necessary to make decisions. The characteristic of the learning curve is that it rises rapidly at first and then quickly begins to flatten out and level off—in other words, learning rapidly reaches a saturation level.* (The following graphs are not intended to be used as a rigorous mathematical portrayal but as a visual image of the dynamics at work).

---

* This simple, graphic portrayal of the learning curve does not visually represent the upward shifts in the curve that might be brought about, for example, by technological change. Consequently, this rendering of the learning curve should be considered a long-run envelope curve that subsumes within it short-run shifts due to technological and human innovations in learning.

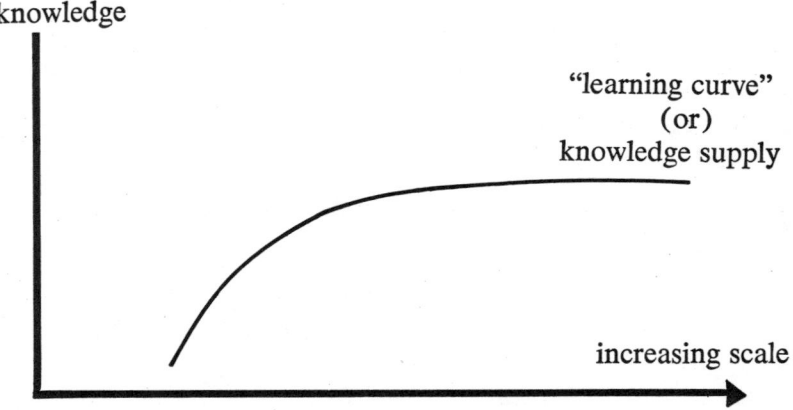

Second, the rate at which knowledge is demanded to cope with the problems of a bureaucracy I will term the "complexity curve," or the knowledge-demand curve. The rate at which the demand for knowledge grows is a synergistic, or multiplicative, product of at least three factors: 1. as the size of the bureaucracy increases, there will be a greater number of decisions to be made and therefore a greater amount of knowledge is likely required; 2. as the complexity of the bureaucracy mounts, the depth of knowledge required for effective decision-making will also grow; and 3. as the interdependence of the bureaucracy increases, the span of knowledge will increase as well. The demand for knowledge is thus a multiplicative product of these three factors and will tend to mount exponentially as the bureaucracy grows in size.

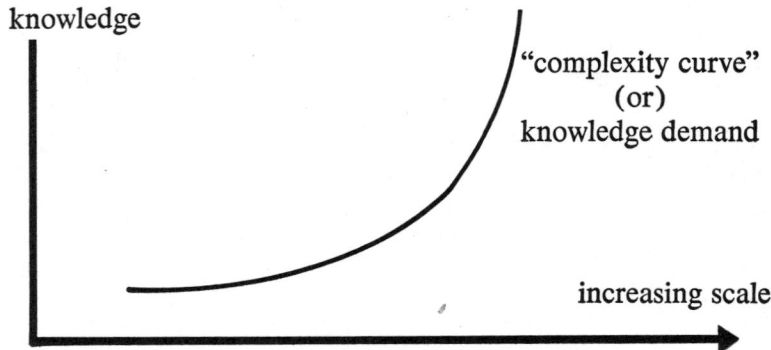

Both the complexity curve and the learning curve have a characteristic shape that reveals the nature of the dynamic problem that emerges when bureaucracies grow to great size. Combining these two curves by overlaying them upon each other suggests the following dynamic relationship between the relative "supply of knowledge" (learning curve) and the relative "demand for knowledge" (complexity curve) as a bureaucracy grows in scale.

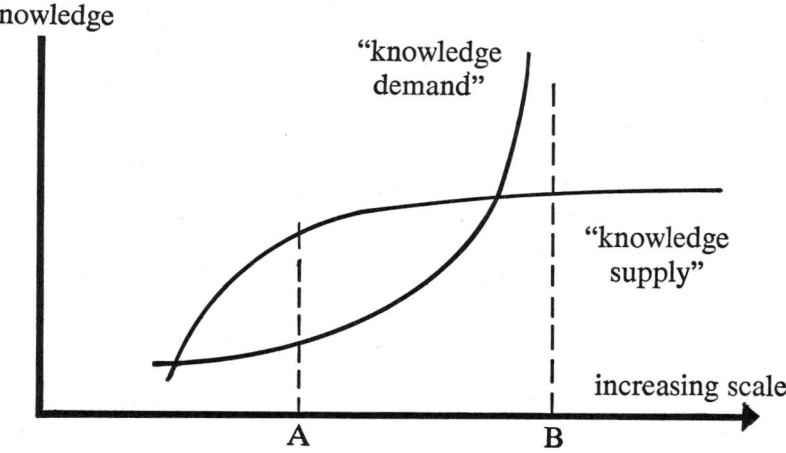

These two curves reveal a very important relationship between knowledge supply and knowledge demand. At point "A," the knowledge supply greatly exceeds the knowledge demanded by the complexity of the bureaucracy. All is well and the decision-maker can readily cope with the problems of the bureaucracy. However, when the force of the exponential increase of complexity becomes manifest (point "B"), then the knowledge demanded by the bureaucracy can greatly exceed the knowledge that can be supplied (as characterized by the learning curve). This figure illustrates another very important point. When the knowledge-demand curve (complexity curve) begins to turn sharply upward, then even a large upward shift in the learning curve will be of little or no use in coping with the extreme levels of complexity that have emerged.

The foregoing suggests that for an extended period of bureaucratic growth, there will be no shortage of knowledge relative to that required to manage the growing bureaucracy effectively. However, within a very short span of time (or within small increments of growth in the scale of the bureaucracy) the knowledge demanded can rapidly overtake, and greatly surpass, that which can be readily supplied. In a very brief period of time we can lose the race with mounting complexity—the knowledge demanded will completely outstrip that which can be supplied. In turn, overly simple solutions will be applied to increasingly complex problems and the overall performance of the bureaucracies will begin to drop precipitously. The declining performance of the bureaucracy will exacerbate the problem of mounting complexity and soon even the most able decision-makers will be utterly overwhelmed through no fault of their own.

Already there is considerable agreement that many of the major bureaucracies in the United States have reached this condition. For example, the seasoned government bureaucrat Elliot Richardson stated: "For a free society, the ultimate challenge of the foreseeable future will consist not simply in managing complexity but in keeping it within the bounds of understanding by society's citizens and their representatives in government." [2] Or consider the comment of U.S. Senator Adlai Stevenson who said: "We're frantically trying to keep our noses above water, racing from one problem to the next." [3] Comments such as these are now commonplace. They reveal that our power to create large and complex bureaucracies does not automatically confer upon us the ability to control them. Indeed, we seem to have already reached a level of social complexity where our bureaucracies exceed our capacity to comprehend and to manage them.

We have been exploring the basic problem of mounting complexity. To further develop the underpinnings of the four-stage model, I want to turn to examine twelve problems that often accompany the emergence of bureaucracies that are of extreme size and complexity.

Problems of Large, Complex Bureaucracies

My intention is not simply to list some of the major problems of large bureaucracies, but also to 1. understand the *pattern* of problems that arise as bureaucracies grow very large, and 2. understand the dynamic changes in that pattern as growth occurs. In order to accomplish this, a four-stage model of growth will be developed that characterizes the life cycle of a bureaucracy.

Since a number of important conclusions will be drawn from this model, it is appropriate that some care be used in developing the logic of this description of systems growth. Therefore, we turn to examine the underpinnings of this model; namely, a discussion of an illustrative range of problems that are characteristic of very large bureaucracies. Once we have considered these problems in relative isolation from one another, we then will explore the dynamic pattern of problems that arise in the life cycle of bureaucratic growth.

The following problems are hypothesized to arise as a bureaucracy grows to extremes of size, complexity, and interdependence:

1. *The bureaucracy will become increasingly difficult to comprehend and therefore commensurately difficult to manage*—This is the central problem spoken of at the outset. As the size and complexity of the bureaucracy increases, the rate at which problems become complex will exceed the rate at which knowledge can be acquired to cope with them; consequently, the bureaucracy becomes increasingly incomprehensible and unmanageable.

2. *Constituency participation in the bureaucracy will diminish*—As the size of the bureaucracy increases, the perceived significance of an individual's participation in the decision-making, for example through voting, is reduced by the par-

ticipation of large numbers of people in the process. The cost, particularly in time, to become an informed participant in decisions is so substantial, and the perceived return is so minimal (one vote among thousands or millions), that a seemingly rational response is to remain ignorant and passively defer to the decisions of the leadership.

3. *The constituency's access to leadership will decline*—Regardless of the size of his or her constituency, there is only one mayor, one governor, one U.S. President, one corporation president, and so on. As the number of persons under his or her jurisdiction grows, an inevitable consequence is a reduction in the amount of time that can be spent with any one person or group. Beyond some size of bureaucracy, access to the leader and his or her staff will, for all practical purposes, be eliminated.

4. *The costs of coordinating and controlling the bureaucracy will grow disproportionately to increases in size*— Initial increases in the size of an organization allow greater efficiency by facilitating specialization and division of labor and by allowing the use of advanced technologies which may become cost-effective only for larger organizations. Yet, at some threshold of size, the number of parts in the bureaucracy will grow so large that the costs of coordinating and controlling the interactions of all those parts will be more than offset by any increases in efficiency that accrue from the larger scale.

5. *Depersonalized interactions with the bureaucracy will be required of the constituents*—The more uniform and predictable the interaction of the person with the bureaucracy, the more efficient can be the system in coping with the demands of large numbers of people. Thus, a powerful means of coping with growing complexity is to reduce the variety and diversity of human interaction with the bureaucracy.

6. *The level of alienation will increase*—As the bureaucracy grows ever larger, the person within it or interacting with it

feels his or her identity being submerged (as only one among countless other individuals). Further, the lack of direct access to leadership, the high levels of specialization, and the growing incomprehensibility of the overall system will intensify the feeling of isolation and estrangement.

7. *The number and significance of unexpected outcomes of policy actions will increase*—To the extent that the sophistication of a policy response is not equal in the long run to the complexity of the problem that it addresses, then the outcomes of that policy action will be increasingly uncertain. Overly simple solutions will be applied to increasingly complex problems and the results will be increasingly unpredictable. Further, with large-scale bureaucracies that are tightly coupled with other bureaucracies, an inappropriate decision can have far-reaching effects—its disruptive potential is increased to embrace a much larger area.

8. *The bureaucracy will become increasingly rigid and inflexible*—As the bureaucracy grows in size and complexity, it will be locked increasingly into a vast and intricate maze of relationships with other elements in the system. Attempts to fundamentally restructure the bureaucracy are exceedingly difficult since it requires change in the whole interlocking structure everywhere at once. Further, to maintain efficiency, interactions must become highly rationalized and standardized (the proverbial mountains of paper work and red tape). The bureaucracy becomes brittle through excessive rationalization; it loses the flexibility necessary to keep from becoming vulnerable to disruption.

9. *The creativity and diversity of policy responses will decline*—As the bureaucracy becomes more complex, the range of creative policy responses will tend to become constricted. Innovation is confined within the narrowing boundaries of what the rigidifying system can assimilate without undergoing fundamental change.

10. *The legitimacy of leadership will decline*—Constituency expectations for effective leadership may be quite high at the same time that the relative capacity to make informed decisions is declining (Problems 1 and 7). Leaders, in an attempt to be elected or assume control, will try to persuade their constituency that they have the "right" and "true" answers to solve the mounting problems of systems malfunction. A doubly dangerous situation is created: There is the appearance of understanding at the same time that the ability to comprehend the system is diminishing. As the gap between constituency expectations and reality grows more pronounced, the legitimacy of the leadership will decline.

11. *The vulnerability of the bureaucracy will increase*—As a bureaucracy becomes more inflexible through excessive rationalization and standardization (Problem 8), it will become increasingly vulnerable. The whole system is no stronger than its weakest link. If one part fails, the effects can reverberate throughout the entire system. This is exacerbated by loss of predictability and control (Problem 1) and by the number and significance of unexpected outcomes of policy actions (Problem 7).

12. *The performance of the system will decline*—As the bureaucracy becomes extremely large and complex, its performance will decline for all of the reasons listed above: declining comprehensibility, increasing vulnerability, escalating costs of coordination and control, loss of legitimacy, and so on. Further, when individual problems reach a critical threshold and begin to collectively reinforce one another, the rate of decline in performance will be accelerated.

Are these problems connected with one another or do they arise independently from one another? Since we are considering systems problems—where, by definition, everything is connected to everything else—it seems logical that we would find a coherent pattern of interconnection among them.

Stages of Growth of Social Systems

In order to describe *patterns* of systems problems that arise as a bureaucracy grows through its life cycle, we require a common frame of reference from which to search for that pattern. A single common denominator exists among these twelve problem areas—each is defined so that it changes with variations in size or scale. Scale, then, provides a consistent frame of reference from which to explore relationships among these problems.

Before we can infer the patterns of problems that might emerge as a bureaucracy grows in scale, we must first describe the nature of the basic pattern of systems growth itself. Indeed, the description of the nature of social-systems growth that we select will strongly condition what pattern of problems will be perceived. In this regard, there exists a widely used concept in economics that lends itself well to clarifying our understanding of the life cycle of growth that occurs as a bureaucracy grows to extremes of size or scale.

There are only a few laws in economics. One is the "law of diminishing returns." One application of this law asserts that at some size or scale of activity, no further advantages can be derived from further increases in scale. Moreover, if scale nonetheless continues to increase, diseconomies of scale will emerge.*

---

* Although the law of diminishing returns is traditionally applied to the description of variable factor proportions, it can also be applied to exploring the implications of using productive systems of growing scale. As applied to the output of a company when the input of one resource only is varied, the law states that ". . . if the input of one resource is increased by equal increments per unit of time while the inputs of other resources are held constant, total product output will increase, but beyond some point the resulting output increases will become smaller and smaller. If input increases of the variable resource are carried far enough, total product will reach a maximum and may then decrease." [4] By varying all factors of production in proportion to increases in scale, we can make scale itself the variable factor and thereby observe the law of diminishing returns translating into diseconomies of scale.[5]

In other words, the system will reach a size where efficiency will actually decrease as the organization becomes larger.

The difficulty in applying the law of diminishing returns to the growth of bureaucracies is that economic theory assumes that the rational organization will recognize when it is growing too large (is experiencing diseconomies of scale) and choose to halt its growth at that point. However, there are a number of reasons to think that bureaucracies may grow far beyond their most efficient size and then be unable and/or unwilling to retreat from that overly large and inefficient scale.

The reasons why bureaucracies may inexorably grow too large are numerous. A few key reasons are summarized below in what can be called the "ratchet effect" of bureaucratic growth:

1. *The bureaucratic imperative*—If the size of a bureaucracy that a decision-maker manages is considered an important source of status and power, then decision-makers may attempt to foster the growth of their bureaucracy in order to secure greater benefit for themselves, even at the cost of a decline in overall systems efficiency. If many bureaucrats pursue this behavior (the search for a larger budget, larger staff, greater responsibility, and so on), the collective effect could be the production of an overly large and inefficient scale of operations.

2. *Something for everyone*—Bureaucracies employ the art of compromise in order to provide something for everyone —attempting to insure that no important constituency will be alienated or angered. The bureaucracy defends its own interest group and draws support from the many persons who depend on its continued existence. A pattern of expectations and demands arises that tends to inhibit the reduction of bureaucratic activity which, once instituted, becomes the norm.

3. *Growth is good*—A central value-premise in the industrial world view has been that growth is good. This has cre-

ated a climate in which a concern for the bigness of our bureaucracies would be less likely to be challanged.

4. *The technological imperative*—Technology (ranging from computers to photocopying machines to the telephone) allows the possibility of vastly expanding the scale of systems and this possibility, in turn, is often translated into apparent necessity. Bureaucracies designed to reap the maximum benefits from potent technologies may find that the system has exceeded its most efficient size (particularly in regard to the human element of the system).

5. *Responding to the needs of a given population*—Many government bureaucracies are obliged by law and/or by egalitarian principles to respond to the needs of an entire population or population segment (for example, all old persons, all school-age children, all poor persons who may be in ill health, etc.). There may be little choice as to the size of the bureaucracy if it is largely dictated by the size of a system needed to respond to a given population segment.

6. *Imprecise means of measurement*—Bureaucracies must attempt to measure the efficiency of their operations via a number of often conflicting and ambiguous measures of performance. With virtually no clear-cut measures of systems performance—particularly when the system is exceedingly large and increasingly incomprehensible as a whole—then the bureaucracy can grow to excessive size without decision-makers' knowing that has occurred.

Even if a bureaucracy were aware that its size was excessive and its efficiency declining, the ratchet effect could strongly inhibit retreat from that scale of activity. Further, there is great inertia in large bureaucracies that have enormous psychological, economic, and political investments in the system as it is constituted. Also, the system may have become sufficiently incomprehensible and yet so seemingly indispensable as to defy its dismantling or fundamental change. The notorious difficulty in eliminating or restructuring a government agency or program seems a manifestation of the ratchet effect. Overall, then, it seems unlikely that the major bureaucracies of the industrial era would voluntarily arrest their growth.

With the ratchet effect driving the growth of bureaucracy, it becomes necessary to extend the application of the law of diminishing returns to include the range of severe diseconomies of scale and beyond. By extending the range of organizational performance considered under this law we may derive a four-stage description of the life cycle of the growth of bureaucracies. The four stages of growth in the life cycle of bureaucratic growth are an initial stage of high growth, a second stage of great efficiency, a third stage plagued by diseconomies of scale, and a fourth stage of bureaucratic crisis. A visual portrayal of this growth curve is shown below:

FOUR STAGES OF GROWTH OF BUREAUCRACIES:

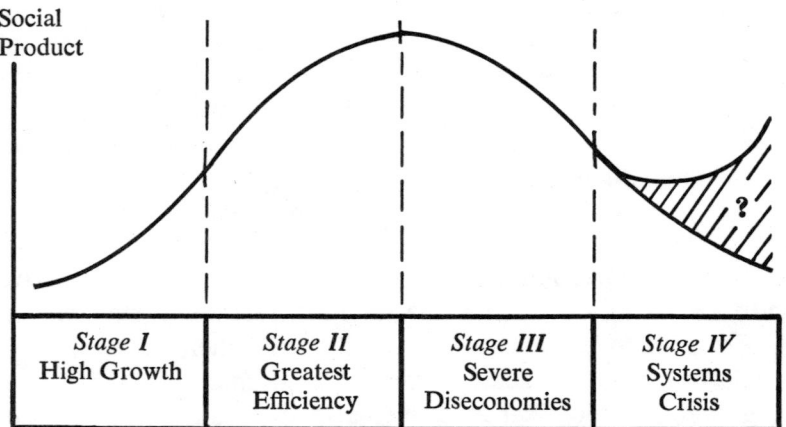

We are now ready to add more flesh to this skeletal model by meshing the four-stage growth curve (developed by expanding the law of diminishing returns) with the twelve problems that arise in the growth of large systems. A matrix format is used to illustrate how each of these twelve problems would likely become manifest in each of the four stages of growth (see following figure). The result provides a highly compact description of the dynamic pattern of bureaucratic growth through a complete life cycle: from inception to demise (or transformation). Admittedly, this is an incomplete model of growth relative to the complexities inherent in the evolution of social bureaucracies; nonetheless, it offers some important clues into the nature of that process.

This four-stage description of the life cycle of bureaucratic growth gives us a useful tool for understanding the present status and the future evolution of a number of the largest, and presumably most vital, institutions in modern society. In summary, what this model, or description of growth, suggests is that large institutions are unlikely to reach a place of equilibrium and rest there. Instead, institutions are likely to grow too large and then—like a rubber band stretched to the limits of its elasticity—lose the resilience necessary to cope with crises flexibly. When this occurs, the institution (or interlocking web of institutions) will encounter a stage of "system crisis" where it will be forced to either: 1. adopt highly authoritarian modes of regulation and control; or 2. fundamentally reconstitute itself in a way that has more resilience and adaptive potential (the nature of such restructuring is discussed in Chapter 8 and Appendix V).

If an authoritarian social system were the outcome, I think it likely that it would be only temporary. The reason is that the onslaught of social complexity knows no ideological boundaries and would impinge, perhaps with nearly equal force (when it begins to mount exponentially upward), on democratic and authoritarian systems alike. Further, the rigidity of authoritarian modes of control lowers the resilience of social systems and thereby makes them more brittle, vulnerable to disruption, and prone to early extinction. Overall, an authoritarian outcome

PROBLEMS OF LARGE SYSTEMS ARRAYED BY STAGES OF GROWTH *

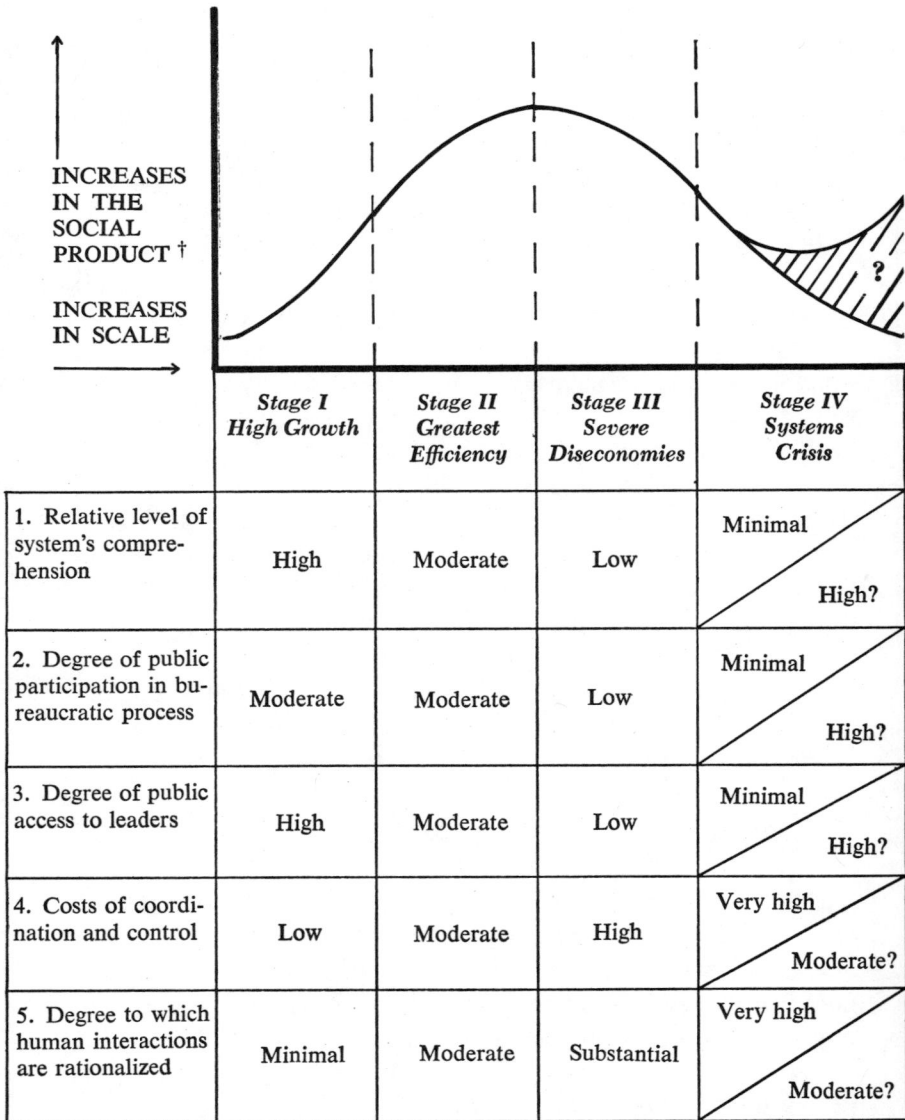

	Stage I High Growth	Stage II Greatest Efficiency	Stage III Severe Diseconomies	Stage IV Systems Crisis
1. Relative level of system's comprehension	High	Moderate	Low	Minimal / High?
2. Degree of public participation in bureaucratic process	Moderate	Moderate	Low	Minimal / High?
3. Degree of public access to leaders	High	Moderate	Low	Minimal / High?
4. Costs of coordination and control	Low	Moderate	High	Very high / Moderate?
5. Degree to which human interactions are rationalized	Minimal	Moderate	Substantial	Very high / Moderate?

	Stage I High Growth	Stage II Greatest Efficiency	Stage III Severe Diseconomies	Stage IV Systems Crisis
6. Level of aliena-tion of constituency	Low	Moderate	High	Very high Low?
7. Degree of coun-ter-expected sys-tems behavior	Low	Moderate	High	Very high Moderate?
8. Degree of sys-tem's rigidity	Low	Moderate	High	Brittle Low?
9. Degree of diver-sity or innovation	High	Moderate	Low	Very low High?
10. Legitimacy of leadership	High	High	Low	Very low High?
11. Degree of sys-tem's vulnerability	Low	Moderate	High	Extreme Moderate?
12. Level of sys-tem's performance	High	High	Declining rapidly	Very low High?

* Large complex systems tend to decline in performance after they reach a certain size. Eventually they enter a stage of "systems crisis," which may lead to very different results: On the one hand, the systems may move toward total collapse; on the other, the systems may be transformed. The far right column suggests the shift in the character of a system if it is to successfully resolve the problems of Stage IV.

† Note: The "social product" of a bureaucracy may be defined as the im-provement in well-being of the clients of a system. The social product might be health care, education, or some other goods or services.

seems likely to delay, but not halt, movement into a Stage IV region of systems crisis and the need for more fundamental restructuring.

Already we can see evidence of major bureaucracies moving into the latter stages of growth. As of 1980, a number of the dominant bureaucracies in the United States are plagued by high costs of coordination and control, wasteful administration, faltering performance, unexpected problems, mounting vulnerability to disruption, and many more ailments. In short, many vital bureaucracies seem to exhibit behaviors characteristic of a system either in Stage III (severe diseconomies) or possibly intruding into Stage IV (systems crisis). Thus, the problem of bureaucratic "limits to growth" seems increasingly critical, and given the built-in momentum toward ever greater scales of activity via the ratchet effect, it seems likely that more and more bureaucracies will encounter these limits in the decades ahead. If this rough estimate of the situation is accurate, then it seems likely that at the same time that the United States approaches resource and environmental "limits to growth," we will also reach institutional limits to growth imposed by the growing malfunction and declining performance of our largest bureaucracies.

Stages of Civilizational Growth

We have been exploring the underpinnings of the four-stage model of growth in order to understand how it might apply to the growth dynamics of industrial civilization. To employ this four-stage model to describe the growth dynamics of an entire society requires that we assume that all sectors of society will *tend* to move and grow together as a relatively integrated whole. Is this a warranted assumption? I think that it is. By considering the United States as one giant supersystem comprised of a number of key subsystems (economic, political, social, environmental) we can employ this four-stage description of growth to help clarify the dynamics of civilizational change. Although there may be leads and lags among these sectors, it seems no accident to find that the U.S. society is simultaneously dominated by big business, big labor, big government, big technology, big cities, big educational institutions, and so on. In addition, it seems no accident to find that we now confront critical problems in every sector of society. The economy, the environment, the political apparatus, the culture, etc., are all showing evidence of breaking down at the same time (see the list of "critical problems" in Chapter 3). In short, it seems warranted to assume that the United States and other industrial nations will tend to behave like an integrated "supersystem." In turn, the stages-of-growth model seems to offer useful insights into the nature of industrial era dynamics of growth.

Conclusion

Does the growth of social complexity present an insurmountable obstacle to further social development? I think not. However, we have created forms of social organization that, if not creatively adapted, will inhibit our continued growth. Therefore, if we are to meet the challenge of complexity successfully, we must begin to vigorously explore new approaches to 1. reducing the growth of social complexity (by experimenting with new social forms and social processes that are much more efficient and well adapted to our changing circumstances); and 2. increasing the knowledge supply (by enhancing our pace of social learning). Let's examine a few of the opportunities that exist for each of these.

First, how might we achieve a quantum increase in our pace of social learning? In Chapter 8, I discussed the immensely important, and grossly underutilized, medium of television. With creative use of this tool of mass communication we could easily achieve a quantum increase in our pace of social learning. Another opportunity for achieving a quantum increase in our learning is emerging through the micro-electronics and computer revolution. These technologies can reduce mechanical barriers to learning by providing much easier access to information—both to decision-makers and the citizenry. Another way that our learning can be greatly enhanced is by educating both sides of our brain. Traditional education has emphasized left hemisphere brain functions (analytical, logical, and linear thinking) while tending to ignore right hemisphere brain functions (pattern recognition, intuition, and nonlinear thinking). With right hemisphere learning, we would have an enhanced capacity to absorb densely packed information as patterns or gestalts—we could begin to approach our problems and their solutions as whole systems rather than isolated elements. What these three opportunities illustrate is that there exist largely untapped potentials for major increases in our rate of social learning. There seem to be no intrinsic "limits to learning" that prevent us from coping successfully with mounting systems complexity.

Second, we require a quantum decrease in the complexity of our institutions in both the public and private sectors. How might this be achieved? Two major opportunities come to mind. The complexity of our bureaucracies could be significantly reduced if they were reconstituted at a scale that invited our understanding of them, and encouraged our participation in them (this topic is discussed in Appendix V). Another way to reduce bureaucratic complexity is through lessening the need for these institutions in the first place. For example, if people within major corporations were more environmentally conscious, it would reduce the need for parental bureaucracies to intrude into their workings with extensive regulations. Or, if people within local communities were to take it upon themselves to provide for the disadvantaged and poor, it would reduce the need for a federal or state bureaucracy to involve itself in the affairs of the locality. If we are to ultimately reduce the need for massive bureaucracies, we (as individuals, citizens, producers, and consumers) must learn to work and live in ways that contribute to the well-being of the whole. In doing so, we can begin to substitute mature self-regulation for further bureaucratic growth (this opportunity is discussed further in Appendix IV).

Overall, I conclude that we *can* achieve a quantum increase in our pace of social learning. Furthermore, we *can* restructure our bureaucracies and adapt our daily lives in such a way as to significantly reduce the growth of institutional complexity. There are no fundamental barriers that prevent us from effectively coping with the problem of mounting social complexity.

APPENDIX IV

THE EVOLUTION OF CONSCIOUSNESS AND THE TRANSFORMATION OF POLITICAL-ECONOMY

The problems of Western industrial societies are of such a tightly interwoven and profoundly difficult nature that they will require an equally profound response if we are to cope with them skillfully. Although a number of responses to a time of civilizational breakdown have been suggested in our discussion of voluntary simplicity, there is one response that is of such importance that it deserves separate consideration; namely, a shift from embedded to self-reflective consciousness as a new basis for social relations. Why is this change so important?

A social system is composed of individuals. Thus, the behavior of our social systems must of necessity mirror and embody the behavior of the individuals who inhabit those systems. A person acting within the context of embedded consciousness tends to behave in an habitual, automatic, and preprogrammed manner. In turn, the programmed behavior of the individual tends to find its collective expression in the programmed or highly regulated social processes that are now characteristic of large, complex bureaucracies in both the public and private sectors of Western industrial societies. Thus, a highly regulated social order seems a predictable expression of a social system where embedded consciousness is the prevailing norm. In such a setting, even a modest movement by many individuals toward self-reflective consciousness implies that corresponding changes in the nature and behavior of social systems would emerge.

The purpose of this appendix, then, is to explore the specific relevance of movement toward self-reflective consciousness for coping with the problems of an aging political-economy. First, however, it is useful to recall the definitions of embedded consciousness and self-reflective consciousness.

Consider, then, two different kinds of self-regulating behavior, each of which implies a markedly different experience of "self" doing the self-regulating. One kind of self-regulation arises from the self-experience associated with embedded consciousness. In other words, the "self" that is doing the regulating is so involved with the concerns of the outer world and, simultaneously, is so embedded within the flow of thought-fantasy-dialogue about those concerns that very little conscious attention is given to the moment-to-moment experiencing of the being that is involved in the whole process. As noted earlier, the experience of self that accompanies embedded consciousness is characteristic of the industrial era. This is a "self" that is running largely on automatic. Behavior tends to be governed largely by reflexive, pre-programmed, and habitual patterns of response. Since the "self" doing the regulating responds to situations in a reflexive and automatic fashion, this can hardly be considered a deeply choice-ful basis for self-regulating behavior. This is more a machinelike self-regulation. Even if conditions change drastically and require highly innovative or original behavior, the actions that emerge from embedded consciousness tend to be repeated variations on old behavioral themes.

A second kind of self-regulation arises from the self-experience associated with self-reflective consciousness. The "self" that is doing the regulating is, to varying degrees, consciously attentive to the moment-to-moment unfolding of both worldly happenings "out there" and simultaneously to the being choosing how to respond to those happenings "in here." Actions, then, are less often conditioned by unnoticed patterns of habitual or reflexive response. Consequently, this "self" has increasing freedom to respond in original ways that are uniquely appropriate to each situation.

With this as background, we now can compare these two kinds of self-regulating behavior and note several crucial differences between them:

Self-Regulation Arising from Embedded Consciousness	*Self-Regulation Arising from Self-Reflective Consciousness*
• the "self" is running on automatic; behavior is reflexive, habitual	• the "self" is consciously attentive to both inner and outer worlds; behavior is much more free and choiceful
• the individual intends the pursuit of personal material gain and social status	• the individual intends the balanced growth of both inner and outer aspects of life
• the individual is not encouraged to be conscious of, or responsive to, the needs of the whole	• the individual is inherently more conscious of, and responsive to, the impact of his or her actions upon the larger world

The predictable outcome of self-regulating behavior arising from embedded consciousness is the exploitation of people and the environment, coupled with the rise of a highly managed social order to restrain the adverse consequences of the self-serving pursuit of material gain. In contrast, the predictable outcome of self-regulating behavior that flows from self-reflective consciousness seems to be a more gentle touching of people and the environment, coupled with a more self-organizing social order at the grass roots level. The profound differences between these two modes of self-regulation suggest the following conclusion: a democratic society and a free-market economy are increasingly unworkable under conditions of embedded consciousness. If we persist in approaching the world through the life-denying and self-serving orientation that characterizes embedded consciousness, it will be at the cost of a free-market economy and democratic society.

The widespread development of the capacity for conscious "self-remembering" may seem idealistic. Yet, the alternative (exploitation of people and resources to the point of their exhaustion, coupled with the rise of a highly managed social order that endeavors to restrain that exploitation) makes it clear that the choice between these two modes of consciousness is not an academic issue but a matter of immediate and practical importance.

This is a fundamental issue requiring our further exploration. In particular, I want to examine the relevance of an evolving human consciousness in two areas: first, its importance in coping with the problem of overwhelming social complexity, and second, its importance in transforming the character of a free-market economy.

The growth of social systems complexity (discussed in the preceding appendix) is making the conscious evolution of consciousness necessary. How is this the case? As a society becomes ever more complex, and demands for self-regulating behavior grow commensurately, that society must begin to draw out of its citizenry more expanded dimensions of human consciousness if it is to cope with that complexity democratically. In short, the growth of social complexity creates the necessity for an unfolding of human consciousness. This means that in order for a civilization that is experiencing growing social complexity to continue to allow individuals to be relatively self-regulating, the individuals therein (as citizens, producers, and consumers) must develop their capacity to be effectively self-regulating at a pace at least equal to that at which the social order is becoming more complex. Without a proportionate increase in the individual capacity to consciously attend to the needs of the whole society, the smooth functioning of the society must necessarily be achieved by ever more bureaucratized and standardized forms of regulation and control (instead of the more resilient and ephemeral process of conscious self-regulation). *Self-reflective consciousness moves from the status of a spiritual luxury for the few in a more rudimentary and fragmented social setting to that of a social necessity for the many in a highly complex and enormously enlarged social setting.*

The severity of the problem of managing bureaucratic complexity seems a rough measure of the magnitude of social necessity that is pushing the widespread emergence of self-reflective consciousness. When some critical threshold is reached in the growth of bureaucratic complexity (a Stage IV, systems breakdown condition), a quantum unfolding of consciousness becomes a social necessity. The alternatives seem to be either social chaos or some form of highly authoritarian society.

Self-reflective consciousness represents both a simple and a complex response to the problems of mounting social complexity. It is simple in that each individual becomes the responsible agent for behavior that is responsive to the needs of the larger social organism. It is complex in the diversity of responses that are allowed by conscious self-remembering as a basis for self-regulation. Self-reflective consciousness allows a complexity, diversity, and freedom of human behavior that could not exist under conditions of a highly managed and pervasively bureaucratized society (the conditions fostered by embedded consciousness). Thus, there is a high opportunity cost if we collectively forgo the actualization of this potential at this critical time in our civilizational growth.

The crucial agent in this response to social complexity is not the federal government; rather, it is millions of individuals as citizens, workers, and consumers. Only by the free choice of autonomous individuals can the potential for self-regulation via self-reflective consciousness be introduced into our collective existence. This is a perfect example of how we are either going to make it together or not at all. We will grow beyond our cultural adolescence into more mature forms of self-regulation only through the collective effects of countless individual transformations.

We have been exploring the relevance of self-reflective consciousness for coping with the problems of social complexity. Now I want to examine the relevance of an evolving human consciousness for transforming the operation of our free-market economy. We can begin by looking at the historical underpinnings of the free-market concept.

In many developed Western nations and in the United States in particular, there has been great reliance upon what has been called the "natural law of the marketplace" to govern human economic behavior effectively. This law emerged at the start of the industrial era and was clearly articulated by Adam Smith in 1776 in his classic economic treatise *The Wealth of Nations*. In accordance with this law, the pursuit of material self-interest was elevated to the status of a virtue. This law assumed that if each person were to pursue *only* his or her own personal material gain, then a process would ensue that would, as if "led by an invisible hand," result in the promotion of the welfare of the larger society. The reasoning was that if each party to an exchange had roughly equal advantage, then, as each person sought his or her own self-interest, the individuals would come to a mutually satisfying agreement which, overall, would leave both parties better off, thereby serving the general welfare. This "natural law" encouraged the unrestrained pursuit of personal material gain and simultaneously relieved the individual of any great need to consciously attend to the impact of those material pursuits upon the larger society (since by virtue of natural law, benefit to the larger welfare was supposed to be automatically assured). Although the free-market system premised upon this law has produced an unparalleled level of material abundance (its primary objective) in the more than two centuries since its formulation, it has major flaws.

This law assumes roughly equal advantage among all parties

to any exchange, but the reality is that great inequalities of advantage exist. Western economies are dominated by a relatively small number of massively large corporations, government bureaucracies, labor unions, and other interest groups that exert a disproportionately large amount of power. Moreover, many parties with vital interests are left out of consideration in exchanges based upon competition between these interest groups (for example, consideration of persons in the Third World nations, future generations, other species, the physical environment, and so on).

After more than two centuries of reliance upon the narrowly focused and self-serving notion of free-market processes, it is clear that these processes are less than an adequate basis for assuring the promotion of the larger social welfare. There are innumerable examples that reveal that a single-minded pursuit of material gain from a context of embedded consciousness does not promote the larger social welfare. A few examples include the massive levels of government regulation necessary to restrain the exploitive pursuit of personal gain, the systematic and callous depletion of nonrenewable resources, the degradation of the natural environment, the lack of conscious consideration for all human beings on this planet, and many more.

The traditional remedy to the distortions and inequities that arise in a self-serving free-market economy is to rely increasingly upon government regulation to attend to the needs of the whole. Yet, as we have discussed, the federal bureaucracies are already of overwhelming size, complexity, and unmanageability. As a consequence, the traditional remedy (of turning to government to restrain the excesses of business) has largely exhausted its potential for insuring the overall welfare. What then is the answer? How are we to cope with a faltering economic order?

The answer is not, I think, to abandon an economy based upon the actions of free individuals, but instead to change the consciousness with which we as individuals participate in such an economy. By moving from embedded consciousness to self-reflective consciousness, our actions (as workers, producers, and consumers) will tend to become much more conscious of, and responsive to, the needs of the larger world; we will be less identified as solely economic entities and will consciously affirm the spiritual dimension of our existence; our behavior will be less programmed and habitual, and we will be able to consume, work, and produce in accordance with what the prevailing conditions suggest is appropriate; and many more. With the unfolding of human consciousness and a commensurate growth in the capacity for mature self-regulation, the whole foundation of a free-market economy would be revitalized and the need for governmental intrusion enormously reduced.

For such a change to occur we need to consider freshly the psychological foundations of Western economic thinking. At present, Western economics is premised on the pleasure-pain principles of an eighteenth-century psychology. This primitive psychology views humankind as little more than a utilitarian robot concerned with nothing more than the gratification to be derived from the consumption or production of the next increment of goods. If economics is a "dismal science," and if that science provides the primary foundation for an increasingly dismal social order, then we need to look at the roots of our economic thinking and see the dismal view of the human being that characterizes its psychological underpinnings. We need to consider freshly who we are as human beings. We need to become conscious of the many dimensions of ourselves that have been left out of the sterile and shallow psychology of Western economics. We need to look beyond the invisible hand of narrow self-interest and embrace a larger guiding principle—that of becoming ever more conscious of, and responsive to, the needs of the larger social organism. In short, we need to move from the life-denying and self-serving orientation of traditional economic thinking to a life-sensing and life-serving orientation that accompanies the emergence of self-reflective consciousness.

The evolution from embedded consciousness to self-reflective consciousness (or by whatever terms we wish to describe this eminently practical process of paying attention to the unfolding of our daily lives) is essential for the revitalization of our faltering political-economy. Instead of leaving the welfare of the whole to the workings of self-interest (the traditional conservative approach) or to the workings of government programs and regulations (the traditional liberal approach), we, the people, could become much more consciously self-regulating.

Many choosing a life of conscious simplicity are asserting their capacity for citizenship (direct participation in political processes) and for entrepreneurship (direct participation in economic processes). As individuals develop their capacity for conscious and direct participation in the political and economic affairs of life, the traditional political polarity of liberal and conservative (concerned primarily with the relative role and power of big government versus big business) will increasingly shift toward another polarity (that of concern for the ability of the individual to determine his or her own fate relative to the enormous power of *both* big government and big business). Traditional political and economic perspectives fail to recognize or promote the most radical change of all in a free-market economy and democratic society; namely, the empowerment of individuals to consciously take charge of their own lives and to consciously begin making changes in their manner of work, patterns of consumption, forms of governance, modes of communication, and many more.

Is it realistic to think that at this time many people could begin to develop this latent faculty (the knowing faculty, or consciousness)? Throughout history, few people have had the opportunity to consciously evolve their interior potentials because much of the evolutionary journey of the human species has been preoccupied with one essential concern—that of survival. The struggle for subsistence has placed substantial constraints on the widespread unfolding of consciousness. The present era of relative abundance (particularly in the Western developed nations) contrasts sharply with the material adversity and poverty of the past. With simplicity, equity, and compassion we can have both freedom from want and freedom to realize our potentials in cooperation with other members of the human family. The industrial revolution may be viewed as a major evolutionary breakthrough that provides the material basis to support the pervasive evolution of both individual and sociocultural awareness.

The cumulative effects of even a modest degree of development of the capacity for self-reflective consciousness would result, in my estimation, in a quantum increase in the effectiveness of self-regulating behavior that is conscious of, and responsive to, the needs of the larger society. The seemingly uncoordinated actions of countless individuals would possess a deeper order and coherence, as they would issue from a shared ground of consciousness. Consequently, actions would tend to coalesce into a larger pattern of coherent and harmonious behavior. We have explored already a pragmatic example of this in the spontaneous manner in which voluntary simplicity has emerged through the independent actions of many individuals.

APPENDIX V

SOCIAL ORGANIZATION IN A REVITALIZING CIVILIZATION

The outer world reveals our inner condition. The living and working environments we create are tangible expressions of our inner values and perceptions. Once created, our living environments are not neutral in their impact—we create our environments and then our environments tend to create us. Our living and working environments daily communicate messages to us, whether we are conscious of them or not. The Nobel Prize winning biologist Rene Dubos put the matter this way: The environments we create are mirrors that reflect the character of our civilization; more importantly, they constitute a book in which is written the formula of life that we communicate to others and transmit to succeeding generations.[1] Our created environments are thus important, not only because they affect the quality and character of our daily lives, but also because of the imprinting influence that they have on future generations.

The question naturally arises: Do the living and working environments that have arisen during the industrial era embody behaviors and values that we wish to transmit to succeeding generations? Not entirely, I think. For example, our huge industrial cities were developed primarily in response to criteria of profit-making and economic efficiency rather than criteria of ecological integrity, human community, and architectural beauty. Thus, as we enter a time of profound civilizational transition that moves from one dominant pattern of values, perceptions, and behaviors to another, it is not surprising to think that the worldly expressions of those values and behaviors may also change. But how might they change? Is there a discernible direction or pattern to the changes that might accompany a revitalizing civilization premised upon the conscious simplification of life? How would institutions, workplaces, neighborhoods, etc., be altered if a life of conscious simplicity were to become widespread in the coming decades? What forms of social and physical organization might emerge to encourage self-reliance, human diversity, human creativity, and mutually helpful living?

One of the most popular current metaphors for describing the social expression of voluntary simplicity is to say that it implies the wholesale decentralization of society. Decentralization, in turn, is a one-way street. To decentralize is to move political, economic, and social activity downward from a large scale to a smaller or more local scale. Despite the popularity of the notion of decentralization, it is, I think, an insufficient metaphor for describing the evolution of social organization. It gives a limited and distorted portrayal of the nature of social evolution that would most likely be at work in a revitalizing civilization.

If decentralization is an inadequate image to describe the richness and complexity of the process of social adaptation that would characterize a revitalizing society, then what metaphor can we use? To answer that question we need to pause and consider the nature of the evolutionary process itself.

Two primary attributes of evolving systems—both biological and social—are 1. a growing degree of *differentiation* (an increase in the degree of diversity or expressiveness of the parts) and, 2. an increasing degree of *integration* (a growing scope of interconnectedness as those parts are linked into a coherently functioning whole). The human body is an elegant example of the balance of integration and differentiation: An incredible diversity of parts (cells, tissues, organs, etc.) are all bound together into an extraordinarily coherent whole (the human body). As this example suggests, evolution seems to be marked by simultaneous increases in both integration (increasing wholeness) and differentiation (increasing diversity). As growth proceeds, it is very important for the two factors of integration and differentiation to remain in a balanced relationship with each other. Let's consider the consequences if they do not.

Increasing differentiation among the parts of a social system without their integration into a larger whole results in chaos and disorder. For example, consider an orchestra wherein every musician intended to refine only the uniqueness of his or her playing without regard for how it might sound when combined with the orchestra as a whole—the result would be noise. Or consider a society in which every citizen intended to do only "his or her own thing" without regard for the impact of his or her actions upon the whole—the result would be social chaos. Clearly, the uniqueness of the parts must be balanced with their integration into a larger and coherent whole.

Alternatively, increasing integration of the whole without increasing diversity among the parts will yield monotony, sameness, homogeneity, and blandness. Consider again the example of an orchestra. Assume this time that each musician endeavored only to integrate his or her playing into ever more complete unity with the entire orchestra without regard for the uniqueness of his or her playing—the result would likely be a monotone utterly lacking in expressiveness. Or consider a society in which only the integration of individuals into a cohesive whole was of concern—the result would surely be a standardized, routinized, bland, and bureaucratized society premised on the lowest common denominator of collective interests. Again, for there to be optimal functioning, integration of the whole must be balanced with differentiation of the parts.

To explore this important notion further, consider again how the human body is constructed. The cells in the body are both integrated (intimately connected with the rest of the body's functions) and differentiated (a great variety of specialized cells exists within the body to perform those functions). Further, at a higher level of bodily organization, the organs are also integrated (each organ is intimately connected with the rest of the body's physiology) and differentiated (each organ performs a highly unique function). At a still higher level, the body itself is integrated (intimately connected with the larger ecology—physical, social, psychological, etc.) and differentiated (each person is unique in countless ways ranging from personality to sexuality). A very important conclusion emerges from this analogy: A healthy organism, whether biological or social, requires a balance of integration and differentiation *within and across* each level of organization.

The foregoing can be restated as a more general principle: *An evolving social organism will tend to be characterized by the balanced unfolding of increasing levels of integration and differentiation, both within and across every level and area of society (from the local to the global scale).* Let's apply this principle to one important domain of social organization—the urban neighborhood—in order to help clarify what it means. For neighborhoods to become more integrated and differentiated, both within and between each major level of social organization, means that they would become 1. more integrated internally (become more autonomous, self-regulating, and self-determining units of social, economic, and political activity); 2. more differentiated internally (contain a wider variety of people, functions, architecture, life-styles, etc.); 3. more integrated externally (relatively autonomous neighborhoods would become important units in the larger urban organization); and 4. more differentiated externally (each neighborhood would perform relatively unique functions on behalf of the larger social organism through some degree of purposeful specialization).

This same evolutionary principle can be applied at the highest levels of human organization. At the planetary scale, it suggests that the next stage of social evolution will involve movement beyond the nation-state and integration into some form of cohesive planetary civilization. Yet, such an evolutionary leap should not be equated with the emergence of a homogenous, undifferentiated, and standardized global social order. The reason is that even greater human diversity will be required in order to accomplish this higher order of social integration. It is vital that important human differences—cultural, religious, political, geographic—not be swallowed up by, and disappear into, a monolithic global social order. We require the simultaneous growth of subplanetary diversity to balance the planetary scope of integration. The creative tensions between these two evolutionary vectors—integration and differentiation—require us to search continually for a skillful middle path that avoids the excesses and imbalance of either extreme (achieving integration at the expense of diversity or achieving diversity at the expense of integration).

Assuming social evolution is characterized by simultaneous increases in integration and differentiation across every level of society, then the enormous complexity, richness, and dynamism of that process reveals how inadequate is the notion of decentralization to describe what is happening. Furthermore, this implies a much more sophisticated response to problems of social systems complexity than a simplistic, "small is beautiful" approach. Indeed, we may find that some of our smallest social systems (such as the traditional neighborhood) are presently too large and, conversely, we may find that some of our largest social systems (such as the traditional nation-state) are too small (to cope, for example, with problems such as Third World starvation and nuclear proliferation). Clearly, there are multiple dimensions of change that must be simultaneously considered and balanced against one another.

With this as background, let's turn to explore the more concrete expressions of voluntary simplicity as they might manifest in the changing structure and character of our living and working environments. We can begin by noting that if we are to take responsibility for the workability and meaningfulness of our lives, then it is essential that our places of living and working be comprehensible to us. If we cannot comprehend our environments, then, despite the opportunity to democratically participate in their functioning, there is not the ability to effectively do so. We have already created living and working environments of such massive scale and bewildering complexity that they are incapacitating; they do not stimulate our participation in their functioning. To hold forth the opportunity to participate while simultaneously diminishing the capacity to effectively do so fosters alienation, cynicism, and despair.

Therefore, one feature of a revitalizing society would be a systematic reduction in the scale and complexity of many of our living and working environments. In particular, those areas that provide the basic essentials of life—food, clothing, shelter, health care, education—would be primary candidates for such innovation. This means that to whatever extent feasible, we would intentionally redesign and rebuild many of our institutions, workplaces, neighborhoods, schools, hospitals, and so on so they are of more approachable size, graspable scope, and manageable complexity. This does not mean turning back the clock in an attempt to retrieve an earlier era; rather, it means developing a whole new level of culture and organization at a grass roots level. This would require bringing sophisticated forms of self-governing behavior into the running of our affairs and designing our living and working environments in such a way as to support that behavior. What might these redesigned living and working environments look like? Some rough guesses are provided below.

As a useful place to begin, imagine a large city of several million persons. This city would be consciously disaggregated into a number of partially decoupled or relatively autonomous townships that, in turn, would be intentionally disaggregated into neighborhood communities or urban villages (with anywhere from several hundred to several thousand persons). Furthermore, at each level in this chain, there would be an attempt to provide as many of the basic necessities of life (food, shelter, energy, health care, human services, etc.) at the smallest scale feasible, given the available human and physical resources. The result would be that instead of a massive and largely undifferentiated city, hundreds, perhaps thousands, of clusters of distinctive neighborhood communities would emerge.

Instead of mass tracts of housing or massive areas of commercial activities, there would be a much greater clustering of activities into *relatively* self-reliant neighborhoods or intentional communities. Each intentional community would contain a diverse range of activities: neighborhood workplaces, community gardens, health-care facilities, child-care centers, cooperative building and repair shops, recycling centers, neighborhood schools, and many more. High levels of social cohesion would be encouraged through the face-to-face contact of many people doing many different kinds of purposeful work together.

With the intermingling of activities into an organic whole, people would tend to feel a much stronger sense of kinship and purposeful community than we do today. Each intentional community would become a microcosm of the totality of life's activities. The result would be a flourishing of architecturally, socially, culturally, and in other ways, distinct or unique communities that have the character of a smaller town. Yet, because these intentional neighborhood communities would be nested within the context of a larger urban region in a communications-rich society, they would not have the parochialism of the traditional small town.

This may seem like an impractical idea, as it would require giving these communities the power of limited taxation, zoning, schooling, banking, planning, incorporation, and many other powers that have traditionally not been given over to neighborhood control. Yet, this level of empowerment at the grass roots level seems essential to a revitalizing society. In their book *Neighborhood Power*, David Morris and Karl Hess describe the democratic underpinnings of such a social order:

> If neighborhoods had any sort of independence, might they not defy the worthy goals of the greater political leaders, the national leaders? Of course they might. But how better judge the wisdom of a larger political goal than by whether or not the people involved will actually support it? Isn't democracy, as a matter of fact, founded upon that sort of test? And where might people better discuss and decide

their support of and role in larger political actions than in the one place where they can debate among themselves as citizens—in their own neighborhoods? [2]

These communities would, to a considerable extent, have to be self-defining, self-organizing, and self-governing. Obviously, this raises enormous issues of equity and freedom. Great maturity and a life-serving intention would be crucial to the long-term success of this manner of social organization. Still, our present neighborhoods represent "tiny, underdeveloped nations" that have enormous untapped potential for enabling people to respond creatively to the stressful and difficult conditions of a disintegrating civilization.[3]

Overall, the trend toward a planetary scope of integration would be balanced by the selective and partial decoupling of social activities—from nation to city to neighborhood—with the conscious intention of accomplishing as much as possible at the most local scale appropriate for that activity. Obviously, there are a number of basic industries and governmental functions that could not be disaggregated to the most local levels. Therefore, this process does not imply the abandonment of the industrial era economy and political apparatus. Instead, it implies a personalizing or humanizing of that which already exists. It would result in a huge step forward in the democratization of life at the local scale. The net effect would likely be a highly eclectic, diverse, experimental, and varied response that would differ from region to region, from neighborhood to neighborhood, and from person to person.

With self-organizing and self-governing activities flourishing at more local levels, a much more flexible and adaptive underpinning to the whole society would be established. The vulnerability of the industrial era society to severe disruption would be greatly reduced by the grass roots resilience that arises with the growth of greater self-reliance and self-determination at every level.

Even this discussion does not fully reveal the structural changes that would likely accompany the emergence of this form of revitalizing society. To more systematically detail some of the important differences between a society moving into a condition of stagnation, in contrast to one involved with intensive grass roots innovation, I refer you to the following table where additional comparisons are made.

CONTRASTS BETWEEN THE STRUCTURE OF STAGNATING AND REVITALIZING SOCIETIES

Stagnating Society	Revitalizing Society
A massive and largely undifferentiated society of overwhelming complexity.	Simultaneous integration and differentiation results in more human-sized social groupings that are of manageable size and complexity.
All sectors of society—economic, political, social, and environmental—are tightly coupled and highly interdependent.	Intentional decoupling encourages local autonomy and self-reliance.
High levels of vulnerability to severe disruption threatens the whole intertwined network —extensive regulation by central authority is necessary.	Lowered vulnerability to disruption due to intentional decoupling of critical sectors of economy and society— centralized regulation is minimized and self-governing activity at the local scale is encouraged.
Undifferentiated growth in a high technology, mass production, mass consumption economy.	Selective or differentiated growth in a mixed economy that combines both high and "intermediate" technology. An emphasis on local self-reliance and living with less.

A strong emphasis on material growth and finding technological means to override resource constraints to growth.

A shift in the nature of growth toward balancing material sufficiency with psychological and spiritual growth in community with others.

Emphasis on centralized energy sources. Heavy reliance on nuclear power, synthetic fuels, and massive coal burning plants.

Emphasis on localized energy sources. Heavy reliance on solar, wind, water, and biomass sources of power coupled with strong energy conservation.

In politics: complacency, inaction, and cynicism prevail. Meaningful choices are made by centralized bureaucracies —a highly managed social order approaching de facto authoritarianism.

High political involvement necessary as choices made at the local level are significant; a life-sensing and life-serving orientation encourages concern for the fate of the larger society and human family. A democratic nation-state nested within an emerging planetary civilization.

Low social cohesion, high levels of social alienation. Low levels of identification with the fate of local community and overall society.

High levels of social cohesion and low levels of social alienation given strong identification with the well-being of the local community (and then beyond to the overall society).

What are the sources of initiative and creativity necessary to sustain the process of a co-evolving integration and differentiation of society? Are our traditional institutions, with their hierarchical or pyramidlike form of organization, capable of initiating and sustaining such a process? Not entirely, I think. To effectively pursue the level of social integration and differentiation required by the problems of our era will require new forms of social organization that supplement more traditional organizational forms. What might these new organizational forms look like? How would they work?

We can gain insight into the nature of a newly emerging form of social organization through the pioneering work of two anthropologists, Virginia Hine and Luther Gerlach.

Hine and Gerlach looked at a variety of social change movements for insight into emerging institutional forms. In looking at the feminist movement, the environmentalist movement, the civil rights movement, and others, they found that regardless of the goals or type of movement they considered, all were characterized by a highly similar pattern of organization. Each successful movement was composed of a whole network of smaller, relatively autonomous, and voluntarily linked organizations. The smaller organizations, or "nodes," were connected in such a way that on an organizational chart, they would look like ". . . a badly knotted fishnet with a multitude of nodes or cells of varying sizes, each linked to all the others either directly or indirectly." [4] The following figure suggests the difference in structure between these two modes of organization:

Hierarchical Organization   Network Organization

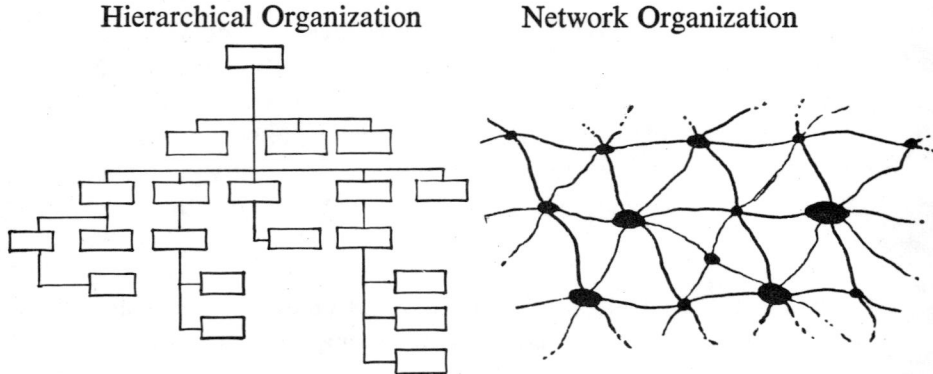

Since each node, or group, within the larger network tends to be organizationally self-sufficient, any one group can survive the elimination of all the others. Further, given the multiplicity of voluntarily linked groups that comprise the whole network, there is no single leader or group that dominates or that is crucial to the continued functioning of the movement.

Hine and Gerlach emphasize that the key to understanding how these seemingly haphazard networks function as a coherent and cohesive whole is by recognizing the power of shared basic assumptions to unify disparate groups. The basic binding force is a deep personal commitment to a few basic assumptions that are shared by all. There can be great controversy within a movement concerning the most appropriate social expression of those underlying assumptions; yet, there exists an underlying "common sense" that provides a potent basis for voluntary association. With voluntary association arises the possibility of mutually beneficial exchanges of information, resources, people, insight, and encouragement.

Overall, these social change movements tend to be structured so that the larger network is composed of many, small, voluntarily linked groups, each with its own leadership, and all woven together into a network of direct and indirect linkages through the unifying power of shared assumptions. This mode of social organization seems to offer a number of advantages of great relevance in coping with the problems of social complexity in the context of a faltering political-economy. Hine describes the key advantages of this form of social organization as follows:

> . . . it encourages full utilization of individual and small group innovation while minimizing the results of failure; it promotes maximum penetration of ideas across socio-economic and cultural barriers while preserving cultural and sub-cultural diversity; it is flexible enough to adapt quickly to changing conditions; and it puts a structural premium on egalitarian, personalistic relationship skills in contrast to the impersonalistic mode of interaction suited to the bureaucratic paradigm.[5]

As the problems of the traditional political-economy worsen, and as the needs for a higher order of social integration and differentiation mount, new forms of social organization will continue to emerge to pioneer change. Networks of the kind described above seem ideally suited to such pioneering inasmuch as they allow people to engage in self-organizing processes to initiate and guide social change toward higher levels of unity and diversity, integration and differentiation.

These "people networks" will be greatly assisted in their work by a micro-electronics and computer revolution that is already diffusing potent new technologies throughout Western industrial countries. Within a decade or two, it is likely that nearly every home will have access to a wide array of communications and information possibilities. These include access to relatively low-cost electronic communication—through computers and/or video—with persons all over the planet; access to an interactive or participatory democracy involving leaders at all levels of government; and access to "electronic universities" where the best of the best educators could teach a vast array of subjects (including the knowledge necessary to build more self-reliant communities—intensive gardening techniques, solar energy systems, owner-built housing, paramedical skills, small business skills, and so on).

This communications-rich environment will promote a vast range of diverse, overlapping, and intertwined communication networks among persons located both far and near. A whole new pastime will likely emerge—that of "networking"—an activity roughly equivalent to a sophisticated, global citizen's band radio. Networking will give rise to new levels and forms of culture and community that will reach global dimensions.

Personally selected networks, with their overlapping associations, will provide an expanded sense of community beyond the immediate physical neighborhood in areas of work, politics, play, research, friendship, the arts, and education. These networks, or "nets," will tend to be self-organizing and co-evolving systems of communication that leap over traditional organizational hierarchies to pass information and learning through society like water passing through a sponge.

At a global level, these networks will be a potent tool for mobilizing grass roots public opinion around critical issues of concern to the entire human family, and for promoting global social cohesion through overlapping networks of association that transcend nation-state boundaries. Furthermore, these global networks will begin to nurture a sense of species-identity, or global social character.

The emerging communications technologies, coupled with the network form of social organization, offer the potential of allowing us to develop a level of social involvement and social cohesion, from local to global scale, far beyond what was imaginable even a few decades earlier. In summary, there already exist (or are fast emerging) both the tools of communication and the forms of social organization necessary to sustain a revitalizing civilization.

REFERENCES

Chapter 1: Voluntary Simplicity

1. The term "simple living" has been used by many folks; see, for example, the book by Arthur Gish, *Beyond the Rat Race*, Scottdale, Pa.: Herald Press, 1973, and the book *99 Ways to a Simple Lifestyle* that was written by the Center for Science in the Public Interest, New York: Anchor Press/ Doubleday, 1977. The phrase "conspicuous conservation" is taken from a speech by Theodore Gordon entitled "Lifestyle of the Future: Conspicuous Conservation," that was reprinted in *Vital Speeches of the Day,* July 1, 1977, published by the City News Publishing Co. in Southold, New York. The phrase "the frugality phenomenon" is taken from an article by the same name, written by Carter Henderson and published in the May, 1978, issue of the *Bulletin of Atomic Scientists.* The phrase "conserver society" was used in the 1977 Canadian report *The Selective Conserver Society,* Canada: University of Montreal, The GAMMA Group. The phrase "creative simplicity" was used in the book *Taking Charge* and was written by the Simple Living Collective of San Francisco, New York: Bantam Books, 1977. Creative simplicity is also a term used by Adam Finnerty in his book, *No More Plastic Jesus,* New York: Orbis Books, 1977. Finally, the phrase "relative poverty" is used by Paolo Soleri in his article, "Relative Poverty and Frugality," that was published in the summer, 1975, issue of the *Co-Evolution Quarterly,* Box 428, Sausalito, CA 94965.

2. Richard Gregg's article, "Voluntary Simplicity," was originally published in the Indian journal *Visva-Bharati Quarterly* in August, 1936. It was subsequently reprinted in two parts in the humanist journal *Manas* in its September 4 and 11, 1974, issues. *Manas* is available from Box 32112, El Serena Station, Los Angeles, CA 90032. Gregg's article was

297

also reprinted in the summer, 1977, issue of the *Co-Evolution Quarterly,* Box 428, Sausalito, CA 94965.

3. Richard Gregg, "Voluntary Simplicity," in the summer, 1977, issue of the *Co-Evolution Quarterly,* p. 20.

4. The attitudinal characteristics of the "voluntary simplicity" world view were drawn largely from the grass roots survey described in Chapter 2. The industrial era attitudes were drawn from prior research on the nature of transformational social change. See, for example, the following reports: *Changing Images of Man,* prepared by the Center for the Study of Social Policy, Stanford Research Institute, Menlo Park, CA 94025 and published in May, 1974; and the report: *Alternative Futures for Environmental Policy Planning: 1975–2000,* Center for the Study of Social Policy, SRI, and published in October, 1975.

Chapter 2: Living on the New Frontier

1. Duane Elgin and Arnold Mitchell, "Voluntary Simplicity," in the summer, 1977, issue of the *Co-Evolution Quarterly,* Box 428, Sausalito, CA 94965.

2. The oration of Chief Seattle was published as an article entitled, "If We Sell You Our Land, Love It," in the *Alternative Celebrations Catalogue,* published by Alternatives, 1924 East Third Street, Bloomington, IN 47401, 1978.

3. This statement of Greenpeace philosophy is available from Greenpeace, 240 Fort Mason, San Francisco, CA 94123.

4. *Ibid.*

5. Quote taken from a letter sent out by the Alliance in November, 1980 (New World Alliance, 733 15th St., N.W., Suite 1131, Washington, D.C. 20005).

Chapter 3: Civilizations in Transition

1. Arnold Toynbee, *A Study of History,* Great Britain: Weathervane Books/Oxford University Press, 1972, p. 360.

2. This listing of critical problems is drawn primarily from two sources: first, *Assessment of Future National and International Problem Areas,* a report prepared for the President's science adviser and funded by the National Science Foundation (Report 4676, published in February, 1977, and written by the Center for the Study of Social Policy, Stanford Re-

search Institute, Menlo Park, CA 94025). Second, *Global 2000 Report to the President,* a report prepared by the U.S. Council on Environmental Quality and the U.S. Department of State, released in 1980 (available from Superintendent of Documents, U.S. Government Printing Office, Washington, D.C. 20402).

3. This definition of absolute poverty was taken from the "Address to the Board of Governors" of the World Bank by Robert McNamara, president, September 30, 1980. (The World Bank is located at 1818 H Street N.W., Washington, D.C. 20433.)

4. Arnold Toynbee, *A Study of History.* I have found two different versions of Toynbee's work to be useful, both with the same title. One is an abridgment that condenses the first six volumes of his massive study into a single book. This version was published in New York by the Oxford University Press in 1947. The second version is a summary volume that represents a further condensation and updating of his work. This version was published in Great Britain in 1972 by Weathervane Books and the Oxford University Press. For an overview of Toynbee's thinking, the second volume seems preferable, and for more detail the former volume is more helpful.

5. This pattern of response to a time of civilizational breakdown is adapted in part from the work on human psychological responses to impending death. See, for example, the pioneering work of Elisabeth Kubler-Ross in her book, *On Death and Dying,* New York: Macmillan Publishing Co., 1969.

Chapter 4: The Relevance and Growth of Voluntary Simplicity

1. Arnold Toynbee, *A Study of History,* Great Britain: Weathervane Books/Oxford University Press, 1972, p. 137.

2. *Ibid.,* p. 137.

3. Toynbee discusses the "Law of Progressive Simplification" in his book, *A Study of History,* Volume I, New York: Oxford University Press, 1947, p. 198.

4. See the publication *Youth and the Establishment,* a report on research for John D. Rockefeller 3rd and the Task Force on Youth by Daniel Yankelovich Inc., published in 1971 and available from JDR 3rd Fund, Inc., 50 Rockefeller Plaza, New York, NY 10020, p. 82.

5. Daniel Yankelovich, *The New Morality: A Profile of American Youth in the 70's,* New York: McGraw-Hill Book Co., 1974, p. 10–11.

6. See the Louis Harris poll entitled "Americans Willing to Change Lifestyle," published December 4, 1975, and available from The Harris Survey, Louis Harris & Associates, Inc., 1270 Avenue of the Americas, New York, NY 10020. Harris's comments on this poll were taken from his remarks before the Democratic members of the U.S. House of Representatives, Washington, D.C., in September, 1977, in a speech, "The Changing Shape of Politics."

7. See the Louis Harris poll entitled "Quality Wins Over Quantity," published May 23, 1977, and available from the address given above.

8. Values and Lifestyles Program, SRI International (formerly the Stanford Research Institute), Menlo Park, CA 94025. An overview of their analysis of population groupings is discussed, for example, in a bulletin of social transformation entitled *Leading Edge,* Vol. 1, No. 1, summer, 1980, available from Leading Edge, P.O. Box 42247, Los Angeles, CA 90042.

9. The Norwegian opinion survey was reported in "News of Norway," Vol. 33, No. 1, January 16, 1976, published by the Norwegian Information Service, 825 Third Avenue., New York, NY 10022.

10. Erik Dammann, *The Future in Our Hands,* New York: Pergamon Press, 1979.

11. Peter Ester, "Attitudes of the Dutch Population on Alternative Lifestyles and Environmental Deterioration," a paper presented at the first meeting of the Alternative Ways of Life sub-project, Cartigny, April 21, 1978, and prepared at the Institute for Environmental Problems, Free University, Amsterdam, Holland.

12. The estimates of the percentage of the population actively exploring a life of voluntary simplicity were derived from earlier work done with Arnold Mitchell (currently the director of the SRI International program on "Values and Lifestyles" mentioned in Reference 8 above). See the article by Arnold Mitchell and me on "voluntary simplicity" mentioned in Reference 1, Chapter 2.

Chapter 5: Appreciating Life

1. Einstein quoted in Lincoln Barnett, *The Universe and Dr. Einstein,* New York: Bantam Books, 1957, p. 108.

2. Bill Broder, *The Sacred Hoop,* San Francisco: Sierra Club Books, 1979.

3. Quoted in Thomas Merton, *Gandhi on Non-Violence,* New York: New Directions Publishing, 1965, p. 68.

4. Nadine Stair's quote was taken from Ram Dass, *Journey of Awakening,* New York: Bantam Books, 1978, p. 5.

5. L. W. Yaggy and T. L. Haines, *The Royal Path of Life,* Chicago: Western Publishing House, 1877, p. 590.

Chapter 6: Living More Voluntarily

1. Roger Walsh, "Initial Meditative Experiences: Part I," *Journal of Transpersonal Psychology,* Number 2, 1977, p. 154. This journal is published by the Association for Transpersonal Psychology, P.O. Box 3049, Stanford, CA 94305.

2. E. F. Schumacher, *A Guide for the Perplexed,* New York: Harper and Row, 1977, p. 119.

3. See, for example, the following sources: P. D. Ouspensky, *In Search of the Miraculous,* New York: Harcourt, Brace, and World, 1949; Arthur Deikman, *Personal Freedom,* New York: Viking Press/Grossman Publishers, 1976; Chogyam Trungpa, "Foundations of Mindfulness," in *Garuda IV,* Berkeley: Shambala Press, 1976; Sri Nisargadatta Maharaj, *I Am That,* Vols. I and II, translated by Maurice Frydman, Bombay, India: Chetana, 1973; also available from Acorn Press, Box 4007, Duke Station, Durham, NC 27706; Joseph Goldstein, *The Experience of Insight,* Santa Cruz, California: Unity Press, 1976; Satprem, *Sri Aurobindo or the Adventure of Consciousness,* New York: Harper and Row, 1968; Nyanaponika Thera, *The Heart of Buddhist Meditation,* New York: Samuel Weiser Inc., 1962.

4. See, for example, Aldous Huxley, *The Perennial Philosophy,* New York: Harper, 1945; as well see the two journals: *Revision: A Journal of Knowledge and Consciousness,* P.O. Box 316, Cambridge, MA 02138; and the *Journal of Transpersonal Psychology,* P.O. Box 3049, Stanford, CA 94305.

5. Paul Tillich, *Love, Power, and Justice.* New York: Oxford University Press, 1954.

6. Naomi Stone, et al., *The Asian Journal of Thomas Merton,* New York: New Directions, 1973, pp. 307–308.

7. The nature of this evolutionary progression is well described, for example, in Ken Wilber's book, *The Atman Project: A Transpersonal View of Human Development,* Wheaton, Illinois: Theosophical Publishing House, 1980.

Chapter 7: Living More Simply

1. I am grateful to Arnold Mitchell for suggesting this illuminating example.

2. These questions were taken from an early version of the book *Taking Charge* that was written by the Simple Living Collective of San Francisco, New York: Bantam Books, 1977.

3. *The Spiritual Teaching of Ramana Maharshi,* Berkeley, California: Shambala Press, 1972, p. 56.

4. James Prescott, "Body Pleasure and the Origins of Violence," *Bulletin of Atomic Scientists,* November, 1975.

Chapter 8: Voluntary Simplicity and Civilizational Revitalization

1. Quoted from the article "Help for a Dying People," *Newsweek,* November 5, 1979.

2. Helen Caldicott, "Waking America Up to the Nuclear Nightmare," an interview with Rob Okun in the fall, 1980, issue of the magazine *New Roots,* Box 548, Greenfield, MA 01302.

3. Quoted in Eknath Easwaran, *Gandhi the Man,* Petaluma, California: Nilgiri Press, 1978, p. 56.

4. *Ibid.*

Chapter 10: East-West Synthesis

1. The resource documents that have been most helpful in exploring the convergence of Eastern and Western views of reality include Barbara Ward, *The Interplay of East and West,* New York: W.W. Norton and Co., 1962; S. Radhakrishnan, *Eastern Religions and Western Thought,* London: Oxford University Press, 1940; S. Radhakrishnan, *East and West,* New York: Harper Brothers, 1956; Lama Govinda, *Creative Meditation and Multi-Dimensional Consciousness,* Wheaton, Illinois: The Theosophical Publishing House, 1976; Gary Zukav, *The Dancing Wu Li*

Masters: An Overview of the New Physics, New York: William Morrow and Co., 1979; Fritjof Capra, *The Tao of Physics: An Exploration of the Parallels Between Modern Physics and Eastern Mysticism,* Boulder, Colorado: Shambala Press, 1975; *Revision: A Journal of Knowledge and Consciousness,* P.O. Box 316, Cambridge, MA 02138; *The Journal of Transpersonal Psychology,* published by the Association for Transpersonal Psychology, P.O. Box 3049, Stanford, CA 94305.

2. Quoted in: Francis Cook, *Hua-yen Buddhism,* The Pennsylvania State University Press, 1977, p. 17.

Appendix III: An Overview of the Stages of Growth Model

1. The "learning curve" is described, for example, in Bernard Berelson and G. Steiner, *Human Evolution: An Inventory of Scientific Findings,* New York: Harcourt, Brace, and World, 1964.

2. Elliot Richardson, *The Creative Balance,* New York: Holt, Rinehart, and Winston, 1976, p. 153.

3. The comment from Senator Adlai Stevenson was quoted from the article "Message from Home—Curb the Bureaucrats," *U.S. News and World Report,* November 10, 1975.

4. Richard Leftwich, *The Price System and Resource Allocation,* New York: Holt, Rinehart, and Winston, 1966, p. 99.

5. Sidney Weintraub, *Intermediate Price Theory,* Philadelphia: Chilton Books, 1964, p. 57.

Appendix V: Social Organization in a Revitalizing Civilization

1. Rene Dubos, *So Human an Animal,* New York: Charles Scribner's Sons, 1968, p. 171.

2. David Morris and Karl Hess, *Neighborhood Power,* Boston: Beacon Press, 1975, p. 3.

3. *Ibid.,* p. 16.

4. Virginia Hine, "The Basic Paradigm of a Future Socio-Cultural System," published in *World Issues,* April/May, 1977, by the Center for Democratic Institutions, p. 19.

5. *Ibid.,* p. 20.

INDEX